THIS SIDE OF HEAVEN

NORMAN N. FELTES

This Side of Heaven: Determining the Donnelly Murders, 1880

UNIVERSITY OF TORONTO PRESS
Toronto Buffalo London

Canadian Cataloguing in Publication Data

Feltes, N.N. (Norman N.)
    This side of heaven : determining the Donnelly murders, 1880

    Includes bibilographical references and index.
    ISBN 0-8020-4486-7

    1. Donnelly family.   2. Murder – Ontario – Lucan.
    3. Lucan (Ont.) – History.   4. Ontario, Southwestern – History.
    I. Title.

    HV6810.L8F44 1999   364.15'23'092271325   c98-932660-8

University of Toronto Press acknowledges the financial assistance to its publishing program of the Canada Council for the Arts and the Ontario Arts Council.

This book has been published with the help of a grant from the Humanities
and Social Sciences Federation of Canada, using funds provided by the Social
Sciences and Humanities Research Council of Canada.

For Elizabeth, Nicholas, Alyson, and Sarah,
who crossed the Peace Bridge at Fort Erie with me,
for good, in August 1969

Contents

Figures

Preface

The story of the murder of five members of the Donnelly family in Biddulph Township, near Lucan, Ontario, in February 1880 is fairly widely known in Canada, mainly because of the trilogy of plays by James Reaney, *Sticks and Stones*, *The St Nicholas Hotel*, and *Handcuffs*, which received the Governor General's Award in 1975. The effect of Reaney's dramas was to make suddenly and widely manifest the myth that had developed around the story of the family and its murderers over the century since the event. Lifting the story out of the popular reminiscence, invented tales, popular songs, and romantic novels that had preserved it, Reaney presented the story as a defining myth of Ontario's historical experience, even of Canada's collective past. I want, first of all, in this book to acknowledge and honour that artistic achievement; had James Reaney not written those works, the story of the Donnelly murders would have remained a sensational local anecdote, to titillate listeners on a winter evening. It certainly would not have been available to me.

While many Canadians have come upon the story of the Donnelly murders through reading Thomas P. Kelley's *The Black Donnellys* (1954) and *Vengeance of the Black Donnellys* (1962), I have not found these books useful for this study. '*Vengeance of the Black Donnellys*,' wrote Kelley in his introduction, 'is fiction and meant to be fiction. Fiction based on fact.' But the relation is never clear (and I'm not here interested in fiction), nor was I reassured by the claim in the introduction to the earlier book that the 'facts' were gathered from 'old newspapers, police and court records, as well as other unimpeachable sources.' In *This Side of Heaven*, I have tried to read critically, if not to impeach, some of these and other sources. There are also able historical accounts of the murders (perhaps to some extent prompted by Reaney's plays), the best of which are William Davison Butt's fine doctoral dissertation, 'The Donnellys: History, Legend, Literature' (University of Western Ontario, 1977), and Ray Fazakas's recently reprinted *The Donnelly Album*, first published 1977 (Willowdale, Ontario: Firefly Books, 1995). A reader interested in the details of the story should turn to one of these.

This book has nothing to add to that story, no new discoveries and no new interpretations; Butt's and Fazakas's accounts are full and convincing, and I am not interested in teasing out critically any possible inconsistencies or contradictions. While I do not spend much time on the story of the murders – James Reaney once said to me, 'I am interested in story; you're interested in structure,' adding generously, 'there's room for both' – I tell it now. The following account is simply a bare-bones re-rendering of the story as I understand it from reading Reaney, Butt, Fazakas, and others. As I explain below, my own book rearranges or re-places this tale in the history of Ontario and Canada in the nineteenth century, according to the particular understandings of that history that I share with other marxists, and other historians, presenting a different idea of that story, and of 'story.'

In 1844, James Donnelly of Borrisokane, Tipperary, emigrated to Upper Canada, joining other Tipperary Irish, Protestant and Catholic, who were building farms in the recently opened Biddulph Township, in the forest of the Huron Tract, about sixteen miles north of London, Ontario. Donnelly squatted on Lot 18 on the Sixth Concession Line, facing what was soon to be known as 'the Roman Line' because it was where the Catholic section of the township began. He was joined in 1847 by his wife, Johanna, and James, their infant son; they were to have six more sons and a daughter in Biddulph. James Donnelly killed a neighbour in a drunken brawl at a barn-raising in 1857 and spent seven years in the Kingston Penitentiary. During that time, the Donnellys were able to keep their small farm, which by the 1870s was moderately successful. During the 1870s some of the sons ran a stage-coach line from London to Lucan and on to Exeter and Clinton. The stage route, in the years before the railway line ran north from London, was fiercely competitive, and the journeys often became races between competing coaches, accompanied by fights and collisions. The Donnelly sons became more and more associated with brawling and were involved in repeated lawsuits, some of them serving short jail terms. Increasingly, cases of arson, theft, and cattle-maiming out on the concessions were blamed on the family by its neighbours, though few of the legal cases against them were successful.

The merchant-magistracy and constabulary of Lucan were certainly, rightly or wrongly, aligned against the Donnelly boys. An early representative climax to the violence occurred in February 1876, an especially turbulent year in Biddulph Township and Lucan. The magistrates decided to serve an outstanding assault warrant on the young James Donnelly, who, with several of his brothers, was attending a wedding celebration in a Lucan hotel. There was a mêlée, people were beaten and shot, and, after the Donnellys escaped, the magistrates called out the militia – the Lucan Volunteers – which searched the farmhouses of the Roman Line, capturing James, John, and Will Donnelly. At the 1876 Middlesex Spring Assizes, the brothers were variously convicted of common assault and shooting with intent to maim and sentenced to jail terms in Toronto.

In the late 1870s, Father John Connelly, the new priest at St Patrick's, the Catholic church at the intersection of the Roman Line with the London Road, formed a 'vigilance society,' made up only of Catholics, to deal with the violence and crime in the community, and in 1879 an offshoot of that group started to meet in one of the rural schoolhouses to deal more directly with what they saw to be the causes. In the early hours of 4 February 1880, a group of thirty-five men broke into the Donnelly farmhouse, murdered the parents, a son, Tom, and Bridget, a niece visiting from Ireland, and burned down the house. The group then went across country to the house of the much-hated Will, called him out, and when John appeared at the door instead shot him dead and fled. A neighbour's fourteen-year-old son, Johnny O'Connor, had been spending the night with the elder Donnellys and had witnessed their murder from under a bed, but the first trial for the murders produced a hung jury and the second an acquittal of the accused. No one was ever found guilty of the Donnelly murders.

When I began this project, two former colleagues, Canadianists, asked me 'what could I hope to say that was original, after all that has been written on the Donnelly murders.' As I have said, I have nothing new to add to the story told by Butt and Fazakas and dramatized by Reaney. While I may momentarily tell one story or another, I am not interested in 'story,' and, as my colleagues implied, the details of the episode are known, from what Johnny O'Connor and Will Donnelly saw on the night of 4 February to William Butt's account of the exchanges between the prosecutors and Oliver Mowat's Ontario government. But I can best explain what might be thought my 'original' view of the episode by telling briefly how I came to write this book.

In March 1992, I presented a scholarly paper to a conference in Louis-ville, Kentucky. I found the conference very unsatisfactory and decided to rent a car and drive to southeastern Kentucky, and over the border to Matewan, West Virginia, the site of a famous labour-organizing struggle about which John Sayles made a fine film. As I was driving into Matewan, I happened to notice on a landscape gardener's truck the name 'Hatfield,' and a few minutes later, on a Prudential Insurance agent's sign, I saw the name 'McCoy,' and for the rest of my trip I mulled over the famous Appalachian feud. When I arrived home, I happened to meet Dennis Duffy, a friend at the University of Toronto, who was originally from Kentucky and who, when I told him of my trip, mentioned that there were several books on the Hatfield–McCoy feud. Indeed there were, and I read one: Altina L. Waller's *Feud: Hatfields, McCoys, and Social Change in Appalachia, 1860–1900* (Chapel Hill: University of North Carolina Press, 1988), a marvellously persuasive social history of the area, from the Civil War to the capital–labour war in Matewan in 1920. In the midst of my excitement over Waller's book, I happened to meet on the street David Sobel, a labour historian, to whom I enthusiastically recommended it. David and I talked about it for a minute, and he said, 'I wonder if one could do that with something Canadian.' We looked at each other in wild surmise and said, simultaneously, 'The Donnellys,' and I have been trying to do that ever since. As well, two other books, Tim Robinson's *The Stones of Aran: The Pilgrimage* (London: Viking, 1986), a historical/geographical survey of the largest of the Aran Islands, off the coast of Galway, and William Cronon's *Nature's Metropolis: Chicago and the Great West* (New York: W.W. Norton, 1991), contributed to my developing sense of what could be done that might be 'original.'

But I knew also that my project must inevitably be original, because I saw it always within a marxist theoretical framework. By writing 'marxist' here, instead of 'Marxist,' I am indicating a particular understanding of history in this book, rather than a political position in general. My title, 'This Side of Heaven,' a phrase taken from the verse on the Donnelly family gravestone, is used here to signal the materialism of my approach. Conventional histories of the episode tended to be narratives of local social disorder and lawlessness and what can happen in those circum-stances, and at least one account attempts to trace the 'feud' back to the 'Whiteboys,' anti-landlord agitators in eighteenth-century Tipperary. From the first I had found it hard to believe that the murders were simply the result of the practices of undisciplined Irish peasants translated to Canada (or what a neighbour dismissed as 'bad genes'), though those kinds of understanding were of course often the very stuff of the romantic stories about the Donnellys. In my book I attempt to go beyond the local and immediate emotions and actions of individuals to consider critically the degree that these were historically determined. In successive chapters I analyse and discuss the geography and physiography of southwestern Ontario and how its original survey appropriated it for settlement; an earlier settlement and then, in the same place, the settlement of Lucan, and the different ideologies of these two communities and their effects; the way in which the locale was crossed by roads and railways, their relation to the Great Lakes–St Lawrence waterway and to the Erie Canal, and the implications of those relations; the development of the 'wheat staple' in southwestern Ontario and its historical implications; and, in a final chapter, Biddulph Township as the social formation that these particular historical structures determined. The term 'social formation,' as I use it in chapter 5, is not, I believe, jargon introduced simply to show my marxist colours or otherwise to pose, but rather is used firmly to differentiate the *structured* social relations that I am exploring from looser, conventional terms such as 'society,' 'community' and 'neighbourhood.' The argument of the book as a whole is that the Donnelly murders and their aftermath, the inconclusive and nullifying trials, can be fully understood only as the effects of these interacting structures – that is, of the social formation that they determine.

It will be clear that I have tried to read 'symptomatically,' to use Louis Althusser's term, the texts that I have used: such diverse 'texts' as railway rights-of-way or the locations (or absence) of grain elevators, but also printed texts such as maps and a disquisition on Harold Innis's alleged 'commodity fetishism.' What does a road 'passable to cannon' mean day to day in a wheat economy? What does the absence of 'country elevators' in southwestern Ontario mean about its grain trade? What does Innis's 'staple theory' signify, if it does not quite locate it historically? What do the decennial censuses tell us about the farms on the Roman Line? I use marxist theory to answer questions such as these as I move towards an understanding of Biddulph as a social formation, in the years leading up to the 1880 murders. Within my theoretical framework, those events were overdetermined – determined, that is, by complex and widely diverse economic, socio-political, and ideological forces; so diversely indeed that I am able to discuss only a handful of the major determinations, those that I have indicated. 'Overdetermination' is thus a central concept for what I am trying to say about the Donnelly murders, and I have tried not to overuse it. But the book's purpose is to demonstrate that, while the people of Biddulph Township in the nineteenth century made their own history, they made it not just as they pleased, but under circumstances that were given them, determining their actions. This is not to profess 'determinism' – that all history is locked in a predestined pattern. In his late work, Althusser discussed also the concept of '*under*determination,' which Étienne Balibar has glossed as the effects of '*virtù*' and '*fortuna*' – individual, personal agency and chance – that is, outside of, escaping overdetermination. While my main concern is with historical determination, unrecognized in the conventional histories of Biddulph (or elsewhere), I would admit the simultaneous play of underdetermination, individual, even idiosyncratic human agency and chance, while simply denying its universal, exclusive causality. My task has been to trace out the play of *over-*, not *under*determination, which previous accounts have ignored, and therein lies this study's real claim to 'originality.' My paragraphs are perhaps longer than is usual these days; they are necessarily so, I suggest, because of this emphasis on the related-ness, the interconnection of different material histories, which is the primary meaning of the book.

Original or not, this book owes an immense amount — more, I'm sure, than I can know — to a great number of people; I learned nothing of the Donnellys at my mother's knee. I am grateful, first of all, and in general, to the staff of the John P. Robarts Research Library, University of Toronto: on every occasion, from renewing my card, through being assigned a book locker, to having a perhaps exhaustedly facetious refer-ence question answered, I was met with efficiency, courtesy, and good will – this during a terrible time for universities and libraries in Ontario. I would like in particular to thank the Reference and Map Library staff, whom I often relied on continuously, and I must specifically thank Mary McTavish, a very fine reference librarian (to understate it), and Joan Winearls, whose Map Library at the Robarts is a major intellectual re-source in central Canada, and who taught me how to use it. I am also very grateful to Theresa Regnier and John H. Lutman, custodians of the J.J. Talman Regional History Collection at the Weldon Library, Univer-sity of Western Ontario, who patiently advised me well. I am grateful to Leon Warmski of the Archives of Ontario, and especially to Carolyn Heald, who not only gave me the benefit of her own historical work on the Irish Palatines in Ontario and her experience as an archivist, but read drafts of two of my chapters and gave me useful criticism. Patrick Macklem gave me extremely valuable comments, twice helping me to reorient a chapter with which I was having difficulty, for which I am very grateful. Professor John Warkentin kindly read a very early draft of a chapter, and I greatly appreciate his comments. Nancy Folbre, too, read a chapter and advised me, for which I am most grateful. I must thank an anonymous reader whose tactful teaching allowed me, I believe, substantially to improve the book's presentation of gender relations. I want also to thank Ann Morrison of the Bora Laskin Law Library, University of Toronto, and Gabriel Pal and Janet Kaufman of the McLaughlin Library, University of Guelph, and Carl Vincent of the National Archives of Canada. And I am grateful to the Aid to Scholarly Publications Programme of the Humanities and Social Sciences Federation of Canada for a grant-in-aid towards the publication of this book.

I have mentioned the crucial interventions in the evolution of this book by Dennis Duffy and David Sobel; I am very thankful for those friendships, which invited such fruitful discussions of the work I was contemplating. And I am, again, extremely grateful to Professor James Reaney for his advice and intellectual companionship. Many persons discussed the book or portions of it with me, or advised me on a specific problem out of their particular expertise. I would like to thank Peter Allen, Elizabeth Braun, Howard Buchbinder, Jack Diamond, Bruce Elliott, Harriet Friedmann, Terry Goldie, Barbara Hanrahan, Linda Hutcheon, Carolyn King, Jim Lemon, Jill Levinson, Joseph E. Lewis, Mary Jane Mossman, Karolyn Smardz, Carolyn Strange, Mel Watkins, Catherine Wilson, and David Wood. I want again to express my gratitude for their help. Also, I read portions or summaries of the work to meetings of the Victorian Studies Association of Western Canada, the University of Toronto Legal Theory Workshop, the Post-Colonial Cultural Studies Conference at the University of Galway, the Conference of the Association for Interdisciplinary Nineteenth Century Studies, and the Society for Critical Exchange, and I am grateful for the general critical exchange that those meetings allowed me.

I want especially to acknowledge the kindness of the Baker Library, Harvard Graduate School of Business Administration, and Dun & Bradstreet for permitting me to quote from the R.G. Dun & Co Credit Ledgers, and to thank Dun & Bradstreet (Canada) for permission to quote from the Dun & Bradstreet Reference Books kept in the Archives of Ontario. And I wish finally to thank Franc van Oort for allowing me to use his etching; I was delighted to encounter it. Against the recurring symbolism of the railway, its directness and regularity, in our cultural past (at least as far back as Dickens's *Dombey and Son*), to imagine (or to find) in Ontario that irregular cross-tie is a fine moment, and the etching seems to me to be the perfect illustration for the cover of this book.

THIS SIDE OF HEAVEN

1

Siting and Surveying

As well as the books by Waller, Robinson, and Cronon that I have mentioned, my first visit to Lucan in 1993 impressed on me the importance of 'place' in the story of the Donnelly murders, the need to think through anew and to clarify historically the notion of the 'place' in which they occurred. 'Place,' or 'space,' is a recurring topic in this book, and among the 'texts' I need to read is the geography of Biddulph Township: the landscape, but the landscape as determined historically – that is, by a particular geological structure, the limestone bedrock, the deposition of unsorted glacial parent material, and the accumulation of topsoil through subsequent aeons of distinctive forests. I would want to make the case, after working this through, that the geography of Biddulph Township, a distinct place read as fully as we can as text, was an important material determinant of the events of 1880. Thus I am interested not in the absolute, ahistorical location of Lucan, easily accessible to a visitor in 1999 (lat. 43°11'N, long. 81°24'W), but in the place understood in a fuller geographical (geological, topographical, and so on) and historical materiality. For *place*, rather than a simple location, is a geographical location 'in difference,' the overlay of a set of differentiating processes, a 'situation,' so to speak. Also, I want initially to distinguish 'place' from 'site' – that is, location also determined in difference but as 'a position of comparative advantage for production, exchange, or transfer'; I discuss 'site' extensively below. Eventually, along with their place and site, I want to examine the *time* of the murders as a similar instantiation, the collocation or literally the coincidence, of a set of differential times, of determinate duration: a 'moment,' if we honour its German sense of process along with its more abrupt English sense, a 'conjuncture.' The time, place, and site of the killings thus shade into one another dialectically, depending on our specific interest at the moment. And so I use the outlandish materials of many disciplinary specialisms to apprehend what forces shaped the time and the place of the Donnelly murders – that is, why they happened at all.

As a historical place, Biddulph Township must first be situated within a millennial time-frame. No more than the town of Lucan is the township, even geographically construed, to be seen as a mere setting for the events of 1880. Just as the Central Hotel building or the Swamp School, though their buildings still stand on the old locations, have no immediately apparent historical meaning, neither does the rise of land on which Lucan sits, nor the pleasant, rolling countryside now given over to agribusiness. Just as it is not the survival of the Grand Trunk roadbed that is historical, nor the market square preserved as a baseball diamond, but rather the transformations begun in the mid-nineteenth century that these traces commemorate, so it is not the topography itself of Biddulph but the material transformations to which that topography alludes which has helped make Biddulph one specific historical place and not another. We must so escape notions of setting as to be able to talk of 'place' as the particular complex result of geomorphic processes specific to this part of our planet, modified but still symptomatically readable, active if mysterious influences on what could and could not be contemplated and done in Lucan in 1880.

The Geography of Biddulph Township

The history that made and makes Biddulph a specific place began thousands of years ago. William Cronon, in his history of Chicago, writes of that city's geographical setting in a way that alerts one to the distinctivenesses of the very different terrain across the Lakes to the northeast:

The lands around [Chicago's original settlement] already carried a complex set of natural markers, each with its own meaning and story: gravel and stone, rivers and lakes, clay and loess, grasses and trees, flock and herd. The glaciers had given this landscape its flatness, its fertility, and its easiest corridors of movement ... Glaciers, bedrocks, and plant communities had together inscribed thousands of square miles with other, subtler divisions – between glaciated and unglaciated regions, between well and poorly drained watersheds, between fertile and less fertile soils, between eastward- and southward-flowing rivers, between grasslands and forests. Each of these natural legacies left patterns on the land, and each would have a part in shaping the history of [the region].

Some geographers are content to divide Canada (and Ontario) into single-factor regions, segregated according to certain dominant characteristics, whether landform, climate, vegetation, or soil, conceiving southwestern Ontario, for instance, in a single way as 'an entity for the purposes of thought,' an intellectual construct, a mental image, presenting a regional consciousness or personality. I am wary of such idealist categories and would rather, while drawing on the various specific analyses of these same geographers, read the terrain and the geology of southwestern Ontario not as a personality, but historically, as the effect of multiple material processes, recognizing the diversity but seeing the relationships within the diversity as productive of change, and ultimately seeing the interplay of changes as productive of the larger unity we may then choose to recognize as a region. Cronon's account emphasizes 'markers' and 'inscriptions,' those subtler divisions which, while producing separation, yet imply a complex common history, not only patterns but, significantly, active shaping differences. If we bring such an analysis to bear on nineteenth-century Ontario and see a geographical region as a more complex identity than is given by its simple, positive difference in climate or forest cover from, for example, Québec, as being rather the overlay of active shaping differences, we can read the historical effects, indeed the social and political effects of the region's landforms, climate, vegetation, and soils. And so I want to read briefly some of the processes of, to be precise, the last 30,000 years, so that I can attempt to locate, in my last chapter, mid-Victorian Biddulph Township as a terrain for particular human actions.[1]

There appear to be two major controls of the physical landscape of southwestern Ontario – its geological history and its climate. The area (Figure 1.1) is located, first and earliest, to the southwest of the Canadian Shield of Precambrian igneous metamorphic rock that covers 48 per cent of Canada, including most of Quebec, Ontario, northern Manitoba, and Saskatchewan, and extends into the United States to form the Adirondacks and the Uplands of Wisconsin and Minnesota. 'An area of modest relief' dipping gently towards Lakes Huron and Erie, it is indeed geologically a different region: it is the St Lawrence platform, the 'build' constituting the overall geological structure of southwestern Ontario. For it is composed of a wholly different bedrock from the Shield in northern and eastern Ontario and was produced from sedimentary rocks, sandstones, shales, and limestones deposited much later by the intruding sea during the Palaeozoic era. Its more precise geological designation is as 'the Norfolk formation: grey and brown limestone, calcareous sand-

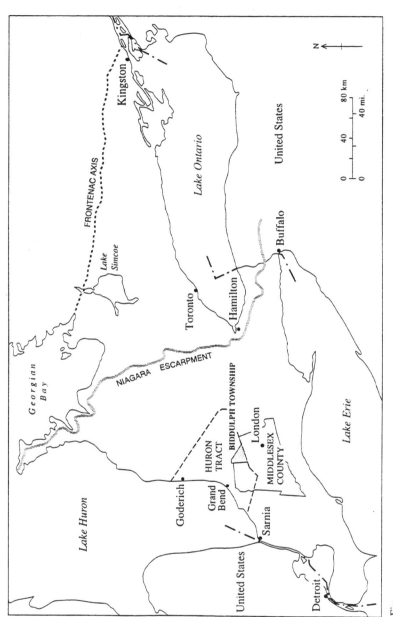

Figure 1.1
Siting southwestern Ontario

stone, chert, small quantities of gypsum.' By the time of human settlement, along with other factors, this bedrock would allow an agriculture very different from elsewhere in Canada. The southwestern portion of this area may be seen as isolated from the rest of Canada and the United States by topographic barriers, one of which is the Niagara Escarpment, an edge (or 'cuesta') of limestone which rises as high as 200 feet to front the Shield on a line from Niagara Falls up to the Bruce Peninsula on Lake Huron (and, importantly, down into New York state).

The Escarpment (just west of Toronto) is the practical eastern physical boundary of southwestern Ontario. There are gaps in the barrier, such as the Dundas valley or the gap at Waterdown, and these, as in 'a great wall through which there are only a few good "gates,"' are (in Cronon's phrase) the easiest corridors of movement, attracting roads and railways, limiting and concentrating the early transportation routes into the region. The Escarpment marks the eastern boundary; otherwise the bounds of southwestern Ontario, again providing both barriers and gateways, were the Great Lakes – 'the central lakelands, extending downward to the great St Lawrence waterway.' Its peninsula divides the upper from the lower Great Lakes; indeed, as an American commentator rather resentfully puts it, 'Canadian territory is thus interjected into the vitals of the United States in the vicinity of Lake Erie.' The Great Lakes also gesture historically to the glaciers that modified them thousands of years earlier and which produced the complex landscape of the region.[2]

At least four successive glaciers covered almost all of Canada (and much of the northern United States) during Pleistocene time; only the last, the 'Wisconsin' glacier, and its behaviour 14,000–13,000 years ago, need concern us. In its progress south, deep into Ohio, Indiana, and Illinois, this glacier had of course, like its predecessors, scoured the earth surface and left as its traces the characteristic scratches on the exposed bedrock. Its retreat, leaving Lakes 'Whittlesey' (Erie) and 'Algonquin' (Huron), produced also the distinctive landscape of southwestern Ontario, and especially of Biddulph Township. Retreating, the glacier divided into two 'lobes,' the 'Lake Huron lobe' and the broad tongue of ice in the lowlands of Lakes Ontario and Erie, the 'Erie lobe.' It is the retreat and local advance of the first of these that is especially significant, for this ice mass did not simply recede steadily to the north: 'It was as though the retreating ice front underwent continual oscillations in which it took two steps backward and one forward over and over again, the result being that, on the whole, the front of the ice retreated in a northerly direction. These are known as the stadial oscillations of the ice front.' These stadial oscillations were amazingly precise processes, precise in their timing and precise in their effect on their site. For there was never a real pause in the advance of the ice front, merely a set of conditions whose effects might give the impression of a pause: 'The ice was always moving slowly forward, but it was also melting. The melting of the ice always tended to drive the front back and it was only when the rate of melting exactly balanced the rate at which the ice advanced that the front became, as we say, stationary. At these times the ice front paused or halted, though the ice itself kept moving, and it was only during these times that terminal or marginal moraines were built.'

I want to emphasize these apparent pauses in the glacier's stadial oscillations, not only the scientific explanation that (again) dispels appearances, but also the exact determinacy, in a time scale of thousands of years, of its moment of balance, and its *locating* effects, the terminal moraines of which Taylor speaks: 'Whenever the ice front halted a marginal deposit of some kind was made, for the ice nearly always carried in its lower layers more or less dirt or detritus gathered from the surface of the ground or of the rock over which it moved.' As a result, as Taylor points out, southwestern Ontario 'is covered with a series of these terminal moraines, all made at climaxes of readvance during the general recession,' and each marking an exactly balanced 'pause' in the geomorphical processes forming the surface of what was to be Ontario. One such set of terminal moraines is the series of complex ridges called the 'Horseshoe moraines,' morainic ridges 'composed of pale brown, hard, calcareous, fine textured till, with a moderate degree of stoniness,' formed around the southeastern corner of the Lake Huron lobe and up around to the Erie lobe. Three of these, from west to east the Seaforth, the Lucan, and the Mitchell Moraines, as well as the spillways that ran along the face of the glacier, cross and determine the landscape of Biddulph Township (Figure 1.2). As one geographer puts it, 'The fundamental elements of the scenery of southern Ontario were in existence by the end of the Tertiary period,' 6,000 years ago. This is, of course, much more than a matter of scenery.

The moraines of Biddulph are formed of 'till,' a heterogeneous mixture of clay, sand, pebbles, and boulders, deposited directly on the limestone bedrock by the glacier. They stretch down across the whole township, broad ridges of heavy brown clay approximately fifty feet high interspersed by till plains ('the moraines and the till plains differ in form ... but are the same with respect to material') and by two glacial spillways, one of which is now followed by a branch of the Little Ausable, angling southwest from the site of what was the Donnelly farm and west of Lucan

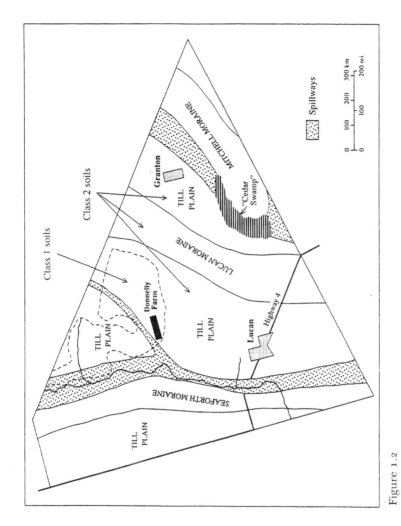

Figure 1.2

Biddulph's physiography and soil. Class 1: 'no significant limitations in use for crops';
Class 2: 'moderate limitations'

to empty eventually into Lake Huron, the other a broad valley, half a mile wide, of sand and silt leading southeast down through what was the 'Cedar Swamp' in the nineteenth century to Medway Creek and the Thames. Thus the Lucan Moraine is the watershed for the township. If the bedrock is the 'frame' or 'build' of Biddulph, these glacial deposits form the basis for what we normally think of as the soil of the township, to be trodden and worked by humans. For 'the depth of the overburden, the gentle slopes, and the high content of limestone and clay are responsible for the development of some highly productive and durable soils.'[3]

The final layer – the topsoil – is the effect of the primeval vegetation, and ultimately of the climate. All weather systems must pass over water to reach southwestern Ontario, a circumstance that produces thirty-five inches of rainfall and eighty inches of snow annually in the snow belt from the lee of Lake Huron across to London. With this amount of snow, spring, the period between the leaf buds and the flower, lasts only about three weeks in southwestern Ontario. The average January temperature is minus 6°C and the average July temperature, 21°C.* But the rapid change from winter to summer also allows a minimum average frost-free period of 140 days, and this modified continental climate permitted, during the period after the last glacier, what some plant geographers would call the achievement of a 'climatic climax' for a certain kind of forest – a state of relative equilibrium 'when the optimum vegetation of a particular long-term plant-succession is left undisturbed in a particular physical environment,' continually reproducing itself over the seasons, while its passing generations decay into topsoil. Like the glacial pause, this climax, the effect of the interaction of temperature, vegetation, and time, brought about the distinctive overburden on the land, inscribing on southwestern Ontario the specific interplay, as it were, of the prevailing mid-continental weather systems and the encircling Great Lakes.

Again, as by the apparent pauses in the glaciers' retreat, I am fascinated by this apparent moment of equilibrium, of climatic climax in the vegetation of the region. A leading ecologist concludes that the classical 'facilitation theory' of plant-succession, enforcing directionality, provides 'a good description of glacial moraine succession,' but his more general

---

* In southwestern Ontario there are 2,000 'mean annual growing degree days' (annual total number of degrees above 5.6 degrees celsius), the highest in Canada; R. Cole Harris and Geoffrey Matthews, eds., *Historical Atlas of Canada*, vol. I, *From the Beginning to 1800* (Toronto: University of Toronto Press, 1987), plate 17.

conclusion is that, despite the continuous fluctuations of climate, 'the climate of an area has clear overall control of the vegetation but within each of the broad climatic zones there are many modifications, caused by soil, topography and animals, that lead to many climax situations.' His hesitating between one climax and many signals a large debate among plant scientists.[4]

That over the millennia the climate and other material processes conditioned the vegetation and thus the distinctive soil of southeastern Ontario is not really at issue. But it is interesting to explore for a moment the implications of this notion of climax, even Krebs's 'many climax situations.' The debate among botanists over plant-succession and climax, like the discrepancy between the appearance and the real process in a glacial pause, raises issues that, I feel, have implications for my larger historical project around the Donnelly murders, problems of what is thought to be usual and what aberrant, what is inevitable and what contingent; issues, ultimately, of determination and agency in human history. The notion of climax, some ecologists argue, like the notion of a glacial pause, is unhistorical; it ignores the historical complexity of an ecosystem. The functionalist emphasis on succession and climax casts certain kinds of change as simply aberrations, disturbances of ordinary, 'natural' processes. Similarly, another writer, discussing the kind of forests that greeted the early European settlers in North America, speaks of catastrophes related to changes of climate or 'conditions of special stress': fire, windstorms and tornadoes, insect outbreaks, and disease epidemics.

The first people in southern Ontario – 'the fluted point people' – did not arrive until about 9000 BC, but William Cronon makes the historical point very clearly: 'Just as ecosystems have been changed by the historical activities of human beings, so too have they their own less-recorded history: forests have been transformed by disease, drought, and fire, species have become extinct, and landscapes have been drastically altered by climatic change without any human intervention at all ... There has been no timeless wilderness in a state of perfect changelessness, no climax forest in permanent stasis.' While I certainly can add nothing to the debate among botanists and ecologists, I am persuaded by those who deconstruct the notion of a stable end-point to a plant-succession, a climax vegetation, since 'the overwhelming evidence from palaeoecology is that communities are ever-changing over time': 'The ideal of a balance between climate and community is something that there will always be a tendency towards, but the time scales of distributional adjustment and of climatic change are such that a truly stable balance may rarely if ever be met.'

As with the glacier, nothing pauses and no climax is reached; instead, what appear to be pauses or climaxes are historically speaking the coincident effects, the overdetermination, of countervailing processes: melting/ice-flow, plant-succession/species change. These historical processes might be more closely specified:

Why a tree of a given species grew where it did was the result not only of ecological factors such as climate, soil, and slope, but of history as well. A fire might shift a forest's composition from one group of species to another. A windstorm might blow over the mature trees of an entire tract of forest and allow the saplings growing beneath them to form a new canopy. Even a minor catastrophe, like the toppling of a single large tree, might create a microenvironment in the shadow of its uprooted base or in the sunlight of the newly broken canopy into which new species might move. Which species grew where in any particular place was thus the result of a cumulative sequence of ecological processes and historical events. The complexity of the precolonial ecosystem was one not merely of space but of time.

To be precise, it seems that we can acknowledge that the forest that covered southwestern Ontario when European (and African) settlers first arrived was indeed the result of a succession, but one that was historical, in Cronon's sense of the word, as well as botanical. The climate was a massively complex determinant of the landscape. Another ecologist describes the general historical outline: 'After recession of the ice, the weathering of parent material from which soil would be formed began. Invasion by plants moving in from the unaffected area south of the Wisconsin glacial boundary began. The amount and nature of this invasion was in part controlled by the character of the mineral surface or substratum – the bare area onto which plant propagules came. Under the combined influence of weathering and a vegetation cover (at first sparse, later continuous) soil development proceeded. Invasion was in part controlled by climate, gradually changing as the ice receded farther and farther northward and finally disappeared.' The slowly changing temperature encouraged first one vegetation and then another: 'The cool moist climate which followed the recession of the ice from its more southern borders favored the establishment of a coniferous forest – a spruce-fir forest such as now occupies a broad band north of the Great

Lakes ... Further amelioration permitted the entrance of more southern species [by 5000 BC].' Because of that history, the forest achieved was distinctive, and the soils produced by thousands of annual cycles of this overdetermined succession of vegetations were also distinctive, both in their distribution over the landscape and in their capabilities as soil. These are less easily recovered histories than those of the glacial moraines that the vegetation overlay, but histories none the less, texts with markers, as Cronon says, as well as their effects as soils on past and present human life.[5]

North of a line drawn east from Grand Bend, on Lake Huron, to Toronto evolved what regional geographers call the Great Lakes–St Lawrence Forest, a transition zone in the Cool Temperate ecological division, made up of conifers, white pine, red pine, and white spruce, with some deciduous trees: red and sugar maple, beech, and red oak. Biddulph Township lies south of that line, in the Niagara section of the Temperate ecological division, where are found as well such trees as black walnut, scarlet oak, sassafras, and sycamore: 'On well-drained till plains, sugar maple, beech, basswood, walnut and oak are common, while on clay plains, silver maple, ash, hickory, and, until recently, elm.' The section on forestry of the *Ausable Valley Conservation Authority Report* (1949) draws on the survey that Dr William ('Tiger') Dunlop made for the Canada Company in 1827 to describe the original forest cover, many of whose species are seldom or never found elsewhere in Canada: 'The main forest cover is described as mixed hardwood, with sugar maple the principal growth followed by beech, elm and basswood. Sometimes, but not often, there was more beech than maple. Hemlock predominated near the streams and interspersed all through were cherry, butternut, various species of oaks and birch.'

I return to these species of tree below (not so much as a historically determined vegetation but as signs of its determination), but here I want to consider the soil that their litter had developed. For that same line on the map, from Grand Bend to Toronto, marks a difference in soil (and, it goes without saying, a relatively stable difference in climate, in summer temperatures), the southern Niagara Forest vegetation having created a 'gray-brown luvisol,' distinct from the 'humic-ferric podzol' of the northern, Great Lakes–Niagara forest. 'Podzolization' – the leaching of minerals from the topsoil – is the dominant soil-forming process in southern Ontario, creating sour, infertile soils, but the grey-brown soil of the southwest is not so highly acid, having, as we have seen, a good supply of lime in the subsoil and 'a greater degree of natural fertility in the form of available mineral nutrients.' This latter is the richest soil in Ontario, 'fertile, deep, ... versatile and productive,' a soil profile that had a profound influence not only on the region's agriculture ('Gray-Brown forest soils and warm summer growing seasons are favourable for most middle latitude crops of European origin') but on its more general social and economic history. I return below to other consequences of Biddulph's location south of the Grand Bend–Toronto line, covered as the first settlers arrived by the primeval Niagara hardwood forest, but I want here to emphasize the fitness to European agriculture of the soil which that forest had produced.[6]

Biddulph especially benefited from the processes that produced the soil of this southwestern region, a benefit arising in part from its morainic subsoil and limestone bedrock. Mostly silty clay loam on and between the moraines (with more or less silt and clay, and with drainage ranging across the township from good to poor), the township also has several sections, especially to the southeast along the old glacial spillway leading to Medway Creek, characterized by sandy, gravelly, or cobbly 'glacolacustrine deposits,' again well to poorly drained. While the small-scale map of soil capability again shows the effect of the old glacial spillway on organic soils, producing 'muck' near the old Cedar Swamp in the southeast, both of the maps that show soil capability for agriculture indicate the generally mixed capability of Biddulph's soil, ranging from 'Class 1,' having 'no significant limitations in use' and 'moderately high to high in productivity for a wide range of field crops,' to 'Class 3,' with 'moderately severe limitations,' such as steepness or the pattern of slopes restricting the range of possible crops. In the nineteenth century, to take an example almost at random, James Donnelly's farm was on a small lobe of *un*limited class-1 soil coming down from the north and crossing the Roman Line, gently sloping, nearly level, silty clay loam, deposited by glaciation from the Lake Huron basin. And so the limestone bedrock differentiated southwestern Ontario from the Shield and eastern Ontario; the climate and the resulting vegetation produced over thousands of years a rich and distinctive topsoil different from the lands immediately to the north, and the glacial deposits, till, moraine, and spillway differentiated the soils of the Huron Tract and the soils within Biddulph: eventually, with settlement, farm from farm. In 1863, a hard-pressed farmer from Ripley, Huron Township, sixty miles to the north, might with his brother walk down to Clinton, where they caught young Jim Donnelly's stage to Lucan: 'At Lucan they cradled grain in the area, returning with ten dollars each at the end of the season via the Donnelly Stage.'[7]

Another historical point can be made about these soils and the ecology of Biddulph in the early years of its settlement. The forest, generated as we have seen by the climate, terrain, and other factors, not only produced over the millennia the soils, distinctive in Canada, of southwestern Ontario but signified to the knowledgeable eye where the best soils lay. The *Ausable Valley Conservation Report* quotes a writer in 1831 – *Hints on Emigration to Upper Canada (Huron Tract)* – on the relation of this forest to the soil: 'The nature of the soil may be invariably discovered by the description of the timber it bears. Thus, on what is called hard timbered land where the maple, beech, black birch, ash, cherry, lime, oak, black walnut, butternut, hickory, plane and tuliptree, etc., are found, the soil consists of deep black loam. Where fir, hemlock and pine are intermixed in any considerable portion with other trees, clay predominates; but where they grow alone, which is generally on elevated situations, sand prevails.' As the report points out: 'these early descriptions along with the vestiges of the primeval forest which remain to-day enable us to form a fair picture of what the original forest was like ... The till moraines and till plains which comprise most of the watershed were covered with sugar maple-beech forest with hickory, black walnut, and black cherry ... intermixed.' Most European wheats, we now know, will grow where rainfall is adequate (fifteen to forty inches annually) and summer temperatures average between 15°C and 23°C. While this scientific knowledge was not available to nineteenth-century European settlers in Upper Canada, the forests themselves provided the necessary information about soils. The Loyalists who arrived between 1784 and 1812, as R.L. Jones points out, were already frontiersmen, and 'long observation had convinced the frontiersman that the native vegetation of a region furnished a reliable indication of its agricultural possibilities': 'Few pioneers were deceived by land speculators if they were able to tramp over the lots offered for sale. Classifications of soil on the basis of the kinds of trees that grew on them were made everywhere along the frontier, and as a matter of course found their way into the immigration literature.' Jones quotes a remarkably exact classification from E.A. Talbot's *Five Years' Residence in the Canadas* (1824): 'Land, upon which black and white Walnut, Chestnut, Hiccory, and Basswood, grow, is esteemed the best on the continent. That which is covered with Maple, Beech, and Cherry, is reckoned as second-rate. Those parts which produce Oak, Elm, and Ash, are esteemed excellent wheat-land, but inferior for all other agricultural purposes. Pine, Hemlock, and Cedar land is hardly worth accepting as a present.' The Swedes, Finns, and Germans who had cleared and settled Pennsylvania, however, 'directed their efforts especially to stands of hickory, beech, maple and ash, for they found the moist conditions these required resulted in a rich, black, humus-laden soil ideal for farming,' and Gentilcore refers to 'maple and beech trees, well recognised by mid-century as the best guides to productive soils.' One writer quotes a passage in John Murray's *Sketches of Canada by a Backwoodsman* (1832): 'The timber is such as in this country indicates the best land: and it is necessary that you should, in the choice of land, be aware of what kind of timbered land is the best. A mixture of maple, basswood (a kind of lime), elm and cherry indicates the very best soils; an intermixture of beech is no objection; and the black walnut is found on first-class soils.' The Germans who left Pennsylvania for Waterloo County in Upper Canada were able to be even more exact: 'The Germans in selecting their land in Upper Canada followed the trail of the black walnut. Because this type of tree grows best on limestone soils and this was the kind of soil the Germans preferred, the black walnut tree made the selection easy.' It was also easy to judge the depth of the topsoil: 'The land that grew the tallest trees must be the best land.' And so, while this sort of knowledge was perhaps not always available in a Canada Company land office in York or Hamilton, British settlers moving from the United States to Canada adopted these German methods. These techniques might easily have been found out, as he moved west, by a shrewd Irish squatter seeking the best farmland, durable, versatile, and productive, in Biddulph Township in the Huron Tract.[8]

What I have chosen to describe thus far is what Cronon, following Hegel (and Marx), calls 'first nature,' 'original, prehuman nature,' as distinct from 'second nature,' 'the artificial nature that people erect atop first nature.' An original, first nature certainly existed (and exists) in southwestern Ontario, but, because I have wanted to emphasize the distinctiveness of the place and to anticipate my own idea of the second nature there, I have already called attention to certain features, such as the gaps in the Escarpment, the moraines, and the soil capabilities. Even during my own initial visit, driving up the Roman Line trying to read the moraines, I was necessarily imposing an initial definition on whatever the first nature may be; there is no innocent reading of landscape. As Alfred Schmidt writes, 'Consciousness always enters as an active spirit into the reality reproduced by it.' Whatever nature I could have been looking at was/is socially mediated, and while I am anticipating no geographical determinations of specific events in nineteenth-century Biddulph (though fallen snow does record footprints), my attention to certain features clearly anticipated the systems of agricultural production, mercantilist and capitalist, that I planned to explore historically. Production is always social, Schmidt reminds us: 'It is always "the appropriation of nature by the individual within and *through the mediation of* a definite form of society," even if the individuals at first pursue their private labours independently of each other.' But in Marx, he goes on, 'nature is not *merely* a social category. It cannot be totally dissolved into the historical processes of its appropriation in respect of form, content, extent and objectivity. If nature is a social category, the inverted statement that society is a category of nature is equally valid.'

Cronon's idea of ecological history similarly begins by assuming a dynamic and changing relationship between environment and culture, one as apt to produce contradiction as continuity: 'Moreover, it assumes that the interactions of the two are dialectical. Environment may initially shape the range of choices available to a people at a given moment, but then culture reshapes environment in responding to these choices. The reshaped environment presents a new set of possibilities for cultural reproduction, thus setting up a new cycle of mutual determination.' This was as true for the Native peoples, who might appear not to have affected the landscape of southwestern Ontario at all, as for the settlers who replaced them. But the chert beds (i.e., flint) along the Niagara Escarpment presented the possibility of tools and weaponry, to which responded, in the seventeenth century, that people known as the Neutrals, who may possibly have owed their neutrality to their custodianship of this resource. Complex historical pressures eventually led the Iroquois to eradicate the Neutrals. The Huron then hunted and cultivated in their own ways in this empty space, which then, emptied again by treaty, presented a new set of possibilities to the imperial government and the Canada Company. In each period, the interactions between first and second nature were dialectical, with the opportunities presenting themselves to a cultural eagerness, and this is the first point that I want to emphasize.

My second point gives a rather stronger sense to the categories and their interaction: it is a relation, but it is a *determinate* one. Sebastiano Timpanaro speaks of 'the conditioning which ... the "natural terrain" exercises over man even after the formation of the "artificial terrain,"' and he quotes Antonio Labriola (from whom he takes his terms) to the effect that 'nature is always the immediate subsoil of the artificial terrain of society, and the ambiance which envelops us all ... We experience [natural forces] continuously.' When Raymond Williams reviewed Timpanaro's *On Materialism*, he took issue with what he saw as still the passivity of these formulations; 'it leaves much unresolved,' Williams pointed out:

There is indeed an 'external situation' which is beyond human choice or control: the far and middle reaches of our environment. It is right to emphasize this, while adding that there are near reaches, even at this level, which are already interactive with human industry and politics. And it is right to describe all these reaches as *conditions* ... They are necessary conditions and as such necessary elements in the relations of all life. But then what can properly be described as an 'external situation' modulates, in complex ways, into what is already an 'interactive situation,' and then, crucially, into an area of material conditions in which it is wholly unreasonable to speak of 'nature' as distinct from 'man' or to use the (political) language of 'impose on' and 'exercise,' now terms of a (dualist) relationship which misrepresent the precise *constituted materiality* which the argument began by offering to emphasize.

As Williams insists, the interaction between first and second nature is not only dialectical but constitutive, a matter of necessary conditions, Cronon's 'cycle of mutual determinations.' It is this cycle, which Williams calls in another place 'a complex and interrelated process of limits and pressures' between first and second nature, that ultimately defines or locates place – the Huron Tract, Biddulph Township, the Roman Line.[9]

Second Nature and Surveys

'The Huron Tract,' 'Biddulph,' 'Roman Line' – terms that have directed the discussion so far – are not, of course, given in first nature but are the effects of European control and comprehension. I am talking not about settlement here – I do so in the next chapter – but about how those lands were first viewed as places, surveyed and appropriated for settlement by Europeans (and, in one instance, by freed African slaves). After the American Revolution, the northern shoreline of Lake Ontario, the Niagara Peninsula, and the Grand River Valley had begun to be settled, as we have seen, by war veterans, by other Loyalists, by Native émigrés from the American colonies, and by Germans and other Europeans from Pennsylvania who preferred to live under British rule. In the first half of the nineteenth century, the British government was concerned to define administratively and defend what remained of its colonies in eastern North America. The area known comprehensively as Quebec, stretching from the Atlantic to wherever it encountered the American border or lands controlled by the Hudson's Bay Company, first was divided administratively in February 1791 into Lower and Upper Canada, which were then renamed Canada East and Canada West in 1841, with the latter becoming Ontario at Confederation in 1867. From the beginning, the defence of these lands was prepared by Lieutenant-Governor John Graves Simcoe's construction of military communication roads to the west (Dundas Street, 1793) and north (Yonge Street, 1796) of York (Toronto).

Simcoe concluded that Dundas Street, and its terminus, London, his proposed capital of Upper Canada, should be located inland, away from (and, as Goodspeed points out, strategically equidistant from) Lakes Erie and Ontario, which constituted such a long, permeable border with the occasionally hostile Americans. There were other reasons for the siting of London, but I want to emphasize the concern for defence and the practice of backing off from the border with the United States, for Simcoe considered Ontario, Northumberland, Durham, and York counties, along the north shore of Lake Ontario, and Norfolk and Suffolk, along Lake Erie, to be '"sensitive" from the military standpoint.' While Simcoe had encouraged Americans to settle in Upper Canada, after the War of 1812 the government's strategy was to promote loyal settlement, which meant that when the original stream of Loyalists from the United States had dried up, settlers were actively recruited in Britain and Ireland (more precise notions of Irish nationhood had not yet complicated Irish loyalty). Again leaving 'settlement' for the next chapter, I want now merely to summarize very briefly the familiar story of the development of the Huron Tract, a part of this strategy.

In 1825, the British government had bought from the Chippewa an immense tract of land (the impossibility of such a purchase cannot be at issue here) running west to Lake Huron from the lands already being settled in the Grand River Valley, and as far north as the present town of Wingham. In 1825, for profit and for the patriotic purposes that I have mentioned, a private concern, the Canada Company, was formed by John Galt and other monied Scottish and English gentlemen to buy for proprietorial settlement 1.1 million acres of this land, backing on Lake Huron in a rough triangle whose base was the townships of London, Nissouri, and Zorra, which were gradually being settled in Middlesex County (Figure 1.1). The well-known story of the exploration of this Huron Tract, starting in 1828, its leading figures, Galt, Dr William 'Tiger' Dunlop, Colonel Anthony Van Egmond, and the surveyors Mahlon Burwell and John McDonald, need not concern us in its details. Galt and his team laid out the town of Guelph in 1827, and then Burwell, Dunlop, and McDonald surveyed a colonization road through the dense forest across the top of the tract, the Huron Road (Highway 8), to Lake Huron, where they established Goderich as the administrative centre for the tract. Burwell also suggested, 'with great submission,' a line for a canal (never undertaken) connecting Lake Huron with Lake Ontario at Burlington Bay, a short cut to the Upper Lakes that avoided the militarily vulnerable narrows around Detroit. In 1831, McDonald then surveyed another road, inland but aligned with the Lake Huron shoreline, south to where it could meet the Proof Line road coming north from London. From these two colonization roads the Huron Tract was settled, and I want to turn now to the deciding structures of that settlement, the assumptions controlling the successive surveys, by which the land was appropriated for sale by the Canada Company and then disbursed.[10]

The surveys of the Huron Tract were official, 'cadastral' surveys, 'primarily concerned with the location and size of parcels of land ... in connection with transfer of ownership or their evaluation for tax and mortgage purposes': we might contrast these to the surveys for military purposes of the shorelines of Lakes Erie and Huron and Georgian Bay, which Lieutenant Henry Bayfield conducted from 1817 to 1826. Cadastral surveys may take two forms; these are what might be thought of as survey ideologies – that is, each in its time may be thought of as inevitable and natural, but each is clearly constrained by that period. The first of these are 'metes and bounds' surveys, also known as 'unsystematic,' 'indiscriminate location,' or 'subsequent' surveys. The phrase 'metes and bounds' simply indicates why this kind was unsystematic or indiscriminate, the signification of 'mete' seeming originally to have oscillated among 'measure,' 'goal,' and 'boundary stone.' It is thus an ad hoc sort of survey, which is why it is often also 'subsequent,' 'a closed traverse around a property,' measuring for cadastral purposes boundaries or landholdings already established, marked by ancient landmarks that are assumed to be permanent – a stream, a boulder, or an old tree. Hence a metes-and-bounds survey often followed on the conquest of settled lands; the Domesday Book surveyed metes and bounds, as did the surveys of Ireland following Cromwell's conquest.

In the 1650s, the Cromwellians, dividing the landholders of Ireland into English Protestants and Irish Papists, transplanted to Connacht and Clare in the west of Ireland all Papist landowners who had been involved in or had held command in the 'rebellion,' as well as those who had not manifested 'constant good affection' to the parliamentarian interests. The lands of these Irish, in twenty-seven counties (among them Tipperary), were to be confiscated and awarded to Parliamentary soldiers and adventurers, and to this end two surveys were conducted in 1654–5. The Cromwellians first undertook a preliminary survey, the Civil Survey, by inquisition rather than by mapped measurement, a stock-taking in which the lands to be confiscated were identified and described. This was followed immediately by the Down Survey, its mapped expression, which was to 'admeasure all the forfeited lands according to their natural, artificial and civil bounds.'

These efforts (which were not to be superseded until the Ordnance Survey of 1842) were classic metes-and-bounds undertakings. Unsystematic, indiscriminate, and self-consciously subsequent, each portion was termed, significantly, a 'scituation' or a 'surround,' enclosing patches of land of different, foreordained shapes. These assumptions (this ideology) we can read, for example, in the Civil Survey's report of 5 September 1654 on the Parish of Borres near Borrisokane, Tipperary, from which James Donnelly, William Hodgins, and several others were to emigrate to Biddulph less than two hundred years later: 'And first beginning in the brooke of Keiloganny in the parish of Ardcrony from thence along ye sd brook to the Castle of Beallafinvoy ... to the foord called Beallaghane bounded on the south west with the lands of Killeagh ... from the sd Foord of Beallaghana [sic] by a ditch to the pathway ... by a shrubby old ditch to a village ... by a little gutter through the middle of a redd bogg, ... to the brook of Killoghany where wee first begunn.'[11]

The 'southern system' of early American colonial surveys similarly involved metes-and-bounds assessments of 'indiscriminate locations whose bounds were determined largely by natural objects, a tree or a stream bed,' but the kind of survey that most immediately concerns us is the systematic, rectangular survey system that displaced metes-and-bounds. In contrast to the boundaries of metes-and-bounds surveys, which do not impose new boundaries on empty space, the boundaries in rectangular surveys (as in Upper Canada) are consequent, presuming eventual townships, concessions, and lots. We have occasion below to note unexpected historical consequences. The general differences between the two survey ideologies are clear: the one comprehends inhabited lands and, while describing them for new purposes, yet does so, it might be said, according to custom. The other comprehends what are perceived as vacant lands, or lands recently vacated, which, while explored, are unknown: there are no pertinent customs beyond those of the survey itself. The governing lines in a rectangular survey are thus systematic and arbitrary. One historian notes: 'Some persons accustomed to the rectangular method of land subdivision indicate that they experience a sense of disorientation when they go to areas of unsystematic surveys. Conversely, people used to a landscape developed under a metes and bounds survey find the gridiron pattern of the rectangular system, where straight roads stretch out interminably before them, most unappealing.'

As well, while metes and bounds might be said to defer to the landscape, as in the case of the boundary of the parish of Borres following a brook to a ford, the rectangular survey merely overlays the landscape, as did the Tenth/Eleventh Concession line in Biddulph, overlaying the Cedar Swamp. Indeed, Biddulph's Fourth/Fifth line was known in the nineteenth century as the 'Ausable Line' for the way it crossed and recrossed six times the branches of the Little Ausable River. The charge to the surveyors of the Huron Tract specified this kind of mathematical regularity while at the same time acknowledging, as would a metes-and-bounds survey, that there was a long irregular lakeshore along one boundary: 'The block shall be marked out by the Surveyor General or his deputies, and shall be approximate to the form of some regular mathematical figure as nearly as may be, consistently with preserving any well defined natural land marks or boundaries.'[12]

But within the rectangular system, which Upper Canada shared with the expanding United States, there were also significant differences, resulting from their different histories and land formations. American expansion beyond the Appalachians originated from distinct colony-states with distinct histories, and settlement was originally licensed (when it *was* licensed) by those particular state governments. Similarly, the settlers, after the wave of Revolutionary War veterans, pursued their individual purposes, often continuing the search for very personal freedoms, religious or political. In Upper Canada, by contrast, unsettled land was first purchased by the British government, the only party allowed to treat with the Native peoples, and became crown land and then was parcelled out in various ways to settlers, at first to reward military service and to indemnify those who had suffered in the wars, and later, as we have seen, to shore up the defences of British North America.

Again, intrinsic to the American settlers' search for freedom had been the notion of a right. One had a right, like Joseph Smith, to lead a group of settlers into open space, establish a township, and wait for 'civilization' to catch up, perhaps then moving on. This process was the distinctive practice of the doctrine of 'manifest destiny,' of 'the frontier.' In Upper Canada, in contrast, there was no equivalent individualist ideology of a right to settle, to freedom, and Canadian destiny was believed never to be manifest in the same way, but rather arduous. Because of the practice of prior land purchase and the limitations on who might buy from the Natives, Upper Canadian land surveying tended to be incremental, moving west and north, but contiguously to surveyed land: as John Galt led the Canada Company's surveyors towards the Huron Tract, he first established Guelph as a sort of base camp. And, while Canadian settlers often moved again further west, they were not as typically following the frontier. Indeed, that term characteristically had a quite different signification in Canada. 'Frontier' meant one thing for Upper Canadians – the political boundary with the United States. The terms that typically signified the incremental Canadian practice of settlement, in contrast to the American ideology of the 'frontier,' were 'front' and 'back': the 'front' being that which faces known, settled land, be it the frontier with the United States or the 'back' of an earlier township: 'back' meant simply 'away from habitation,' whether the 'back' of a concession lot or the Canadian backwoods.

This difference in national ideologies of settlement shows itself not only in the implied contrast between a 'homestead' and a 'lot' in a 'concession,' but in the differences in terminology and practice in the actual (rectangular) surveys in the two countries. The American scheme for a rectangular survey of an area first established a principal north–south meridian (paralleling a map meridian) and then a base line crossing it at right angles to establish an initial point. The area was then divided into townships, each six miles square, measured in all four directions from that initial point: 'The townships are numbered to the north or south commencing with number 1 at the base, and with range numbers to the east or west beginning with the number 1 at the principal meridian.' This procedure reproduces the traditional plan of the central nucleus of the New England township, with 'a radial pattern extending out from the centre.' In contrast, the surveyors of Upper Canada did not strike a cross at an initial point; rather, they typically 'ran a base [or 'proof'] line' from an already established point (such as 'the rear of Wilmot' on the eastern edge of the Huron Tract in the case of the Huron Road), on to which line the townships, yet to be surveyed, would front. Thus what characterized the surveys of Upper Canada in general was incrementally and contiguity (metonym instead of metaphor), fronting always on the known and dependable.[13]

Surveying the Huron Tract

We can see the effect of these practices in Upper Canadian surveying in the plan of the townships of the Huron Tract. A colleague once pointed out to me as we looked at a plan of the townships that Biddulph, judging from its shape, was clearly 'a leftover chunk.' When I compared the two proposals for the layout of townships in the tract, I could see why this would appear to be so. In the surveyor John McDonald's first draft in 1828 of a plan (Figure 1.3a), he laid out the northern townships to front on the Huron Road and then laid out the western townships to front on the projected London–Goderich Road. The southern townships, however – what were to become McGillivray, Biddulph, and Blanshard – were to front *to the south*, along the border of the tract with Middlesex County. In this scheme, Usborne Township, the triangle in the centre, is the 'leftover chunk.' The obvious difficulty with this plan was that the southern boundary of the Huron Tract was at that time only an abstract (cadastral) line; there was no colonization road contemplated for that line (though today Highway 7 runs there – a significantly later decision). In a dense forest, inland and utterly dependent on roads for initial access and supplies, and eventually to market their produce, settlers would be reluctant to take up land in those hypothetical townships.

And so the township plan changed. Its new design (Figure 1.3b), like the first, has most of the townships fronting on the two roads but rearranges those townships to the south. A second tier, Usborne and Blanshard, now fronts on the backs of those townships along the Huron Road, which, it might be presumed, would rapidly fill up. Biddulph is now in the 'leftover,' triangular shape but continues to front on the London–Goderich Road, which indeed will soon angle through the township to the Proof Line in Middlesex. All the townships now fronted on lands administered by the Canada Company; indeed, the 'leftover' shape of Biddulph inscribes not only the direction from which the Huron Tract was settled but the precise purposes of roads in the settlement of inland tracts of the Upper Canadian forest. These sorts of determinations, as we see below, became in time even more specific, touching

Figure 1.3 (opposite)
Township plans for the Huron Tract. A: From 'Draft of the Huron Tract belonging to the Canada Company shewing the Communication Road from Guelph to Goderich Harbour ... and proposed by Mr. Galt as the Base of two Tier of Townships.' John McDonald, 1828. Archives of Ontario (Winearls no. 1030[a]). B: From 'Draft of the Huron Tract ... Showing The Communication Road from Goderich by Wilmot with the Tier of Lots on each side thereof and the Line of Road communicating therefrom to the Talbot Settlement, together with a tier of Lots in like manner on each side and a Proposed Arrangement of

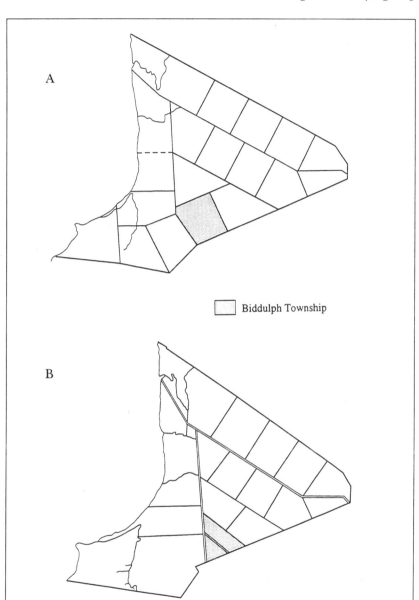

A

B

Biddulph Township

the Townships by which almost all abut on these two roads.' John McDonald, 1829. Archives of Ontario (Winearls no. 1031)

directly on the relations between the Donnellys and their neighbours in Biddulph in the 1880s, when the forest had all but disappeared.

The township as the distinctive unit of land settlement in Upper Canada was historically and geographically produced. In the seventeenth century, as is well known, Quebec was settled according to the 'seigneurial system,' whereby the Company of One Hundred Associates, roughly equivalent to the Canada Company, granted large tracts of land, or *seigneuries*, to individual *seigneurs*, who were required to bring them into agricultural production: 'The original base line for subdivision was the St Lawrence River. For the boundaries, parallel lines were run perpendicular to the river frontage. In order that as many settlers as possible might have access to the water, lots were narrow and long.' Another historian adds: 'With some exceptions the seigneuries were subdivided into *rangs*, or ranges, of long narrow lots running back from rivers ... As a system of settlement the seigneuries offered several advantages. They were easy and cheap to survey and subdivide. Every farmer had direct access to the water which afforded an easy method of transport for produce both in summer and winter. The narrowness of the lots made for closeness of neighbours, while each farmer got a fair share of different types of terrain.' The primary concerns in this long-lot division of land were obviously giving river frontage to a maximum number of owners, but also closeness of neighbours – that is, 'community.' These considerations were also paramount in the early surveys of Upper Canada after the Conquest. But there the main unit of settlement was not to be the seigneurie but the township, an English and American unit of land division introduced into Upper Canada by Governor Haldimand to resettle the first waves of Loyalists near present-day Kingston in 1783. The most effective size and shape for a township and its lots, and their internal arrangement, were to be the major concerns in the surveys of Upper Canada for the next fifty years, and I want to consider the significance of these questions very briefly and in the contrasts between two township systems: the 2,300-acre, single-front township with 200-acre lots that Haldimand established near Cataraqui (Kingston), and the 1,000-acre, double-front, 100-acre-lot townships into which the Huron Tract was to be subdivided fifty years later.[14]

We can easily see the influence of the seigneurial system on Upper Canada surveys in the single-front system (Figure 1.4a). Like the *seigneuries*, these early single-front lots were deep and narrow, and while in both these systems, as Gentilcore notes, the lot is aligned to the water frontage, there is 'an obvious relationship between the dates of the surveys and the distance from water frontage.' Put another way, as the surveys

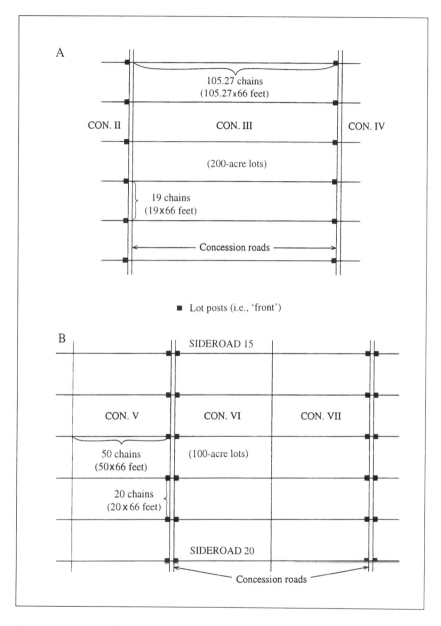

Figure 1.4
Basic methods of the Upper Canada land survey. A: 2,300-acre single-front
system (1783–1818); B: 1,000-acre double-front system (1835–1906)

moved inland from the water the survey system had to change. The single-front lots that fronted on roads became broader, eventually a standard thirty chains (1,980 feet). But this broad frontage made neither for community nor for easy road maintenance, that being a responsibility of the fronting property-holders. Moreover, the wild side of the road (the 'back' of the next concession) tended not to dry out, but to become soggy and break down. And so, as settlement moved west and inland from the St Lawrence and the Lakes, new provision for transportation and community needed to be found. The double-front township system (Figure 1.4b) introduced by the Canada Company in 1835 (and after 1850 used for all crown surveys until 1906) shows the preferred solution. Just as the shape of Biddulph Township and the disposition of the others in the Huron Tract indicate both the dependence of lots on roads and Goderich as the preferred terminus, so the arrangement within the township, the size of the lots, and their placement on the north–south concession roads inscribe a supplementary meaning. While the single-front system, as we have seen, had not made for cohesive settlements, the double-front, 100-acre-lot system not only meant cheaper, more manageable lots for immigrant settlers but also hastened road opening and made for easier road maintenance, since the lot had only one quarter-mile frontage on a concession road, instead of two. Above all, the single-front survey fostered community, since double, facing lots would produce a denser concentration of settlers.[15]

The Huron Tract was surveyed and first settled, then, from the north and from the west, initially along the Huron Road to Goderich and south along the Goderich–London Road, and soon by settlers coming up the Proof Line from London. This history of the survey of the Huron Tract is traced in the numbering of the lines of Biddulph Township, the north–south concession roads being numbered from the west and the east–west sideroads from the north. Goderich is thus inscribed as the point of origin of its survey as well as the real terminus of the two colonization roads (though they actually intersect at Clinton). In 1829, when John McDonald surveyed the road south to London, he marked the corners of the planned townships and laid out the frontposts of the lots that would face the road. For two years the road was not cleared of logs, let alone turnpiked (cambered with earth), but settlers were already using it. By 1832 settlers had reached the present Centralia, on the west side of the London Road, opposite the northwest corner of Biddulph (named, like the other townships, after a director of the Canada Company).

McDonald's party began its survey of Biddulph in 1836, one year after the introduction of the double-front system. His field notes, now in the

Archives of Ontario, record the manner of proceeding in the survey of the township as well as his impressions of the geography that I have described. Working south along the London–Huron Road, when the party reached the Sideroad 25 it would seem to have surveyed east along that sideroad, at each concession surveying north to the township boundary, then retracing their steps to the sideroad and surveying to the township's southern boundary. Thus, as it surveyed north on the line between the Sixth and Seventh Concessions, McDonald commented on the physical features of the landscape, as he had been instructed to do (and with an accuracy that we can now recognize). At what was to be Lot 18 (i.e., three lots south of the Sideroad 15), looking at the two frontages, west and east, he noted 'Good level land Elm Black Ash & Birch swale.† Good level land – Timber Elm Beech Maple Bassd.' In the following decades, Biddulph's Sixth and Seventh Concession line, because of its settlers' religion, came to be known as 'the Roman Line,' and within ten years of John McDonald's survey, Lot 18 would become the farm of James and Johanna Donnelly.[16]

By now, I would hope, we can begin to read some of the determinations even of that particular place on which the Donnelly family squatted – Lot 18, Sixth/Seventh Biddulph Township, in the middle third of the nineteenth-century. The Donnellys found themselves at that time in that place not only because of the attraction of cheap land and a greater degree of personal freedom for Irish Catholic farmers, but more specifically because of a certain kind of land, which allowed (and with the climate allowed *only*) a certain kind of agriculture. It was a place in the North American space and in early industrial time that allowed only certain corridors for particular kinds of transportation and hence, for the settlers, created certain kinds of dependencies. This segment of southwestern Ontario, moreover, was continually reminded of its directions of origin and its administrative capital by the lines on its map. It was, finally, a place in which the assumptions and intentions of its survey method encouraged a certain kind of settlement. The village of Lucan was surveyed after the township and has its own history, which I discuss below, but Biddulph Township was already developing its communities in determinate ways. The double front settlement of concession lines was expressly intended to foster social coherence, community, and in Biddulph it did: it produced the Roman Line, setting again certain conditions of

---

† 'Swale' means 'a depression in regions of undulating glacial moraine'; *The Encyclopedic Dictionary of Physical Geography*, ed. Andrew Goudie (Oxford: Blackwell, 1985), 418.

possibility. Just as the limestone, the Great Lakes, and the particular vegetation ordained the distinctive shape of the land and its soils, so the imbrication of a particular second nature, initially a sequence and method of appropriating that land in a nascent capitalism, determined particulars of the social order raised on that land. We could say, for instance, that but for the double-front survey system of 1835 there would have been no Roman Line in Biddulph Township, with the diverse potentialities of a close community, in the latter half of the nineteenth century. What other conditions of possibility that engaged, and the precise nature of their overdeterminations, we can now explore.

2

Ideologies of Settlement

In a determinate way, then, its survey appropriated the Huron Tract for settlement, one important consideration being the necessity to encourage loyal immigrants in order to resist the influence of American settlers. But even within this particular determination there are again distinctions to be made, such as how loyalty was to be ensured, what its practices might be. Nor can the settlement of Biddulph Township be represented in a simple narrative, by an easy summary, as:

- From 1827, the Canada Company surveyed the tract, and it sold off the land over the next fifty years in different amounts and different locations, accepting payment according to different, successive plans.
- While there were settlers of European stock from the start, the earliest group to settle in Biddulph were free African Americans from Cincinnati, Ohio, who founded the colony of 'Wilberforce' roughly where Lucan stands now.
- These settlers eventually left (though a few families stayed, some to this day), to be replaced, from the late 1830s on, by Irish emigrants, first Protestants, then Catholics, who gave the township its particular character and reputation.

The easy succession of this account (like the glacial pause and the forest's climax) elides the historical constraints on the settlement of Biddulph. Migration theory is the equivalent in the history of settlements to the theory of climax vegetation. Like that theory, it escapes from historical (including ideological) influences into positivist abstraction; it is no accident that E.G. Ravenstein's well-known papers on 'The Laws of Migration,' with their discussions of the 'absorption' and 'dispersal' of the 'migratory current,' were first read in 1885 and 1889 to the Royal Statistical Society. More recently, Everett S. Lee's 'A Theory of Migration,' in its discussion of 'origin and destination factors and intervening obstacles in migration,' ignores not only the various assistance schemes that initially determined all three of these factors but the shifting ideologies of colonization of which the schemes are merely the practices. Just as the meaning and the effects of a survey, for example, derive only from its limiting specificity, so settlement realizes itself only in specific settlements and their ideologies of settlement. Much of the great value of Bruce Elliott's *Irish Migrants in the Canadas* (1988) derives from his painstaking analysis of the specifics of genealogy, birth and marriage records, land titles, and the like, so that when he structures his study around the concept of 'chain migration' we recognize that each category draws on empirical work. Elliott carefully examines specific kinship groups, place of residence in Ireland, and place of residence in Upper Canada; we can see the process of chain migration in the comment of one of the Canada Company's commissioners about an inhabitant of York intending to move in 1831 to Colborne Township in the Huron Tract: 'The settlement of this person is considered important to the interests of the Company, as he is an old experienced emigrant, possessed of considerable property, and his family, relations, and friends, who have already gone to Goderich and its neighbourhood, in consequence, exceed in number fifty persons.' But even this process, convincingly grounded in the specifics of a 'chain,' is in certain ways unhistorical: while it can locate the decisions of individual Irish Protestants, for example, to emigrate from York, or Tipperary in 'the taut political atmosphere preceding and surrounding Catholic emancipation in 1829,' and relate the timing of a decision to 'domestic economic and social conditions,' the interplay of kinship and local economic pressures still manages to ignore larger historical processes at work.[1]

The hypothesis that I test here against the particulars of the settlement of Biddulph Township is that while its immediate process is surely as Elliott describes it, that process is heavily overdetermined by developments in early British capitalism, as these affect the political life of Upper Canada. Rather than (as Norman Macdonald described it in 1939) the interplay of assisted and unassisted settlement ('assisted' alternately by the British government and by parishes), the historical dialectic in early-nineteenth-century colonization policy is a projection of particular struggles on the ideological level of the early-nineteenth-century British capitalist social formation: Benthamite free enterprisers against the landed interests and residual mercantilist colonial policy. This struggle manifests itself in the sequence that other historians describe as, first, a system of land grants, assisted and unassisted, which gave way in 1826 to, second, a system of purposefully using the colonies to solve British population problems ('shovelling out paupers'), which then again gave way in the 1830s to, third, 'systematic colonization,' solving these problems by 'a plan which would pay for itself ... by means of a fund from the sale of colonial lands at a price so fixed as to keep available land, capital, and labour in proper proportion.' Moreover, this British sequence played itself out in Upper Canadian conditions as a problem of 'responsible government' – 'whether the complaint originated in the land policy, or in the clergy reserves, in the schools, or in the bank monopoly, or in the state of trade, or perhaps in some personal injury, or in jealousy at expulsion from office.'

The resolution proposed for this transatlantic (while in Upper Canada very *provincial*) set of contradictions was, of course, the Durham Report of 1839, in which the trials of Upper (and Lower) Canada were addressed by the new Benthamite, free-market thinking of Durham, his colleague Charles Buller, and, behind Buller, Edward Gibbon Wakefield, bringing to bear in colonial affairs the capitalist market solution to social problems (and more). This progression is the widest historical dimension of the settlement of Biddulph Township in the Huron Tract, working itself through in distinct practices of settlement. And the impact of these on the history of the Irish in Biddulph can perhaps best be demonstrated by the contrasting ideology determining the earlier community of Wilberforce.[2]

Practices of Settlement: Wilberforce

In 1829, because of the influx into Cincinnati of fugitive slaves who competed with increased numbers of free Blacks and white immigrants in the unskilled labour market, as well as the deference of Cincinnati business interests to the ways of their southern customers, the trustees of Cincinnati Township announced that they would henceforward enforce the Ohio Black Laws of 1804–7. These laws required 'blacks and mulatto persons' moving to Cincinnati to produce certificates of freedom and to post a $500 bond for good behaviour, and it punished businesses that hired Blacks who did not have the proper papers. In October 1829 there was a three-day riot (or 'sporadic fighting') by whites in the Black section of the city, and as a result agents for the Cincinnati Colonization Society, an affiliate of the American Colonization Society, which was promoting colonies of freed slaves in Liberia and on the Ivory Coast of Africa, approached Sir John Colborne, the lieutenant-governor of Upper Canada, and the Canada Company, to ask whether Black settlers would be welcome there. Colborne famously answered, 'Tell the Republicans on your side of the line that we Royalists do not know *men* by their colour,' and the Canada Company agreed to sell to the Cincinnati settlers four thousand acres for $6,000, to be paid by November 1830.

While between one thousand and two thousand Blacks fled Cincinnati, only 460 went to Canada, and of those only five or six families, joined by fifteen families from Boston, settled in Biddulph. Robin Winks writes, 'At no time did the tiny Negro community of Wilberforce ... rise above a population of two hundred, with perhaps eight hundred more in the general Lucan–Biddulph area.' The only reference to Wilberforce on a map that I know of is on the Upper Canada map in *Tanner's Universal Atlas*, published in Philadelphia in 1833–4, which shows the 'Wilberforce Tract' as a one-mile-square around the London–Goderich Road at Clandeboye. The Colonization Society provided the settlers with no capital to meet the land payments, and in the end only 800 acres (the equivalent of eight lots) was purchased, with donations mainly from American Quakers. 'Confidence in their ability to prosecute the business successfully was impaired,' Benjamin Lundy recorded in his diary, and partly because of this default (and partly, as we see below, because of racial prejudice and the political shift in Britain) the Canada Company refused any future land sales to Black settlers. Financial problems continued to beset the Wilberforce colony; dependent for capital funds on further contributions from abroad, the colony in the early 1830s sent to the United States and to Britain agents who, while they collected large amounts of money, conveyed none of it to Biddulph. Nevertheless, the settlers paid part of the purchase price of their lots by building the Goderich–London Road across Biddulph from Clandeboye to Elginfield, 'through seven miles and a quarter of very thickly and heavily timbered land.' They cleared and farmed the land along this road and built their houses, a tavern, a general store, and a grist mill.[3]

There was 'considerable friction,' as Fred Hamil put it, between the Wilberforce colony and white settlers and administrators. Hamil records a petition from the Western District (an area perhaps especially susceptible to what Landon calls 'nearby American influences') opposing the removal of the Amherstburg garrison because of 'the very numerous and troublesome black population daily coming into the District from the slave states.' Benjamin Lundy, in contrast, claimed in 1832 that while the 'Yankee' settlers in Biddulph and London Townships retained 'their abominable prejudice against the coloured race,' Canadian-born residents were quite friendly, and the Irish 'are often heard to say they prefer the people of colour as neighbours' to the Yankees. But in this contradictory situation the Canada Company feared for land sales, while some of the new settlers seemed to fear for their land values.

Much later, and after the disappearance of Wilberforce, Samuel Gridley Howe, in his report to the Freedman's Inquiry Commission following a tour of Upper Canada in 1863, was to discount the theory of the 'contagion' of American prejudice and to suggest a more structural explanation: 'The truth of the matter seems to be that, as long as the coloured people form a very small proportion of the population, and are dependent, they receive protection and favours; but when they increase, and compete with the laboring class for a living, and especially when they begin to aspire to social equality, they cease to be "interesting negroes," and become "niggers."' Howe's perception of a symptomatic relation between dependence and 'competition' is very important for our purposes; indeed, the primary (if overlooked) signification of 'colony' is precisely dependence. Howe makes this very point; criticizing the systematic congregating of Blacks into colonies and their disciplining into dependence on outsiders, he concludes: 'Taken as a whole, the colonists have cost to somebody a great deal of money, and a great deal of effort; and they have not succeeded so well as many who have been thrown entirely upon their own resources.'[4]

Thus Wilberforce was crucially determined by its own problematic, the central assumptions under which it was constituted, for it was not simply settled but rather conceived and constituted as a colony. The histories of Wilberforce seem to me to overlook the significance of this fact, whether they speak of the internal problems of the settlement or of its affiliation with the American Colonization Society. Fred Landon notes without comment that Benjamin Lundy visited Wilberforce in his travels to seek locations 'where large groups of Negroes might be placed on the land.' Landon also noted that 'there was too much paternalism in [the scheme] to produce the best results,' and so Wilberforce was 'a failure almost from the start,' and he makes no theoretical connection between the fact of the large groups and the fatal paternalism. But my intention here is to distinguish between the Black colonization of Biddulph and the later Irish immigration; colonization was a particular kind of settlement whose specificity allows us more clearly to characterize that later kind, which I shall call 'market settlement.' To settle a country by colonization meant originally (in 1622) 'to plant or establish a colony' (*Oxford English Dictionary*). That is, in its earlier sense, 'colony' meant precisely a collectivity planned elsewhere; only later, in the nineteenth century (and we can be more historically and theoretically precise about this shift), did 'to colonize,' shifting from the transitive to the intransitive mode, place its emphasis more generally on the process of settling, 'to form or establish a colony or settlement,' this latter sense moving towards what I want to signify by 'market settlement.' Colonization, as applied to African Americans in the first third of the nineteenth century, was certainly understood in the earlier sense. This was the central set of assumptions of the American Colonization Society. The colonization movement was inadequately conceived and 'not altogether sincere,' as W.E.B. DuBois said, since it kept the laws of 'the singular institution' (in a contemporary's phrase) '*unreproved* in their wickedness.' Whereas William Lloyd Garrison and the Abolitionist Movement sought the eradication of an evil, the Colonization Movement merely sought the solution to a problem, and its solution was the planned, voluntary transportation of large groups of Blacks to Africa or, since (as an anti-colonization convention put it in 1831) 'here we were born, and here we will die,' to Canada.[5]

The events of 1829 did not allow the Black population of Cincinnati time to debate the issues between abolition and colonization; the colonization apparatus was in place, hence the approach by the Cincinnati Colonization Society to Sir John Colborne. The Cincinnati Blacks moved as 'an organized Negro community,' a term usually defined against such utopian communities as Nashoba in western Tennessee. But I think that it is more historically accurate to recognize Wilberforce as a *colony* in the original sense: the administrative apparatus that conceived and arranged the settlement was the Colonization Movement; the Cincinnati group negotiated with the Canada Company and the province of Upper Canada, albeit through agents, *as a group* ('J.C. Brown & others,' the Land Records say); the eventual 800 acres was purchased *wholesale*, as it were, for the colony. These details, the patronage, those headstart provisions that the colonists did have, and their continuing and contentious dependence on fund-raising are primarily symptoms of their affiliation with the Colonization Movement. Clarence Karr speaks of what he calls 'hot-house' or assisted methods of settlement, in which 'the proprietor undertook to build roads and houses ... , to clear land and to establish complete towns in an attempt to force the opening [of a new territory].' The Wilberforce colonists, of course, never received any of that sort of assistance, but the founding assumptions of their colony are entirely consistent with it, deriving as they did from the dominant mercantilist ideology of colonization. The failure of Wilberforce should not then be seen as a moral failure but at least in part as the effect of the contemporary practices of colonization.[6]

By the mid-1840s (the Peases say after 1836) it was clear that Wilberforce 'no longer existed in an organized sense, although a few of the settlers stayed on.' The causes usually given for its failure, besides Cincinnati's quick reversal in 1830 of its policy towards Blacks, are 'a lack of good leadership and organization' and the Canada Company's refusal to sell more land to Blacks. This last hints that in the end the Black settlers in Wilberforce were, at least to some extent, driven out. As early as December 1830, Peter Robinson advised the provincial government (and the colonial secretary in London seems to have concurred) against allowing the Black colonists exclusively to settle a whole township – a project with obvious political implications and therefore dear to the heart of many of the colonists. While desiring to hold out 'the same encouragement ... to people of colour as to other settlers,' Robinson advised that a Black township might lead to 'a grumbling [he crossed out 'complaint'] of so great a number of persons from the United States as to alarm the present inhabitants, who appear to have a repugnance to their forming communities near them.' A month later, N.S. Price, secretary to the board of the Canada Company, was writing to the commissioners in Upper Canada about 'the doubtful nature of the question whether the Company's interests or those of the Province would be promoted by their [the Black settlers'] introduction' and that 'the Directors are by no means disposed to court the settlement of those People on their Land, at the risk of offending public feeling, or even prejudice, as the injury might be greater than any benefit to be derived.' Less than a year later, he wrote again to Thomas Mercer Jones, one of the commissioners, that 'the Board fully concur with you in opinion that great circumspection and caution are necessary on the ground of deference to public feeling in treating with the Black People for their settlement on the Company's Lands and if they should determine to prefer some other domicile it will not be a subject of regret to the Board.'

While the official position of the Colonial Office continued to be one of even-handed tolerance of any loyal settlers, by the 1840s the antipathy of their neighbours to the Blacks in Wilberforce occasionally took a violent form. The J.J. Talman Regional Collection holds a clipping from the 'Huron Gazette' of the *London* (Ontario) *Times*, which reports on 29

November 1848 'an outrage of very malicious character' in which the barns and produce of three Black settlers were burned in one night; while white suspects and their motives were identified, the three white justices of the peace could find 'no proof sufficient to insure committal.' William Porte's *Counting House Diary* records in August 1865: 'Turner's Barn with all contents burned down last night. An Act of Incendiary.'[7]

Practices of Settlement: Lucan

But the demise of Wilberforce, as a colony, was not caused only by the complicity of the Canada Company and the Colonial Office in vocal, even violent white settlers' racial prejudice, any more than by the simple departure of its members to warmer climes. One important condition, while more diffuse, was directly economic, anticipating the exigencies of the developing market in land that Irish settlers in Biddulph were themselves increasingly to face. The land that the Black settlers (assisted by Frederick Stover of the Quakers) purchased on 20 September 1830 included Lots 2, 3, 5, and 8 along the north side of the road down to Elginfield and Lots 2, 3, 5, and 11 on the south side (Goodspeed cites William Porte's remembering that the important Lots 6, north and south, were included in the original purchase, but this seems to contradict the evidence of the land records). Lots 2, north and south of the road (Figure 2.1), where it crosses the Little Ausable and turns southeast, are the westernmost holdings, and the adjacent Lots 3 are where the vandalism was to occur in 1848. The road angles down between Lots 4, held by Irish Protestants, to Lots 5, again Wilberforce lots, north (Brown, Dutton, and Stover) and south (Peter Butler). The sign of the economic disturbance, or cause, that I have mentioned is the Grand Trunk right-of-way. Whereas the Main Trunk Line of Railway Act of 1851 had declared that the Great Western Railroad, to run from Ancaster (and soon from the Niagara Suspension Bridge) through London to Windsor, was eventually to form the southwestern Ontario section of the interprovincial main line, that guarantee was withdrawn by May 1852. Soon the purchase of the near-defunct Toronto and Guelph Railway, and the Grand Trunk Prospectus of 12 April 1853, made it clear that the Grand Trunk's English bankers and contractors, in G.R. Stevens's words, 'were looking past the Canadas ... to a half-built city at the foot of Lake Michigan which held the traffic of a half-continent in fee': 'Guelph lay almost in the

Figure 2.1 (opposite)
Wilberforce, Lucan, and land speculation (1850–70) on the Roman Line

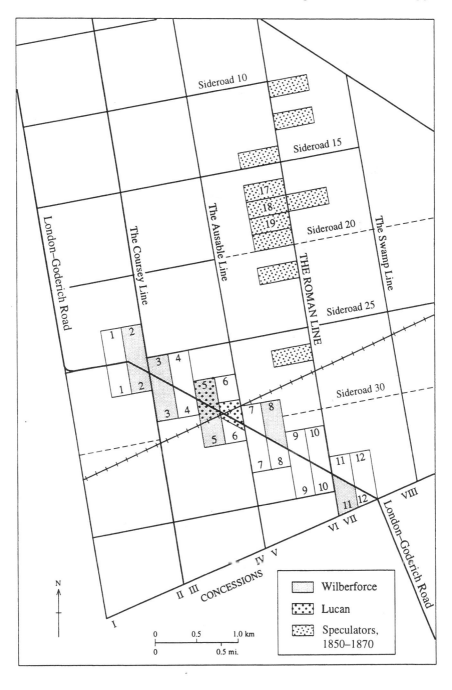

direct line between Toronto and Sarnia and the Michigan boundary was fifty-four miles closer to Toronto at Sarnia than at Windsor.'

And so the Grand Trunk prepared to extend its line, independently of the Great Western, to Sarnia. I return to the history of the railways in the next chapter, but I want here simply to note that Alexander Galt and others in England knew of these new plans by 1852, that the Wilberforce colony was on the direct line between Toronto and Sarnia, and that on 31 August 1853 Donald McDonald 'of the City of Toronto Gentleman' bought Lot 6, on the north side of the Goderich–London Road (which he sold to the Grand Trunk on 16 September 1859), and his cousin, John McDonald of Goderich, the original surveyor of Biddulph Township, on 10 February 1854 bought Lot 29, Concession V, which he in turn sold to the Grand Trunk on 6 July 1860. The contract for the Toronto–Stratford section was officially announced at the Grand Trunk shareholders' meeting in 1854, and the section through Biddulph was surveyed in 1856–7 and opened for traffic on 21 November 1859. The railway crosses the London–Goderich Road just before the Ausable Line (Concession III/IV) in the western half of south Lot 6; by then, Lots 6, north and south, were held by John McDonald. The 1861 Agricultural Census of Biddulph does not mention Lots 6 but does refer to Lot 8, north of the road, and two lots east of the road–railway junction, which John McDonald had bought from Nathaniel Paul of the Wilberforce colony in March 1854. McDonald had not improved the lot in the six years – it is described as 120 acres: 25 under cultivation as pasture, no crops; 95 acres wooded or wild, no tools or implements; and nothing else – and he sold it four years later. This is one face of land speculation, as we see below. As Gentilcore and Donkin wryly comment, 'the whole question of the role of the survey in land speculation remains to be investigated'; 'speculation,' I am suggesting, is perhaps not the precise word here.[8]

As one historian writes: 'No railroad directorate in the period under review [1850–81] possessed the experience, talent or time to cope with the awesome responsibilities of management,' and thus (referring to the Great Western and Northern railways) 'power without accountability rested with the chief engineer working with or controlled by the contractor.' Casimir Gzowski's contract to build the Guelph–Sarnia line stipulates that 'the Contractors shall have the location of the line and may select and determine the course in which the Railway shall be made.' Approaching from the east, the Grand Trunk roadbed rises 32$\frac{1}{2}$ feet from Fish Creek, just over the boundary in Perth County, crossing the Roman

Line ten lots to the south of the Donnelly farm, as it begins its gentle descent across the London–Goderich Road and down along the curve of the Little Ausable into McGillivray Township. There are three shallow cuts as it crosses the Biddulph moraines, and I can find no geographical reason why it should cross the road at one place or another;* indeed, according to the manuscript 'description of the lands intended to be passed over' by the railway in the J.J. Talman Regional Collection, John McDonald also owned Lot 24 on Concession V in neighbouring McGillivray Township, and in order to cross that lot (and, of course, others) the railway appears to have needed to make a slight turn to the north. The contractor's decision to select and determine this particular turn remains mysterious, as does the line to Sarnia as a whole. As late as 1859, in fact, the map appended to the managing director's report to Grand Trunk shareholders shows the line running through 'Ireland' (Clandeboye) not 'Marystown,' which was McDonald's proposed name for Lucan. But my main point is that it is precisely at this place, in *space* (Lot 6) and *time* (1850–60), that the village of Lucan came into existence, replacing Wilberforce, at the intersection of railway and highway. A land speculator would perceive such an intersection as a small but perhaps profitable instance of what I discuss in the next chapter as a 'competitive point'; here we can see it as what Morton called a 'commercial agricultural, or homestead, site,' where suddenly place is determined anew by 'fertility, distance from the railway, and rail freight rates.' Goodspeed records: 'On the plans of the railway company becoming known, Sheriff McDonald and Donald McDonald, of Toronto, purchased Lots 6, north and south, and planned the village in 1854, and in February, 1855, sold many of the lots by auction [i.e., subdivided Lots 6].'

The 'Old Book' of the Abstract Index to Deeds in Lucan ('Abstracts before 1866'), preserved in the Archives of Ontario, records clearly the McDonalds' primitive accumulation of Lucan real estate, while the next volume ('Abstracts 1831–1866') records the subdivision and distribution. The speculative pressure on the other lands along the road, not only on Lot 5, next door, but all along the road down through Biddulph,

---

* 'No country in which most of the surface has a layer of soil over it deserves the name of rough. It needs but a little study and care to get several lines of reasonable cost through it. The art of location consists merely in making a judicious choice – not in getting *a* line, which is always easy in such regions.' A.M. Wellington, *The Economic Theory of the Location of Railways*, 6th ed. (New York: John Wiley and Sons, 1887), 840. The line through Biddulph seems to be an especially judicious choice.

became intense. The Land Registry Abstracts show that by February 1865 the Brown/Dutton/Stover Lot 5, north of the road, was in the hands of Henry M. Atkinson, one of the early Irish Protestant settlers. The railway station adjoined not Lot 5, south, the next lot west of the intersection with the road and Wilberforce property, but Lot 4, south, owned by Patrick McIlhargy. Parts of Lot 5, south, with the railway line running through it, were sold by Peter Butler and others of the colony in 1858–60, both to the Grand Trunk and its builder, Casimir Gzowski, and to the township (for subdivision as town lots), and the rest was sold over the next five years in one-sixth- or one-eighth-lot parcels, to William Frank, Patrick Devinney, William Madill, and so on. William Porte's 'Counting House Diary for 1865' records one such sale: 'Saturday 4 March 1865. Deed from D.M. Harris [a Wilberforce colonist] to B[ernard] Stanley E 1/2 Lot 3 NLR. 32 Acres'; three months later Porte recorded: 'Deed from William Mayo et ux to B. Stanley of 6 1/8 Acres of part of Lot 5 SLR.'

What sorts of bargains were struck is not significant: the historical process that took place in Biddulph in 1856–65 was what Marx called, in his remarks on Wakefield and elsewhere in *Capital*, 'primitive accumulation,' an equivalent, though on a much smaller scale, to the Scottish Highland clearances and English enclosure (or, indeed, the purchase of the land from Canada's Native peoples), as capital sweeps away a community to make way for whom and what is to come. *What* is to come is obvious: a railway, a village, but equally important, a speculative market in land, and we encounter this again on the Roman Line. *Who* is to come is sufficiently indicated by the change of owners' names, from 'Brown,' 'Dutton,' 'Butler,' 'Paul,' and 'Harris,' to 'McDonald,' 'Stanley,' 'Atkinson,' 'Hodgins,' and 'Ryan.' Nathaniel Paul's purchase, on 25 July 1831, of Lot 10, south of the road, between the Roman Line and Elginfield ('Ryan's Corners'), was cancelled in November 1841; Elginfield, of course, is where the Biddulph section of the road joins the London Proof Line road. The decennial census returns for Biddulph also imply something of what was happening, as Black families disappeared (though some individuals remained). The 1851 Census records thirty-nine persons, individuals and seven families, U.S. born and of 'African origin': Butlers, Taylors, Turners, Harrises, and Bells, aged from one year to seventy-three. In 1861, there were fifty-three persons of African origin, and the same families. In 1871, there were seventy-two individuals of African origin, but the Taylors and Harrises had left. By 1881, there were ten Butlers, five Turners, and ten Washingtons, with other individuals and couples. These records and the changes in land ownership indicate the disappearance of Wilberforce as a village, of course, but especially as a colony. The land in Biddulph had become by the 1850s a speculative commodity, as the colonization roads became increasingly channels for the transportation of produce, and then as they in turn were replaced by the railway; greater land speculation was the final solvent of Wilberforce.[9]

Colonization and Ideological Change

This particular historical process in Biddulph in the 1830s was overdetermined by the change that I have mentioned in the ideology of colonization. 'Throughout the entire history of Upper Canada,' Lillian Gates writes, 'the question of what was the best policy to adopt for the Crown lands was debated over and over again with inconclusive results.' Until 1826, the policy had been to grant free land to particular supplicants. These might be discharged veterans of the wars with the Americans, planted to strengthen the physical and political defences of the Rideau area against the Americans, or loyal settlers who had suffered in the wars. The free grant policy also enriched Colonel Thomas Talbot, whose 'palatinate' eventually extended 130 miles along the north shore of Lake Erie, from Long Point to the Detroit River, and north through London Township to the boundary of what was to become Biddulph. The abuses latent in the practice of gratuitous land grants realized themselves in Upper Canada in local struggles over speculation and undeveloped land, political favouritism, and religious discrimination, struggles that produced the campaign for 'reform' and 'responsible government' (I return to the interaction of these imperial tests of local Upper Canadian politics in a later chapter).

The assumptions that evolved in Britain after 1826 continued to shape colonization as a matter of concern mainly for the imperial centre, and hence still in mercantilist terms. While assistance might also be obtained from home parish funds, 'the surplus unemployed of the British Isles were to be transferred, under Government supervision and at Government expense, to Canada, with the double purpose of transforming its waste lands and providing a home for British unemployed.' The oracle of this transitional emigration policy from 1826 to 1831 was Robert John Wilmot Horton, undersecretary in the Colonial Office, who attempted without success to carry through Parliament his plan for 'the carrying out, rationing, and settling of paupers at the expense of the parish or local bodies, individual or collective, to which they were an encumbrance, and the proposal for raising the money by an annuity charged upon the rates.' Wilmot Horton's plan, paternalist and arbitrary, taking again little account of the needs and wishes of resident Canadian settlers, was the last flowering of the mercantilist ideology of settlement. Like the land grants policy, it still conceived colonization to mean, in 1830, the transplanting of a dependent group of people to a colony in the interests of the imperial power. While I have not traced in the records of the Colonial Office or the Canada Company the details of this debate, it seems no accident that precisely at this transitional juncture the Wilberforce colony was introduced into Biddulph and, within the decade, dispersed, to be followed by a wholly different form of capitalist colonization, the practical manifestation of a wholly different ideology of colonization. The British government, ceasing after the Horton experiments to oversee settlement plans for British North America, left those colonies as 'a free field for voluntary, unassisted emigrants.' Gates says, even more forcefully, 'What did settle the country – apart from the assisted settlement – was squatting,' the most radically free enterprise of all.

Throughout the 1830s and 1840s in Britain what was known as the Colonial Reform Movement, developed by Edward Gibbon Wakefield out of Adam Smith's general critique of mercantilism, succeeded in putting Benthamite ideals into practice in British colonial relations. In his critique of Wakefield in volume one of *Capital*, Marx added that Wakefield's theory of systematic colonization furthermore 'aims at manufacturing wage-labourers in the colonies.' Thus a first principle, says Leo Johnson, 'was to attract and create a labouring class in Upper Canada,' or more important, a capitalist labour market. The vogue for the ideas of the Wakefield school around 1840 thus seems to provide the widest context for the contrast between the colonization of Wilberforce and the later Irish immigration to Biddulph. Its most immediate effect in the early 1830s was to criticize the dependence and paternalism implicit in mercantilist colonial relations, and it achieved a notable triumph in the Durham Report. Gilbert Paterson writes of the influence of Colonial Reform in Upper Canada, 'Through his influence with Lord Howick, Under Secretary for the Colonies, Wakefield managed to secure the adoption of his scheme, thus opening out a new policy respecting Crown Lands. In Upper Canada the new regulations were grafted on the old. In March of 1831 Goderich [the Colonial Secretary] informed Colborne that some of the heads of Instructions by which the Commissioner of Crown Lands was governed were open to serious objection,' and, as we see below, the private Canada Company's policies towards its own lands were clearly affected by this change of government policy. 'Systematic colonization' focused on the sale of new land at a 'sufficient price,' which would regulate both the flow of land coming into use in a colony and generate revenues available to assist immigration. Marx saw this policy as 'a euphemistic circumlocution for the ransom which the worker must pay to the capitalist in return for permission to retire from the wage-labour market to the land,' Wakefield's proposals setting 'new barriers to the ownership of land' in the interest of the capitalist labour market. 'The core of Wakefield's theory,' explained one historian, 'is that poor conditions in the colonies result from scarcity of labour, and that scarcity of labour results from the unrestricted alienation of land. Land, therefore, should be distributed in such a way as to prevent labourers from turning into land-owners too soon, and to maintain a proper proportion between labourers and capitalists in the colony. The best method of achieving this purpose was by selling land at a "sufficient price" – that is, a price sufficient to prevent labourers from turning into land-owners before other labourers arrived.' I return to these points below, but here I want simply to examine the proposals on their own terms. The ideological shift involved is from settling a colony *on* the land to regulating the availability of new land so as to attract useful and energetic settlers. In theory at least, Gates claims, a land *sales* policy was in force in Upper Canada after 1826. It encouraged what the Richards Report to the Colonial Office in 1831 had called 'a retail occupation of the wilderness,' lot by lot. As the *Spectator*, the organ of colonial reform, put it, systematic colonization worked 'not by pushing *e*migration from England, but by pulling *im*migration to the colonies.'

Colonial Reformers thus relied on the efficacy of the invisible hand of a constructed market in land, a self-regulating mechanism for colonization. As Winch writes, quoting Wakefield, 'The sufficient price now became the regulator of the supply and demand for labour; the whole system was to be kept in a kind of moving equilibrium. According to the extent of the land sold, would be the increase of demand for labour wherewith to cultivate new land, and according to the extent of land sold, would be the amount of the fund for procuring fresh labour.' Wakefield himself in 1849 would emphasize that he defined colonization only as 'the process by which the colony is peopled and settled,' a generalization that eliminates the earlier emphasis on the dependent group in favour of a free-market mechanism. This change in the guiding assumptions of British colonial policy seems to me best to explain the indecision of this period in the Canada Company's affairs, as well as distinguishing the Irish settlement of the Roman Line from that of the Wilberforce colony.[10]

However indecisive the Canada Company's directors may have been in their early years about its future, by 1842 there was a decisive change of policy, clearly a response to the influence of the Colonial Reformers, which affected the pattern of settlement in Biddulph and throughout the Huron Tract. Earlier, during the aftermath of the change in government land policy in 1826, and during Wilmot Horton's brief campaign to shovel out British paupers to the colonies, the Canada Company had imposed a policy for land purchase in Upper Canada of 20 per cent down payment and 20 per cent payable for each of four years, with the contract then renewable at 6 per cent interest. The government of Upper Canada in those years had itself adopted (and John Galt had recommended to the Company) a different policy, of 10 years' credit at 6 per cent interest. As Clarence Karr points out, this conflicting government policy of sales on easier terms severely restricted the Company's land sales for the next fifteen years: 'For that period the Huron Tract ... would attract only those people who possessed considerable means. Those with less cash were able to purchase land from the government at almost twice the credit period.'

Frederick Widder criticized the purchase terms for the Company's lands, initially introducing a slight reduction of prices when he was appointed commissioner for the Company in 1839. But in 1842 he drastically revised the Company's credit terms. Because he felt that the attraction of the chain of relatives and friends already settled was weakening, he introduced a new leasehold plan. The Company 'would take a note at six percent interest for the down payment and give a settler either five or ten years to raise the total price of his land. As long as the settler each year paid the six percent interest charges he was left alone. What this amounted to was that for a five or ten year period a settler was really renting his land at six percent of the cost price.' Gates summarized the change: 'The settler could lease the land for ten years at a rent equal to the interest on the value of the land, with the option of purchasing at any time during the lease at a fixed advance upon the price at the time of leasing.' This leasing system geared to the price of land, Karr says, 'permitted thousands of almost penniless, often illiterate pioneers to locate on the Company's lots.' As the Ausable Valley conservancy history describes it, 'Poor immigrants could lease land for ten years, with the option of converting the lease to a sale at any time by paying the full price of the lot. In this way, the company's continuing title to the land would be incontestable, and the settlement would be speeded up because of the attractiveness of the system to men without much capital.' By 1840, according to Commissioner Mercer Jones, Biddulph was the fourth most populous township in Huron County, and Karr's figures show that by 1844, though less of its land was as yet *under cultivation* than at either end of the Huron Road to the north, Biddulph Township had the second highest percentage of acres *sold* in the Huron Tract. While the differential between these two statistics is perhaps again one face of speculation, the statistics themselves can be quite precisely situated historically.[11]

Settlement of the Huron Tract

Clearly the new leasing system served the Canada Company's immediate purpose of settling the Huron Tract and could be alleged to be a purely pragmatic decision. But historically, in the context both of the development of colonial policy and of the political economy of Upper Canada, the new system was determined by the Colonial Reform/Wakefieldian theory/Benthamite free-enterprise movement of those years. Moreover (and more empirically), the change in land policy, as an effect of this change, coincided with the new Irish Roman Catholic settlement of eastern Biddulph Township, the Roman Line, and beyond. We have looked at the relation of this shift to the Irish Protestant (and speculators') displacement of Wilberforce from the London–Goderich Road and the replacement of a colony by Lucan, and now I want to relate the change to the constituent role of this ideological shift in the founding of that new kind of community, central to this study – that group of Tipperary Catholic settlers along and clustered near Biddulph Concession VI/VII, the Roman Line. Bruce Elliott's detailed analysis of the migration of Tipperary Protestants into Biddulph Township begins in 1818 with Richard Talbot, assisted by the British government, leading a group of Irish settlers to London Township, 'then on the northern fringes of civilization.' The result of this migration was two 'group settlements' (i.e., 'colonies'), the first located in the south of the township and the second five miles away, in the northwest corner near the boundary of the Huron Tract. Elliott's mastery of the histories of the families making up these groups allows him convincingly to demonstrate the process of chain migration, as these settlements, or 'ethnic clusters,' developed. Thus the Tipperary Protestant settlement spreading across the Huron Tract boundary and up the first three concession lines in western Biddulph can indeed be seen simply as 'an extension northward of the quite solid Tipperary cluster in the northwestern corner of London Township.'

'The acquisition of land, however,' as Leo Johnson points out, 'was not merely a matter of individual preference and initiative.' To trace the migratory chain through its successive terminal clusters understates equally important considerations: the facts of the Upper Canadian wilderness and its entries, and of the land survey and the arrangements for the appropriation of land; that is, the evolving 'market conditions.' The 'Memoranda and Suggestions in Regard to the Huron Tract' that the directors of the Canada Company sent to John Galt in 1827 had presumed easy access into the border townships of Biddulph from Zorra, Nissouri, and London Townships on the south, and indeed settlers extended their holdings across the township boundary into Biddulph as early as 1832, and the first Tipperary settlers in Biddulph – the Coursey family – bought their lots a year later. That is perhaps still a 'chain,' but other things were also there: Biddulph was already established as *Biddulph*; the land had been surveyed, and the Second Concession Line was to become known as the 'Coursey Line.' As well, the earliest settlers occupied the lands along the roads built by the Canada Company (and the Wilberforce colonists), for chain migration (and 'gravitation migration' towards areas with people of similar origin) took place (as Elliott would readily admit) within the context of the Company's slow development of the whole Huron Tract. Thus James Hodgins, an early immigrant, was both a Tipperary Protestant and, from 1835, the Canada Company's Biddulph agent, increasingly serving not only his connections in Ireland but a land market in the tract, in which roads, for example, were crucial.

Whereas the Wilberforce colony was a community originating in the trials created by racial persecution and it disappeared as a community partly because of the new market in land, the Irish Protestant community in western Biddulph to some extent, and certainly the Irish Catholic community on the Roman Line, having suffered different trials, migrated individually or as families, as participants in the very land market whose structuration had dissolved Wilberforce. The emphasis on prior acquaintance or family connection, or chain, ignores changes in economic doctrine but also ignores the situation encountered in Biddulph – the road, the proposed sideroads, variations in soil and drainage, that is, differential lands in an arbitrary appropriative structure, i.e., the shape of its market.

The Huron Road across the top of the tract was completed in December 1832, and in 1840 a military map records it as among roads 'which tho' often far from good may be considered as militarily passable at all seasons,' in contrast to, for example, the Port Franks Road (the present Highway 83) connecting it with Fullarton, which in 1840 was 'generally but not at all seasons passable by guns' nor, I assume, by wagons or coaches. Scott's *The Settlement of Huron County* records that by 1837 there were only 385 persons settled in the whole Huron Tract, but a year later there were 1,168, and in 1842 the population of Huron County was 7,190 (or, as Thomas Mercer Jones, the Canada Company's commissioner, estimated, 5,905). Most settlers in the early years who were going as far west in Upper Canada as Huron County headed directly for Goderich: 'They would take the old Dundas road through to Guelph. Here they would check their holdings at the Canada Company offices and proceed along the Huron Road.'

'The most orderly process of settlement,' Scott writes, 'followed the roads,' and so in the late 1820s and early 1830s the Huron Tract was in the main being settled at each end of the Huron Road: from the east, North and South Easthope Townships, Downie, and Ellice (there is a cairn commemorating Andrew and Eva Seebach, the first settlers in Ellice, 1829), and then east from Goderich and south along the lake to Bayfield, and as the road south from Clinton opened in 1832, down into Stanley Township (1833), Tuckersmith (1833), and the villages of Exeter (1831) and Centralia (1832). W.H. Smith has traced the gradual growth of population and the increasing production of wheat, oats, potatoes, and maple sugar along the road up to 1850. And so, whereas the general movement of the Irish into Biddulph, as Elliott notes, was northward from London along the London–Goderich Road (the route that James Donnelly took in 1845), that migration encountered these other settlers moving down along the same road: indeed, mixed settlement characterized the London–Goderich Road on the western border of Biddulph's First Concession. As the road opened across Biddulph itself, from about 1836 on, the lots remaining on the first four, westernmost concessions filled up, primarily as the Protestant Irish settlers continued to move north from London Township, the relations of kinship and ethnic group inevitably underlain by the pattern of the survey and the roads. Thus the roads at this time were primarily for access, but by 1839 there was a mail route, '1 time' a week, along both the Huron and London–Goderich roads, and there were 'post towns' at Stratford, McKillop, and Goderich, and at Clandeboye ('Ireland') on the boundary with Biddulph (as well as, according to the 1840 military map, 'T. Hodgins' and one other inn).

Stanleys, Hodginses, Atkinsons, and others were on Biddulph's first four lines by 1836, as far up as lots 12 and 13. By 1842 the western half was filled and the Catholics were arriving on Concessions VI, VII, and VIII, as we see the effects of the change in the Canada Company's sales policy. Whereas the vast majority (twelve out of fifteen) of the early contracts for lots on Concession V, the easternmost Protestant concession at this time, were in the form of sales, all but one of those for lots settled in the 1840s on the next concession east, Concession VI on the west side of the Roman Line, were in the form of the new leases. Like the earlier concessions, those fronting the Roman Line were settled from the south, up from the lots along the London–Goderich Road. On Concession VI, initial leases (some of which were not renewed) were issued in 1842 up to Lot 25 and then, in 1843, up to lot 12, and on Concession VII up to Lot 14. The shift in the Canada Company's land policy is marked on the Line by the different contracts signed for Lots 19 and 17 on Concession V, immediately to the south and north of what was to become the Donnellys' lot (Figure 2.1). On 4 August 1843, John Quigley bought Lot 19, the southern lot, with payments to be made over twelve years of £2, £3, £4, £6.5, £8, £9, £10.5, £11, £12, £13.10, £14.10, and £16.10. A little over a year later, Thomas Broderick leased Lot 17, to the north, for ten years at an annual rent of £3 7/6, with the right to buy at any time for £68.15.

It is difficult to infer the individual considerations (beyond the influence of the 'chain') that determined this scramble. I would presume that they were primarily *use*-values for these Irish Catholic farmers in the early 1840s: that is, the perceived quality of the soil on a lot, or its proximity to the London–Goderich Road or to a planned sideroad (every five lots). Lot 18 on Concession VI, the Donnellys', is an example of what W.L. Morton termed a 'squatter site, ... a function of natural advantages for subsistence agriculture.' The land on Lot 18 seems to have been highly valued even in its early, relatively unimproved years, and the Tax Assessment Roll for 1862 shows that both the north half (which had by then been for fifteen years, one way or another, the Donnellys' land) and the south half had received the highest assessments ($265 each) on Concession VI north of the Lucan sideroad. Across the line, Lots 17 and 18 similarly had the highest evaluations on Concession VII. I presume, again, that these judgments reflect the assessor's awareness, however arrived at, of the narrow strip of 'Class 1' soil, which, as I mentioned in the last chapter, crosses the Line at that place, also presumably a value in the scramble twenty years earlier. Several of the leases of the early 1840s, as I have said, were soon abandoned, for whatever reasons, but in 1862, twenty of twenty-four lots on Concession VI and fifteen of twenty-three on VII were still occupied by the families of their original settlers, and in 1878 fifteen lots on the Line were still held by the families of settlers, who had farmed (*used*) the land for three decades. Others moved elsewhere on or near the Line, or had simply moved on, to Michigan or to western Canada. This then – the acquisition and exploitation of use-values on the land (whose extreme instance is the squatter) – is one (perhaps chronologically prior) aspect of the process of the market settlement of the Roman Line.[12]

Speculation on the Roman Line

One P. Fogarty had taken a lease on Lot 18, Concession VI, in late 1843, thus indicating some interest in the land, but his interest had lapsed, and in 1846 the Canada Company sold the lot to John Grace. Grace paid £11.5 down and £9 a year for the next five years for Lot 18. By 1865, when the Company transferred to Grace the deed to the lot, the Donnellys were squatting there. In December of that year Grace sold the southern half ('50 acres more or less') to Michael Maher, and eleven months later he sold the northern fifty acres (more or less) to James Donnelly, who had been squatting and improving the land for nearly a decade. Grace never himself resided on or improved Lot 18; in 1842 he had leased and settled on Lot 31, further down the Roman Line, taking the deed in 1854 (Figure 2.1). Lot 31 had certain advantages ('externalities' in the economics of land) that Lot 18 did not: to the north it adjoined Sideroad 30 (eventually the Lucan Sideroad), on the south it bordered the lots on the London–Goderich Road, and it faced on the west another roadfront lot, one of the Wilberforce lots, into which Lucan would eventually expand. By 1862 Grace had sold the northern half of Lot 31, but the southern half, where he lived, was now assessed at $30 more than even the Donnellys' valuable half lot to the north.

John Grace had settled in Biddulph, and on the Roman Line, but he clearly had a keen eye for exchange-value in land; in his handling of Lot 18, the Donnellys', he was in a small way a speculator in those values. Though not quite rough and ready, the notion of land speculation that I am positing here is less sophisticated, in several senses, than certain other understandings of the term, resting not at all on moral gradations of interest and opportunity in land matters but on evidence of a preoccupation with exchange-value. As Michael Doucet puts it: 'The notion of speculation revolves around holding land because of its potential increase in value rather than because of its productivity. Speculators, then, are interested in land because of its exchange value rather than because of its use value.' I consider this distinction (original neither to myself nor Doucet) more useful than that made by Randy Widdis between 'inherent value' (the speculators' view of land) and 'without value' (the 'serious farmer's' view of land) or his distinction between 'classical speculators' and 'land bankers' and Donald H. Akenson's suggestion that collectively speculators acted simply as 'a mechanism for passing land on to new owners.' For my purposes it suffices that John Grace *used* Lot 31; he did *not* use Lot 18 in that sense and therefore was for a brief time a speculator.[13]

I am here interested in Grace himself only as a symptom of the early, determining presence on the Roman Line of a more widespread land speculation, a presence that had of course even earlier foreclosed the possibility of Wilberforce's continuing as a community. Historians of the frontier point out that in those conditions land speculation provided the only opportunity for the sort of capital accumulation that brought social status and political power, a point not lost on the lawyers, merchants, and politicians, for example, in the village of London, Ontario. Doucet remarks that 'control over the timing of development on much of the North American frontier lay not in the hands of the hardy agriculturalists of [Frederick Jackson] Turnerian myth, but with the urban commercial and industrial elite.' Unlike John Grace, certain other speculators on the Roman Line from the 1840s on never had any interest in the opportunity of residing there. In 1859, J.B. Strathy of London leased Lot 20 on Concession VI, buying it in 1867, the same year that J. Meredith bought Lot 17. In 1860, Crowell Willson, president of the Agricultural Mutual Assurance Association of Canada and, after Confederation, M.P. for East Middlesex, purchased Lot 19, and W.R. Meredith, a London lawyer (who was to be counsel for the defence in the Donnelly murder trial), became interested in 1873 by buying half of Lot 9, near the township's northern boundary.

But by far the most interested and active land speculator on the Roman Line in the 1850s and 1860s, buying lots and offering mortgages, was George Jervis Goodhue. By the end of the 1850s, Goodhue owned Lots 18, 13, and 11 on Concession VII and half of lot 12 along the northern boundary, and in the 1860s he bought Lots 27, 22, and 15 on the western side of the road, on Concession VI. 'A representative of the shrewd speculating type,' as Fred Landon put it, Goodhue was a London merchant, postmaster from 1830, and first village president, who was appointed district magistrate and then a member of the Legislative Council of Upper Canada in the 1840s. He had invested and lost money in Ontario railways in the 1840s but then concentrated on land speculation and mortgages. 'The care of his estate,' the *Dictionary of Canadian Biography* records, 'became the occupation of his life'; it notes as well that the tales of the harshness of his business activities have not yet died in western Ontario folklore; he 'did so well at usury,' in Orlo Miller's words, that when he died in 1870 he was a millionaire and the richest man in London, 'good for any amount,' as the R.G. Dun & Co credit assessor said in 1858.

While he invested throughout western Ontario, Goodhue concentrated most heavily on London, Middlesex, and the Huron Tract. The *Land Record Index* shows that Goodhue had an interest in twenty-six lots in Biddulph during the 1850s and 1860s, at one time or another holding the deeds to twenty-one of the twenty-six. His mortgage business was very profitable. The *Alphabetical Index to Deeds* records his name as 'grantor' of a mortgage eighty-two times. On 6 October 1859, Thomas Tierney mortgaged Lot 31 on Concession VII to Goodhue for $300 at 24 per cent per annum and while some might think this rate usurious (though legal controls on usury were abolished in Upper Canada in 1858), Frederick H. Armstrong claims that 'the rates he charged would appear to have been reasonably standard for the time and region': 'Sometimes these were very high, at others quite low. The few surviving mortgages from the 1840s show a rate of 6% which remained standard until 1853. In 1854–55 and early 1856 this rate increased to 12% and then dropped to 6% late in 1856 and in 1857. By 1858 there was a spectacular leap to first 18% and then 24% during November, the latter figure remaining in force till the autumn of 1859 when 18% again appears. In the period 1861–64, 12% again was standard. There are few mortgages from the late 1860s but there is one for 16% dated 1866 and another for 6% in 1869.'[14]

Gagan's figures for Toronto Gore Township support Armstrong's contention that these rates were fairly standard for the place and time (especially around the depression of 1857), and this substantiates as well the emphasis that I want to make. Below I comment briefly on a few of Goodhue's specific activities, but I want to insist first that, like John Grace, his significance is symptomatic rather than personal; certainly I consider his speculative activities more complex than to say, as Akenson says of another speculator: 'He did well and thereby new aspirants to farming in the township were enabled to better themselves.' I would rather see his activities as, again, an index to the influence of land speculation at the formation of the community along the Roman Line (and, of course, elsewhere in Biddulph and at other times) and, to the degree that his rates are standard, as an index to moments of crisis on one level of that settler community. Or, to make the point more concretely, we might again contrast what we (and the Colonial Office) saw as the dependence of the Wilberforce colony – dependent on donations from American Quakers, which dependence disappears forever along with Wilberforce – with the new settlements, such as Lucan and the Roman Line, which emerge in Biddulph. As we have seen, Wilberforce was destroyed, at least in part, by the new speculative conditions of Bidduph's land market, and these same conditions structure from the very start the Roman Line as a market settlement. That is, the Roman Line and eastern Biddulph were not somehow magically *in*dependent; rather they were dependent in a new way, through mortgages, on the money market in London, as (in Doucet's phrase) that village-town-urban elite takes control over the timing and development on much of its Huron County frontier. The sheer scale of Goodhue's land investments, rather than merely making him, as Widdis would have it, a land speculator or not, or a 'classical speculator' rather than a 'land banker,' makes him a very concrete instance of the influence of speculative capital on the inception of the Roman Catholic community in Biddulph Township. Goodhue's is an example of what Marx referred to as 'the mobile wealth piled up through usury – especially that practised against landed property – and through mercantile profits.' Describing the 'prehistory of the bourgeois economy' in the *Grundrisse*, Marx writes, 'Usury, trade, urbanization and the treasury rising with it play the main roles' in the 'formation of money-wealth' (another edition translates 'treasury' as 'government finance').

James Donnelly (constrained by other circumstances that I examine below) did mortgage his land, beginning in 1859 when he was in Kingston, with a Sidney B. Tripp, and the northern half of Lot 18, Concession VI, was mortgaged continuously until after the murders, with the surviving sons discharging the last mortgage in 1893. Donnelly took mortgages with Tripp, James Burgess, the Ontario Savings and Loan Society, and twice with a Constantia Mills. There is no record of either the Donnellys or their closest friends, the Keefes, ever having any financial dealing with

George Jervis Goodhue, whose speculative presence, as we have seen, was so prominent on the Roman Line in the 1850s and 1860s (Goodhue's rates in 1859, as we have seen, were 24 and 18 per cent). We explore the significances of the Donnelly relations with mortgage capital in more detail below, for it is in these troubled waters that the Tipperary immigrants immediately on arrival needed to learn to swim. David Gagan, having studied closely mortgaging practices in Toronto Gore Township in these years, indicates in general the potential effects of the speculative development of land: 'Mortgage debt may have been a prime cause of dislocation in the best of times and, for the imprudent borrower, an invitation to disaster in periods of rapid economic change.'[15]

Gender and Property on the Roman Line

Thus I ask, in chapter 5, what the particular pressures of market settlement might have been in the case of Johanna Donnelly, an immigrant farmer's wife, nine years in Upper Canada in 1857, left to raise seven sons and a daughter on a fifty-acre farm, when her husband was sentenced to seven years in the Kingston prison. For the settlement of the Roman Line, as of all of Upper Canada, was also gendered from the start. As Joy Parr points out, emigration itself is a gendered process, 'beginning for men with a solitary experiment in distant lands, for women with a long interlude between two worlds waiting for word that it is safe to follow': 'For men the journey has seemed a response to international differentials in the labour market, for women a way to begin or to consolidate a married life. Emigration usually is seen to cast men in active and women in adaptive roles, men being part of a structured system, women living out the consequences of a subjective choice.'

After the emigrant's arrival in Upper Canada, land holding, indeed its possibility, was legally determined by sex in several ways. The records of the mortgages that James Donnelly and Michael Maher took out in 1859 on their separate fifty-acre holdings on Lot 18 list the grantors as 'James Donnelly *et uxor*' and 'Michael Maher *et uxor*,' acknowledging the wives' 'dower right.' Under English common law the husband could not mortgage the land without his wife barring her dower right to one-third of it on his death: 'Anyone who wanted to purchase property from a married man did so subject to the wife's inchoate right to dower, which would attach to the land at the husband's death ... Effectively, the wife's dower right meant that a husband had to have his wife's consent to sell, mortgage or give away his property.'

The gendered restrictions of property law were pervasive, and less favourable to women than even the dower right suggests. Catherine Cavanaugh has suggested that women's interest in family property took two forms: *sameness*, that is, equal rights with their husbands to the property that they had helped acquire (as in the necessity for Johanna's consent to James Donnelly's mortgage arrangements), and *difference*, that is, protection in the event of marital breakdown (as in a husband's death or desertion, or James Donnelly's imprisonment). But province by province, Canada had acquired the English common law doctrine of couverture, or marital unity, and the first act of the legislature of Upper Canada provided that English law, as it stood on 15 October 1792, should govern all matters of property. In common law (and in Blackstone's words), 'By marriage, the husband and wife are one person in law; that is, the very being or legal existence of the woman is suspended during the marriage, or at least is incorporated and consolidated into that of the husband.'

What Dicey calls this 'barbarism of the common law' determined not only that a wife could own no property separately from her husband nor receive her own income but that she had no 'contractual capacity'; she could not bind herself by contract. In England the Court of Chancery had from the sixteenth century on 'waged constant war' against these 'exhorbitant common-law rights' of husbands and by the early nineteenth century had established in equity for married women nearly all the rights over property held by a man or a single woman. But even after the right of a married woman to her own property was established in equity, she was prevented while married by a provision called 'restraint in anticipation' from selling her separate property or charging it with her debts, as, for instance, by taking out a mortgage on it. And this restraint was overdetermined by class: even the reforms in equity did little to assist the woman who was poor. While a rich wife, marrying perhaps with her own property, enjoyed the protection of equity, the poor wife simply bore the barbarism of the common law. In Canada, moreover, the English ameliorations through equity law since the sixteenth century were all but ignored by the courts, and the reforms of married women's property law needed to be undertaken anew in the legislatures.

At least in her dower right, a woman's sameness to her husband was ensured by English common law in Canada, and so the first wave of legislative reform, recovering the rights in equity that Canadian courts had discounted, began with legislation directed towards families in crisis, resulting from marital breakdown. In English common law, if a wife were deserted by her husband, in the narrow sense of his having 'abjured the realm, or [being] banished,' the wife took on the property rights of a single woman. But in Canada, as Constance Backhouse observes, 'the lure of vast expanses of unsettled land caused many men to desert their families,' and so legislators moved to broaden the wife's protection. Influenced by U.S. reforms, legislatures in the Maritimes took the lead. In 1851, New Brunswick passed an act empowering a deserted wife to own fully any property that she had herself accumulated, and this right was broadened in 1859 to include a woman living separately 'not wilfully and of her own accord,' who also might now dispose of her separate property. Prince Edward Island followed suit in 1860, and Nova Scotia in 1866. These statutes did not give women financial autonomy but merely provided relief in time of marital crisis.

In 1859, Canada West was the first jurisdiction to legislate to allow *any* married woman full dispositive powers over her separate property, though the provisions were ambiguous: a husband still had control over his wife's and children's earnings unless prevented by a court order on the grounds of his lunacy, habitual drunkenness, desertion, or, specifically, imprisonment. And even with these restrictions the legislation was diluted by the Ontario judges: 'In their hands the statutes were systematically stripped of their potential, and the dramatic transformation in married women's property rights forecast by the law editors was halted in its tracks. The Judges ensured that the second wave statutes would be properly characterized as "protective" legislation, rather than measures to enhance women's proprietary autonomy.' In this ambiguous and contentious legal context, Wilberforce, the western half of Biddulph, and the Roman Line were, in their different ways, settled; James Donnelly was imprisoned and his wife raised the young family on the fifty-acre farm. The legal sanctions of settlement were in all instances decidedly gendered.[16]

What was possible for a woman and what was possible for a man on Biddulph's Roman Line (or in Wilberforce or Lucan) were matters not just of community mores or culture, but the effects of a particular legal tradition, fought over in Canada in and between courts and legislatures in the first half of the nineteenth century. Indeed, if we are able to speak of the Roman Line as a community at all, then even before we consider its Irishness or its Catholicism we must take into account these material determinations: the features, of course, of the geography and its survey that I discussed above, but more important for its historical specificity as a community, its ideology of market settlement and the form given that market by land speculation and by gender inequity. These particular historical forces bear the more heavily the more closely we look at particular families and individuals, not only the Donnellys, of course, but their neighbours. These complex relations, even more than religion or place of origin, are the historical integuments, the conditions of possibility, of a *specific* community, expressed most concretely, most historically, in alliances, hatreds, and, of course, motives.

3

Access and Circulation,
Delivery and Through Passage

'The most orderly process of settlement ... followed the roads,' wrote James Scott, historian of the settlement of Huron County. Scott's reference here is to the Huron Road and the London–Goderich Road, yet not all settlement, of course, could take place along these colonization roads. As settlers moved inland, the relations between road and settlement became more complex, even reversed. 'Occupance of land,' counters Thomas McIlwraith, 'was not delayed for want of access,' and in another place he writes: 'It is a safe generalization that an opened road was not necessary to the selection of an inland lot, nor was its absence a barrier to reaching that land, but invariably an opened road was an immediate manifestation of land occupance.' The historical relations between road and settlement go beyond their simple presence or absence. Not only the term 'inland,' but 'open' and 'occupance' are imprecise, as we have seen, and the kinds of road, the materials of their construction, and their direction, termini, and way-stations have often quite complex historical meanings. It is not enough to place the development of roads in southwestern Ontario within a general history of transportation, a chronology of modes, routes, and short-cuts. 'Transportation' carries too much empiricist baggage, not least the straightforward progress that the chronology would appear to manifest. Glazebrook, in his *History of Transportation in Canada*, claimed that 'the objects of the system of roads in British North America need little explanation': 'Generally speaking they may be divided into two: long-distance routes for mail, passengers, and light freight; local roads for communication between town and country, to carry farm products to market and to ports, to supply farmers with manufactured articles, to open a way to the mills, and to make possible the settlement of a steadily-increasing area.' Straightforward as this may be, it is far too little explanation of objectives, occluding recognition, for instance, of successive patterns of objective and of whose purposes those served. So far, we have been reading the processes of survey and settlement of the Huron Tract for their historical determination by proto-capitalist and capitalist ideological practices, and here I want to read in a similar fashion the construction of roads, canals, and railways, as signifying historical processes that determined the social formations, the possibilities and impossibilities of particular local societies: Biddulph Township, Lucan, the Roman Line.[1]

Both Scott and McIlwraith speak in the first instance of 'access roads'; I abstract further that concept of Access so as to escape the empiricist limitations to which I have referred and to place it, along with Circulation, among two other abstract categories, Delivery and Through Passage. By organizing my analysis around these categories – Access and Circulation, Delivery, and Through Passage – I hope both to make significant use of the empirical materials (location, modes, and technologies of 'transportation') and simple narrative succession (road/waterway/rail or foot/wagon/barge/train), but at the same time to historicize these materials as symptoms of increased capitalist pressure on the settlement of southwestern Ontario. 'Transportation' can be read thus in closer relation to a specific locality; the relations of the details of local experience – the connection of individual lives and the life of the community in Biddulph Township to the dialectical development of different capitals (and of Capital) – become apparent as we trace, in the interplay and succession of mode, location, and technology over the middle decades of the nineteenth century, these motives and purposes for transportation: Access and Circulation, Delivery, and Through Passage.

We have taken Access to indicate simple entry 'inland,' 'back' from colonization roads by; first, explorers and surveyors, and, second, settlers, as the Irish Catholic settlers, James Donnelly among them, moved up Concessions VI and VII from the London–Goderich Road. With Access I want to associate Circulation, those modes and facilities for movement within and about an embryonic settlement, up and down the Roman Line, whether for companionship and conviviality or for barter and simple exchange. As an American commentator wrote in 1852: 'On Sunday, the farmer can go to church with regularity ... He can live with more friendliness with his neighbours ... He can meet people of his own pursuits more frequently, and converse upon prices current and improved modes of farming. Indeed, all the advantages which result from a road of superior excellence accrue to the farmer. There is nothing which so

much retards improvement as imperfect communications.' While perhaps less conversant with improved modes of farming, a farm woman
would also benefit socially and culturally from a road of superior excellence. Capital, of course, has no interest in improvement on the simple
level of Access and Circulation; there is seldom material profit in regular
Sunday church-going. It is with the next stage, Delivery, that Capital
(originating perhaps in local capitals) begins to show a determining
interest. And it is there that 'transportation' becomes gendered; while
women may be directly instrumental in the historical phases of 'Access'
and 'Circulation' (not surprising, since these categories would associate
initially with the economic phase of subsistence farming), women are
excluded ('sex is irrelevant') in the subsequent (capitalist) phases of
'Delivery' and 'Through Passage.' By Delivery I mean to signify the phase
or level of transportation motive or purpose that indicates cash-crop
staple production, a move beyond subsistence farming to farming for
market exchange, the need both to deliver produce in to a village or to a
railway siding and to deliver in return, so as to make the round trip
profitable, supplies or manufactured commodities. Through Passage, finally, is that (usually, but not always) later transportation purpose where
capitals (usually distant), no longer taking an interest in production or
in a particular locale, simply use the local as a factor in the production of
distant profits, as a roadbed. This is a more complex transition than that
to Delivery, and we need to examine its symptoms and specify its effects
on our particular locale in southwestern Ontario. But these four general
concepts, or motives or purposes, receive historical structure precisely by
their relation to the development of North American capitalism in the
nineteenth century, in a dialectic of place, movement, technology, and
capitalist desire. As organizing concepts, Access and Circulation, Delivery, and Through Passage allow us to articulate the empirical details and
the ideological histories of my earlier sections in a symptomatic reading
of the roads, waterways, and railways of southwestern Ontario. And we
may begin by reconsidering Access in relation to the inland (or 'leftover') situation of Biddulph Township.[2]

'There is a large extent of country,' wrote Thomas Roy in 1841, 'chiefly
in the London and Brock Districts, which is too remote from the Lakes
to be fully benefitted by their navigation.' Rather than rivers down to
Lake Erie, the extensive glacial deltas of outwash and gravel in Norfolk,
Elgin, and Middlesex counties had produced high banks along the shoreline between Long Point and Point Pelee ('high bluffs cut in unconsoli-
dated drift,' or, as John Kenneth Galbraith called it, 'an illogical arrange-

ment of the local terrain') which made the Lake Erie shore difficult of access, the early traders merely coasting it until they reached Detroit. The Thames, giving extended access from the west, none the less tended in an unexpectedly southerly direction, providing only 'a well travelled highway between Niagara and Detroit.' Because of flooding and low summer flow, the Ausable, one of the larger rivers flowing into Lake Huron and draining the Huron Tract to the north (but 'a dull, dirty sluggish stream, crawling with a motion scarcely visible,' said a report in 1858) was never useful as a waterway even to the Native peoples (though a military map of 1838–9 thought to indicate a portage from the Ausable west of Ailsa Craig to the Thames at Komoka).

And so, while 'natural drainage lines are commonly used as routes of ingress,' as corridors for initial occupance, this was not practicable for the inland townships of southwestern Ontario. Their relationship to water transportation, as we see below, was a very indirect, even artificial one; it was not one of Access or even, for many years, of Delivery. The scarcity of major rivers flowing into Lakes Erie and Huron influenced in yet another way the history of the country along the Lakes and south of the Canadian Shield. It was impracticable, until steam-towing and railways altered the situation, to raft timber on the lakes, and so there was, during the first period of settlement, little market for timber, except what the locality itself provided. As Arthur Lower says: 'There was, perforce, concentration on clearing and farming, and as a result, the forest disappeared rapidly and the farm took its place. The process was helped by the fact that it was mainly hardwood country and that pine occurred chiefly on the more barren soils.' What timber was exported went first down the Thames to Chatham, the principal shipping port for the products of the Thames River area, and then primarily to the United States, the only available market for lumber and then available only to those regions enjoying such direct communication.[3]

Access by Road

The very first roads in Upper Canada, as we have seen, had been strategic military roads: Yonge Street, connecting Lake Ontario to Lake Simcoe (and thence by water to Penetanguishene on Georgian Bay, where there was to be a naval station), and Dundas Street, connecting York (Toronto), Burlington, and Ancaster by a road through the Dundas gap in the Escarpment to London and the forks of the Thames (communicating thence by water to Lake St Clair and the Detroit–St Clair Rivers). Dundas

Street became also a major access route to the counties north of the Thames, intersecting at London the Proof Line Road, which became the Goderich Road at Elginfield. In 1809–11 the Talbot Road, to the south, followed a Native path westward along the shore of Lake Erie and, not being disabled by the reserved lands that retarded road improvements elsewhere, soon became known as the best road in the province. Yonge Street in turn became the portage route that replaced the northern French River/Lake Nipissing/Ottawa River waterway, which had served western exploration and the fur trade for over a century: 'The Northwest Fur Company, then [1794] the principal trading company to the Northwest, diverted its cargoes from the Ottawa and French River route to the St Lawrence, to Lake Ontario and to this new portage road, ... and this became the main route for northwest trade in general.' This portage function, as well as the particular military roles of both streets, could be seen as anticipations of the pattern of Through Passage, the placement of roads to connect the far-flung interests of external institutions, whether state or private capitalist.[4]

'Inland' Biddulph Township had an advantage, in that it alone of the Huron townships could exploit both sides of the colonization road that crossed it going from London to Goderich, and soon, as in the rest of the tract, Biddulph's settlement, as we have seen, spread out along its concession roads. So far I have made no real distinction between that main colonization road and these concession roads, but for these last, 'road' often meant only the original road allowance, the path blazed by the surveyors – straight lines, as Patrick Shirriff said in 1833, 'formed by felling trees, the branches and trunks of which have been burnt, or formed into corduroy, and the stumps, from two to three feet in height, left standing,' as on James Donnelly's original path up the Roman Line. McIlwraith defines an 'open road' in the early nineteenth century as simply 'a right-of-way along which trees have been felled leaving stumps short enough to be cleared by the axle of a wagon, to a width sufficient for a team to draw the wagon through.' A road once 'opened' in this way was meant not to be 'closed' again by the forest, but it was often at best 'merely a bridle path in summer and an ox-sled road in winter.' The Board of Agriculture report for 1858 on Huron County remarked that the London–Goderich Road was 'well turnpiked and graded – an excellent summer and winter road, but in the spring and fall nearly impassable.'

Suitable for Access or Circulation, simple 'opened' roads enabled only a subsistence or barter economy, in a market that certainly could put no premium on time. Winter snow and ice, which T.C. Keefer called 'the great democratic elements in the physical constitution of Canada,' allowed farmers to overcome 'the tariff of bad roads,' the effects of the shortage of road labour and the absence of road capital: 'The winter transportation that was possible over the snow roads or on the ice of lake and river was, in fact, one of the main sources of the rapid prosperity of the country: for during this season the farmer was able to take his produce to market and to obtain a year's supplies.' This seasonal rhythm in transportation, of course, was a decidedly non-capitalist temporality, and the merely opened, uncapitalized roads were to become increasingly intolerable: 'It may have been possible to do some clearing and to build a house with only footpath access, but by the end of the first full growing season there was grain to be milled for personal use and hopefully some surplus to be sold for other necessities. Pack-animals were not a part of the commercial scene, and the proverbial pioneer with a sack of grain over his shoulder has been glorified out of all proportion to his significance.' And, as McIlwraith adds, 'non-agricultural commerce could not conveniently wait for winter.'5

 I have emphasized that these roads were uncapitalized. No local capital could yet exist, and, as I have said, distant capitals had as yet little interest in the tiny settlements in the Huron Tract, either as producers or consumers. Thus what roads there were existed as the result of the pioneers' initial settlement duty to clear the roads and their ensuing statutory obligation to maintain them. 'This work required little skill and no scientific knowledge,' wrote William Johnston of statutory road-making in Perth County: 'To have built such roads even as then existed, by taxes levied, would have been impossible, or at least would have made progress extremely slow. There was no money in circulation to pay taxes, and the only medium current in interchanging commodities was energy and muscle. These qualities were at once laid under tribute and made available for taxpaying purposes, thus discharging a levy which could not have been met in any other way. This is the underlying principle of statute labour.' But the amount of labour to be expended was limited by the very laws that required it, and so a road that was washed out might not be repaired until the next statutory period. And because the legislation made no provision for bridges and culverts, the roads built could serve only limited functions. In some important instances, as we have seen, roads served some larger military or corporate scheme: the Queen's Rangers constructing Dundas and Yonge Streets, or the Canada Company, the Huron and the London–Goderich Roads. Such 'grace and favour' took into account only the requirements of Access and Circulation, and the statutory labours of the adjacent settlers were often thwarted by the presence of clergy reserves and the fact that the road-building statutes did not bind speculators. The fund that the Canada Company had promised for improvements was often unwisely expended: much of it was used up on the harbour and roads around Goderich, and since the Company rarely asked for tenders, and since its history of paying contractors in land encouraged higher prices for the work, outlying townships saw little improvement in their roads. In 1852, William Smith wrote: 'With the exception of a few miles on the Huron road, east of Goderich, there is *no good road* in the tract, there is no road fit for a vehicle, between Goderich and Port Sarnia.' The historian of Perth County adds: 'While those in authority at Goderich [the Company officers] may have done something (as was their duty) to facilitate settlement and improve the Huron Tract, it cannot be shown that, with the exception of clearing a road to Goderich to assist travel in that direction, much had been accomplished.' The bitterness apparent here had contributed finally to Perth County's withdrawal in 1850 from the United Counties of Huron, Perth, and Bruce, and the first act of the new Perth county council when it took office in 1853 was to borrow £20,000 for improvements to leading roads.[6]

What I have called Delivery is intended to mark the transition in the relationship of the early roads of Upper Canada to the pressures both of the eventual growth of surplus grain production for market and of non-agricultural commerce, the suppliers of manufactured necessities and so on. Over time the needs and purposes of the settlers in the Huron Tract had shifted to the point that the roads had to change also, and the means, technology, and capital were now available. We can read the records of the kinds and condition of the roads to locate that socio-economic change fairly accurately: 'Farmers and joint stock companies built roads if the anticipated exportable surplus and associated imports were sufficient to justify the cost ... Roads, therefore, were much more the result than the cause of the economic opportunity provided by the wheat economy.' The transition in southwestern Ontario from Access and Circulation to Delivery is thus the interaction of three histories: the change from road construction and maintenance by statutory labour to capitalized construction by contract labour; the shift from subsistence agricultural production within a local market to staple production for export; and the attempt to meet market requirements independent of weather and climate. It is the interaction of these three factors registered in road construction and materials that locates dialectically a particular

date or period in the development of Biddulph Township, or alternatively, shapes for a time the life of the communities there (to be later
again transformed by the dialectical change that I am labelling Through
Passage). I want to examine the interplay of these three histories that
triangulate road Delivery, looking at particular details and focusing finally on the building of Port Stanley, as a way of moving into the new
transportation modes and the final change.

As John McCallum remarks, 'The early settlers in Ontario had little
agricultural surplus since only five to ten acres of land could be cleared
each year'; after the first full growing season there might be '*some* surplus,' McIlwraith concurs. Again, the earliest attempt 'to concentrate the
bulk of native products to transportable proportions' and to establish
'the greatly-to-be-desired staple' was the reduction of timber to potash, as
the land was cleared for wheat: 'The southern hardwood forest was good
for nothing except firewood or potash and there was, therefore, every
incentive to destroy it as quickly as possible in order to get at the soil
under it.' But even the planting of wheat did not lead immediately to
wheat export. The rapid settlement of Biddulph and neighbouring townships meant that into the 1850s little wheat was exported: 'The new
arrivals provided a ready market for older farms. In 1841, a traveller
states that "but little surplus grain is at present available for exportation.
All that the farmer can produce is bought up by the incoming settlers".'[7]

Capital and Delivery by Road

The transition out of such a subsistence economy is indicated by changes
in the system of road-building and the kinds of roads. Thomas McIlwraith
described the stages in road development as proceeding from their opening through the forest through successive attempts to grapple with the
problem of water, eventually best solved in the nineteenth century by
macadam. An alternative chronology is suggested by the opening of stage-
coach travel from Queenston through Ancaster, Brantford, Burford, and
Oxford to Sandwich (Windsor) in 1828. This was a four-day trip available
once a week, and there was regular stage-coach service from Hamilton
through Galt, Guelph, and over the Huron Road to Goderich by 1841;
the Donnellys, as we know, were to have an interest in this endeavour by
the 1870s. While these are certainly steps in the transportation of mail
and passengers through the province, the through stage-coach seems to
me primarily to indicate the legislative assembly's somewhat parochial

priorities as it intervenes to grant a monopoly, since 'the country was scarcely able to support the line of stages through Western Ontario.'

More significant historically than passenger traffic, I have suggested, is the necessity of the move towards exportation or Delivery, which occurred in the 1840s and 1850s. A military map of the Huron Tract prepared in 1840 distinguishes 'roads militarily passable at all seasons' (the Bayfield Road, the London–Goderich Road, and the Huron Road – though the last remained 'chiefly mud or corduroy until long after the middle of the century'). The map contrasts these to the Port Franks Road and the extension from Clandeboye south to the Egremont Road, which were 'generally but not all seasons passable by guns,' that is to say, also passable by loaded farm wagons. Ten years later a map records that neither of the two colonization roads was planked or gravelled. While gravelling a road (with material from streambeds or glacial deposits) might be undertaken by unskilled statutory labour, planking and macadamizing could not; such all-weather roads, adapted to Delivery in both directions (and incidentally passable by guns), required skills and materials that only public or private capital could mobilize. As the engineer Thomas Roy remarked in 1841: 'Excavation and embankment, ditching, providing and breaking stone, and some other works, may, and perhaps ought to be done by contract; but forming the metal-bed, laying on the metal [in the sense of 'broken stone used in macadamizing roads'], and finishing the road, ought, in every case, to be done by men permanently employed, who have been well trained to, and are experienced in the business.'

Macadamizing best exemplifies this new stage of all-weather, skilled, and hence capital-intensive road-building. Roy estimates the cost per mile for common road in 1841 to be £220 to £280, and for macadam, £1,370. What this sum bought was some local version of J.L. McAdam's techniques. A raised foundation for the road was to be prepared and, 'having secured the soil from *under* water,' 'the road-maker is next to secure it from rain water, by a solid road, made of clean, dry stone, or flint, so selected, prepared, and laid, as to be perfectly impervious to water: and this cannot be effected, unless the greatest care be taken, that no earth, clay, chalk, or other matter, that will hold or conduct water, be mixed with the broken stone; which must be so prepared and laid, as to unite by its own angles into a firm, compact, impenetrable body.' This is no common road. And so James B. Brown could celebrate in 1843 the establishment, after passage of the Act of Union for the two Canadas, of the new Board of Works, stimulated by a loan of £1½ million guaranteed by the British government, of which over £200,000 was set aside for public improvements ('harbours, lighthouses, roads and bridges, but chiefly roads and bridges') west of Lake Ontario; 'the country,' said Brown, 'altogether already affords evidence of being very greatly indebted.'[8]

In 1837 Upper Canada had in the first session of the new legislature granted funds to macadamize Yonge Street, Hurontario Street, Dundas Street from Hamilton to Brantford, and the road from Dundas to Waterloo, with more money to be granted in the second session to complete these projects. J.H. Aitchison labelled this an orgy of spending of scarce capital, a 'period which the challenge of the St. Lawrence and the promoters of the Welland Canal were chiefly responsible for initiating.' By 1843 there were twelve macadamized roads in Canada West, all of them in the Home, Gore, and Niagara Districts and deemed 'necessary to connect the Roads of the Home and Western Districts with the Niagara Frontier' (we shortly examine the influence of the Erie Canal). In February 1845, the London District council petitioned the governor general that the road to Goderich be either macadamized or planked (Goodhue signed the petition), and in March, Hamilton Killaly, chair of the Board of Works, added his support. Then, at a series of meetings in April and May 1849, the London Proof Line Road Company was formed to gravel or macadamize the road north. The first twelve miles of Yonge Street north of Toronto had also been macadamized by the late 1830s. The rest of Yonge Street was planked in 1835, the first use (on the continent perhaps) of what was to become a more common if still (at a cost of £850–£1,050 per mile) capital-intensive technology. Though J.J. Talman noted that the *Globe* in 1855 called the plank roads in York County 'detestable,' 'a disgrace to all connected with them,' even 'a public imposition,' in 1846 Sir Richard Bonnycastle had been impressed by the novelty, so un-English, of the planked Yonge Street: 'Fancy rolling along a floor of thick boards through field and forest for a hundred miles. The boards are covered with earth, or gravel, if it can be had, and this deadens the noise and prevents the wear and tear, so that you glide along pretty much the same as a child's go-cart goes over the carpet.'

While the advantage of plank roads was that the material was readily available, and 'only a sawmill and some rough carpenters were needed,' the work was to that extent skilled, laborious, and hence expensive: 'The subgrade once established, longitudinal trenches were dug in which sills consisting of three-inch plank four and eight inches wide were placed, and on them were laid the planks, three inches thick and eight feet long, at right angles to the direction of the road. The sills were set slightly below the surface of the ground, and the planks were pounded down ... and it is reported that it was hard work to take one of them up.' Hard work, yet work that was soon necessary, since plank roads needed to be rebuilt within seven years. Nevertheless, this 'interesting but passing phase in the history of Canadian roads' is, with the early macadamization, especially significant in the history of Upper Canada. The macadamization of the Niagara roads and the planking of Yonge Street, of Dundas Street, and soon the road from London to Chatham and beyond not only acknowledge, as I have suggested, the presence of the Erie Canal but might again be seen to prefigure the Through Passage to come. Plank roads elsewhere might merely signify preoccupation with Delivery. James Brown spoke of the benefits to be derived if, as he expected, the London–Goderich Road were soon planked: 'This road, cutting quite through the township of London, and extending onwards through the richly fertile district of Huron, is one the improvement in planking which will confer great advantages upon many rapidly growing settlements, and also much benefit the town of London.' 'On planked roads,' he writes, 'double the old loads is likely to be drawn with less expenditure of animal power, and in less time, and always with complete certainty, whatever may be the state of the weather.' The values of a specifically *capitalist* agricultural road system could not be more pointedly expressed. 'The farmers, thus encouraged, will be stimulated to produce more than they do now, and the good effects to the market towns, as well as to the producers themselves, and therefore, of course, to the whole country, must soon become very apparent.' In Hugh G.J. Aitken's words: 'The opening up of the Huron Tract depended very directly upon the improvement of transportation facilities, both to bring out settlers and their effects and to provide a remunerative market for their produce.' The plank road from London to Port Stanley was an integral part of this vision of staple wheat production and the kinds of Delivery that it required. Commenting on construction of the London–Port Stanley Road, one historian wrote: 'These years might be regarded as a transitionary period leading up to the capitalism which began in the late nineteenth century and continued on into the twentieth.'

I would date the advent of capitalism somewhat earlier but agree that the Port Stanley Road was intimately connected with its restructuring of southwestern Ontario. As David Hall goes on to say, the main pattern of road development in the late 1830s and early 1840s was north–south, not east–west, 'in an attempt to create improved transportation facilities for the produce of the farm and forest,' but 'the economic importance of these roads did not last for more than one or two decades.' An explanation of these facts is afforded, I am arguing, by seeing them within, first, the transition from Access and Circulation to Delivery, and then, the transition to Through Passage – the very form of the impact of capitalist transportation on southwestern Ontario.[9]

The Place of Port Stanley

'Form,' or orientation; we are trying to read what William Cronon would call 'the geographical orientation' of the Huron Tract's or Biddulph Township's 'physical networks' for what they can tell us of the capitalist transformation of southwestern Ontario. As I have mentioned, immediately following the end of the War of 1812 a reconnaissance survey was done of all the Great Lakes, and in 1816 and 1817 Lieutenant Henry W. Bayfield surveyed Lake Erie, noting all the creeks along the inhospitable north shore. In 1826 a Select Committee of the Upper Canada House of Assembly proposed a port at Kettle Creek, due south of London, 'considering that the coast of Lake Erie is so deficent in harbours, and that the mouth of Kettle Creek is the natural outlet for an extensive, fertile and populous country, rapidly increasing in wealth; and considering that it is demonstrable that the work ... will be the means of enabling an extensive country to realize the advantages contemplated by the Welland Canal.'

We return below to the advantages associated with the then-not-yet-completed Welland Canal, but I want to continue to consider the relation of Kettle Creek/Port Stanley to the not-quite-populous country being settled to the north by the just-chartered Canada Company (my compounds are intended to emphasize a conjuncture). Captain George Phillpotts, assigned by Lord Glenelg to study the Canadas' inland waterways 'with a view to establish a competent Navigation between Lake Erie and the sea,' reported in 1840 that the current American concerns about the lack of harbours on the south side of Lake Erie were applicable as well to the north shore. The prosperity and rapid growth of the Canadas, he argued, depended very much on having good harbours on the Lakes, 'in order to afford the Inhabitants of the different Townships in the interior a good and convenient opportunity of shipping their produce for Market, and of receiving Merchandize etc in return.'

The arguments for Kettle Creek from the start stressed both the existing transportation on the lake and the agricultural potential of the inland townships. A series of surveys of the north shore of Lake Erie in 1789–91 had established that between Point Pelee and Point aux Pins there was 'no possibility of Landing or saving a Boat in a Storm' because of the 100- to 200-foot clay banks, and to the east the 'small runs of Water are nothing but Ravines' until one reached what was to become Talbot Creek and Kettle River. This last, but for fallen timber, was 'Navigable for Boats for many miles up it' but had a narrow, twenty-five-foot mouth and a sand bar beyond only 5½-feet deep.

In 1826, John Harris, a marine surveyor invited to give evidence to the Select Committee, told it twice that the whole coast of Lake Erie from Long Point did not afford shelter even for a boat (i.e., even a durham boat or a *batteau*) to anchor with safety, while asserting at the same time that Kettle Creek was 'the natural outlet of that country,' a conjunction of first and second nature concurred in by Charles Ingersoll, another witness to the Select Committee in 1826. Ingersoll added, 'There is no flour sent at present from the townships above-mentioned, from the want of flour mills to manufacture it properly, and the expense of transport. The last objection will be obviated by the construction of a harbour at Kettle Creek.' In 1830, James Hamilton, president of the new Kettle Creek Harbour Commission, again made the point that 'Kettle Creek Harbour ... Port Stanley ... is the only harbour between Fort Erie and Sandwich.' Hamilton reiterated his opinion of the difficulties in Delivery five years later when he called attention to 'the excessive high rates of toll imposed, when compared with those enacted at other harbours on either lake – the direct tendency of which is to force the produce of the country into other, more hazardous but less expensive channels.' Less expensive, perhaps, as regards tolls (the object of his argument), but not so as a mode of transportation. As Cronon says, 'Wagons offered few economies of scale, and so set well-defined limits to how far one could afford to travel in them.' As John Harris had told the Select Committee in 1826 – referring to exports of potash which, as the settlers cleared the land, was then the most valuable product – 'the present land carriage is so great, if they send their produce to a safe port for shipment, it swallows up the profit that ought to arise.'[10]

And yet, despite its limitations and even though it was not used by such London traders as George Jervis Goodhue (then in his early career as a merchant), Kettle Creek, the 'natural outlet' for London Township and the country north, was expanding its export and import trade long before its development by the Board of Works as Port Stanley. In 1823, 262 barrels of ashes and 686 bushels of wheat had been exported from

Kettle Creek, and 236 barrels bulk of 'merchandise' and 345 of salt were imported. In 1829, 448 barrels of ashes, and in 1830 530 barrels, were exported, but more important, 2,096 bushels of wheat in 1829 and 17,359 bushels in 1830 were exported, with 1,797 barrels of merchandise and 923 of salt arriving. In 1830, for the first time, 'Bushels of wheat' is the first export statistic reported to the legislative assembly, followed by 'Barrels of flour' and 'Barrels of Pork and Beef,' displacing 'Barrels of pot and pearl ashes.' This shift of emphasis, reflecting the increase in sheer quantity of wheat exported, clearly shows the London District moving out of a settler, subsistence economy in the 1830s to a capitalist wheat-export economy (Upper Canada was the one grain-exporting province in British North America), and the growing Port Stanley planned to provide the major transportation link with the North American and European markets.

In December 1833, 'owners and masters sailing to and from Kettle Creek harbour' protested the expense of loading and unloading cargoes with scows outside the sandbar, and in 1834 a Special Committee on Harbours on the north side of Lake Erie reported to the legislature that 'the harbour formed at Port Stanley, although not so good as is desirable, extends great accommodation to the neighbourhood in which it is situated, by affording the inhabitants, as well as those considerably in the interior, the means of sending their surplus products to market; but it is necessary that a further grant should be made by your honourable House to improve that harbour to the extent that the public interests require.' Throughout the 1830s, the assembly considered several bills for improvements to Port Stanley. But Upper Canada faced other, more urgent problems during those years, and in the political struggles in the legislature several Port Stanley bills died, though early in the decade £3,500 was granted for lengthening the piers. A bill authorizing £2,000 for further improvements was then proposed and passed but was '*not returned from the Council.*' Another bill for improvements was referred to the Committee on Canals and died there, and yet another, to remodel the harbour and complete the pier, sent to a Committee of the whole House, was '*not considered.*' Only in 1839–40, after the resolution of the political crisis, was £2,000 authorized for Port Stanley.[11]

And so, a harbour of refuge since 1838, Port Stanley was being actively developed by the new Board of Works and a 26½-mile plank road constructed from London when James Brown described the town in his *Views of Canada and the Colonists* in 1844: 'Port Stanley is beautifully situated at the mouth of Kettle Creek, which is the outlet of the finest grain country on Lake Erie, and is the port at which are entered all goods for Talbot Street, twenty miles east and west of it, for St Thomas, London, Delaware, and the adjacent countries, and when completed as a harbour, with a plank road to London, may be expected to yield three times the revenue it has ever yet produced.'

The Board of Works Correspondence for February and March 1842 is full of tenders by neighbouring sawmills to supply thousands of feet of three-inch pine plank, twelve and sixteen feet in length; the organization of that procurement would be well beyond the administrative capacity of the settlers themselves. Casimir Gzowski, the new superintendent of roads and waterways in the London District of Canada West, reported that by May 1844 eleven continuous miles had been laid from London, that the rest was in hand, and that seven of the eight toll houses had been erected. An 1840 map shows in detail its course down from London, along the north branch of the Talbot Road, through St Thomas, until, in the next last concession before the lake, it turns down to the deep, steep-sided, flat-floored valley through the hundred-foot bluffs. Port Stanley itself was concurrently being rebuilt as a modern commercial port. Two days after reporting the delivery of planks and scantling for the sills of the road, Gzowski submitted an estimate for the Port Stanley piers, to be built out to fifteen feet of water (one map suggests seventeen feet six inches), indicating the ambitions for the port (before 1850 the Welland Canal had a depth of only eight feet six inches, deepened in 1853 to ten feet). R.L. Jones describes how, because of the differential between the export price of wheat in Upper Canada and the Rochester price, Americans were buying wheat in large quantities at Port Stanley. By the 1850s the village had become one of the most important ports on Lakes Erie and Huron. A century later a local historian spoke of the tradition in the town of 'the long line of wagon-trains bringing grain for shipment,' but as we see below this moment of influence lasted only a decade.[12]

Delivery and Canals

The Board of Works spent £200,000 on harbours, lighthouses, roads, and bridges in the early 1840s, but there was no doubt that Britain's guarantee of the £1.5-million loan for improvement of public works in the new United Province of Canada was intended primarily to be spent on canals. The new Port Stanley was to feed the improved Second Welland

Canal and 'the new generation of waterways.' And the board's new macadamized roads round the head of Lake Ontario, as I have mentioned,
were intended less to benefit the small harbours, Grimsby, Stony Creek,
and Niagara, than the canal: 'The completion of the Queenston and
Hamilton road, a measure of great Public importance, will furnish the
inhabitants in the vicinity of these places, with easier access to a better
market even if these small harbours were repaired.' The projectors of
the Second Welland Canal were very conscious (the success of the Erie
Canal had forced them to be so) of the Welland's international, indeed
continental contexts. Samuel Power, engineer for the Welland Canal
Company, reported in 1844: 'The Queenston Hamilton road ... is not
inferior in importance to any road in Canada, even when viewed alone it
is worthy of attention, as traversing a well settled and fertile district, but
it acquires additional importance when considered in connection with
the roads leading westward from Hamilton towards Detroit ... For no
doubt can exist, but that all persons travelling towards Detroit will select
this route until the Americans complete the line of railways on the Southern Side of Lake Erie, or the people of Canada one which will be 100
miles shorter from Fort Erie to Amherstburgh.'[13]

Power is here thinking about the Welland Canal in relation not only to
a local road but to trunk roads and to railways on both shores of the lake
(even anticipating the Great Western's Air Line of 1873), keeping in
mind not only Queenston and Hamilton but Amherstburg, Detroit, and,
without naming it, Chicago. For our part, we could generalize further:
not only does the construction of Port Stanley and its plank road concretely link the grain farmers of the London District (and soon of
Biddulph Township) to international transport, but the simultaneity (while
no coincidence) of the board's construction in the early 1840s of the
Second Welland Canal and its ancillary roads indicates the subsumption
(under the sign of Delivery) of the district's grain surplus by Capital.
Canadian state capital built Port Stanley so as to intercept and connect
with the grain traffic anticipated from Chicago and the 'Great West,'
which it hoped as well to capture for the St Lawrence waterway. Put
another way, at this moment a narrative of the Huron Tract's historical
shift out of a subsistence and into an export economy encounters both
the narrative of the historical struggle between capitalists in Montreal
and New York (between the St Lawrence–Welland and the Erie Canal)
and another history, of the nineteenth-century grain trade, its places
(Chicago, Milwaukee, Toledo, and eventually the west), techniques (grad-

ing, elevators, and so on), and technology, dictated by what Cronon calls the 'logic of capital.' From this moment on, the logic of capital (including what we might here call 'the logic of capitalist Delivery') will inform the economic (but not only the economic) life of the tract, of Biddulph Township, in major ways.

The logic of Delivery is not arbitrary, but rather an effect obviously of the geographical facts that I have discussed above. The historical markets for the grain of Upper Canada, determined also by its distinctive political history and the vagaries of the American protective tariff, were the Maritimes, Britain, and, to some extent, the West Indies. The northern mid-continent, including the Great Lakes, is separated from the Atlantic Ocean by two barriers, the Appalachians and the Niagara Escarpment, which extends well south into New York state. There are only two natural gaps to sea level in the first barrier, the channel of the St Lawrence River and that of the Hudson, one on each side of the border. Between 1828 and 1846, there was canal construction on a vast scale in the United States between Lake Erie, the Ohio River, and the Mississippi, turning to the north the wheat trade that earlier had flowed the other way. The Americans' decision, when building the Erie Canal in the early 1820s, not to follow the old Mohawk route north of Albany to Oswego on Lake Ontario but to turn west, crossing the Escarpment at Lockport and terminating at Buffalo on Lake Erie, left the Canadians to solve the problem of the Escarpment and Niagara Falls on their side of the border. Thus it seems unproductive simply to classify canals (as did an 1884 report on deepening the Welland) as either a purely artificial waterway, like the Erie, or a 'canalized river ... forming a slack-water navigation connected by canals,' like the Rideau or Trent, or 'ship canals of large capacity,' like the Suez, Panama, or, unexpectedly, the Welland. The St Lawrence–Great Lakes–Welland and the Erie, at least, are best seen as systems and parts of systems; they are connected to more than other waterways. Both are affected, for example, by systems of *weather*: not only 'the gales and seas of Lakes Huron and Superior in the autumn' of which the same report speaks, but the winter temperatures that close both canal systems with ice for four and a half months each year, and which, because of the currents, blocks the mouth of the Erie Canal at Buffalo. More to our purpose, each canal system engages, along its whole length and at each end, an economic system driven by the logic of capital. Cronon describes that logic in relation to the railways and Chicago's 'Great West' from the 1860s, and I should like to apply his

analysis to the very different historical situation of Port Stanley in relation to water transport in the 1840s and 1850s and to those inland
Ontario townships to which Port Stanley was the natural outlet.[14]

The logic of capital worked itself through water transport in Canada
West in the competition between the Erie Canal and the St Lawrence–
Great Lakes–Welland Canal waterway. After the momentous decision by
the builders of the Erie Canal to cross both natural barriers between New
York City and Lake Erie, that canal's history in general is mainly a matter
of adjusting tolls. But the history in general of the Canadian waterway is
rather different, a long story of attempts to maximize the advantage of
short canals and much slack water (where ships could travel under their
own power and at their own speed), and a shorter ocean voyage, by
widening and deepening the canals – those on the St Lawrence between
Prescott and Montreal and the Welland Canal across the Escarpment
between Lakes Erie and Ontario. These are the recurring particulars of
the competition between the two routes throughout the century, a conflict which, in the socio-political setting and in conjunction and competition with railways, makes up in general the empirical history of the two
great water systems.

The construction of the Second Welland Canal (1842–5) exemplifies
this interplay of particular constraints. The locks of the First Canal, pri-
vately constructed, were for reasons of economy built of wood, so the
first priority in the reconstruction was to rebuild the locks in stone. The
objective of the original builders, in the 1820s and before the Union,
had been simply to link Lakes Erie and Ontario (and hence four of the
five lakes), and its locks accommodated only sloops and small schooners,
the class of vessels then navigating the lakes. By the 1840s, the Union of
the two Canadas, the competition of the Erie Canal for the ocean trade,
and the increasing number and size of steamships forced new priorities.
Called on to report on the probable extension of commerce from
Montreal 'through Lake Erie, the River Detroit, Lakes St Clair, Huron
and Michigan to Chicago,' Captain Phillpotts had recommended, in his
first report in 1839, that the Welland Canal be 'at once enlarged to the
size required for large steamers.' Smaller, schooner-sized craft required
trans-shipment, and because of the length of slack water on the whole
waterway Phillpotts foresaw the future to lie in large steamers. But only
the entrance locks of the Second Canal were built to accommodate steamships, hence only laker craft continued to travel the whole canal. In the
lifetime of the Second Canal (until 1885), it became increasingly clear
that improvements in the Welland Canal must be coordinated with those

in the St Lawrence canals. The history on this level is such a one of an interplay of economics, technology, and politics.[15]

The logic of capital, however, dictated by an economic system with its own imperatives, engages the competition between the two waterways generally in three ways. Cronon shows that railway investors needed constantly to take into account their very large fixed costs and operating expenses: 'Ties rotted, bridges collapsed, and rails rusted no matter how few trains passed over them.' Ships, he points out, are intrinsically cheaper to run than railways, 'largely because the buoyancy and lower friction of water travel required less energy consumption. Sail ships had no fuel costs at all, and steamships got more mileage from the fuel they consumed than railroads did.' But a canal, unlike slack water, also had sizeable fixed costs in its channel and locks, and so the carrying trade by water, like the railways, needed ('logically') to minimize these, first of all, by ensuring two-way traffic. Harold Innis cites speakers in the legislative assembly of Canada in the early 1860s who recognized the influence of New York City as a factor in the difficulties of the St Lawrence. New York, 'being the great commercial emporium of the Northern States, controls the bulk of the import trade; consequently, freights rule lower at that port than at any other on this part of the continent.' Most ships returning from Europe to Quebec or Montreal, in contrast, had to make the voyage in ballast. Thus, as Thomas Keefer pointed out, neither its length nor its advanced facilities gave the Erie Canal its competitive advantage in 1863, but rather New York's superiority over Montreal in its ability to supply back freights, a double haul. Canada's disadvantage here – that is, the bias of the logic of capital – showed even on a small scale. Lake carriage east to Kingston, for example, was done only on American vessels; there was no return freight for Canadian boats, while 'the American vessel, after discharging her cargo at Kingston, goes to Oswego [on the Erie Canal] ... and obtains a return cargo of coal at as high rates as down freights.' The struggle between the two systems of water transport could be characterized as 'a competition between the attractions offered by rival *seaports* and *their* ocean aspect, rather than between the inland routes by which these were reached; that when the Canada route would have the patronage of one hundred thousand, the American would have that of one million.' Thus, while Montreal might offer a shorter ocean voyage to Liverpool, New York offered the Europeans instead a huge market for *their* goods, and this guaranteed two-way traffic and produced lower fares and lower insurance rates. The logic of capital dictated, as Samuel Keefer was to point out in 1871, that 'New York being the great centre of the import trade for the West, has hitherto naturally drawn to it the commercial marine of all nations, and vessels carrying wheat, corn, and other products of the grain-growing States, have never wanted return freights. Hitherto, however, the direct foreign trade with the West, *via* the St Lawrence, has been insignificant.'

By mid-century, New York had developed the most extensive trading hinterland and the most powerful financial institutions of any North American port city, and Buffalo, at the head of the Erie Canal and with grain elevators since 1842, was the largest market for grain and flour in North America. An 1884 report to the minister of railways and canals in Canada on the need to deepen the Welland Canal argued further that the trade in grain futures that had developed in New York in the previous ten years ensured that that city would be the preferred destination: 'Wherever this speculation exists trade follows.' Thus, whatever technological improvements in the St Lawrence–Welland waterway Canada might undertake, whether deepenings or widenings, lengthenings or shortenings, the logic of capital dictated in favour of the Erie Canal and its New York City terminus, and this in turn was a condition for the Delivery of Huron Tract wheat out of Port Stanley.[16]

Another of Cronon's instances of the determining influence of the logic of capital on transport by rail also bears on transport by water. Transportation capital values sheer quantity, bulk, on several levels, and 'all of the grain-carrying units increase in size during this period.' Moreover, 'the first principle of railroad rate setting,' Cronon writes, 'was to encourage customers ... to make the longest journey possible on one's own line.' He quotes an observer in 1879: 'The whole tendency of rail transportation is towards the largest shipments without breaking bulk.' 'Breaking bulk' ('to destroy the completeness of a cargo by taking out a portion, to begin to unload' [1692]; *OED*) signifies for the carrying trade anything that might prevent continuous conveyance, specifically the need to transship cargo to another carrier or to another mode. Once loaded, a cargo ideally should not be handled again until it arrives at its destination. 'It is an axiom in trade,' wrote Samuel Keefer in 1871, 'that the nearer you can bring the produce to its market without breaking bulk, the greater will be the saving in freight.' A corollary axiom in the logic of Delivery was that 'experience proves that the largest class of vessels, especially steam, now plying the lakes, carry property at the cheapest rates.' Thus for the rest of the century the lake steamers, as contrasted to the lakers, which were sailing vessels, always exceeded the capacity of the Welland Canal, needing to break bulk at the foot of Lake Erie, to the disadvantage of the St Lawrence waterway and to the (temporary) advantage of the Erie Canal.

Both the emphasis on bulk and the axiomatic resistance to breaking bulk operated against the export of wheat from Port Stanley in the 1860s by either of the competing waterway systems. And while residents of towns along the Lakes such as London, as Jones points out, were less interested in a trunk railway to Montreal than in a feeder line to a harbour such as Port Stanley for transport across the lake to the United States, those interests were soon irrelevant to both the development of the carrying trade by both water and rail and North American wheat production. Grain from Port Stanley was barely loaded, from rail or wagon, when it had almost immediately to break bulk again at the foot of the lake, and 'charges of transshipment in the case of the short lake shipment would be of relatively greater importance than in the case of the longer lake shipment.' Put another way, the sheer bulk of the grain shipped from the American west made uneconomic the handling costs of collecting the addition from Port Stanley; the map-diagram from which I have derived Figure 3.1 does not even bother to list the amount of wheat (in 1868, 80,935 bushels) exported from Port Stanley.[17]

A final axiom in the logic of Delivery also determined the fate of Port Stanley as a centre for the export of the grain of the Huron Tract. Again, Cronon explains it with reference to the railways, and to Chicago. Chicago and other cities often found themselves with more than one railway, and so shippers were able to play off the different lines against each other and drive down rates: 'At "competitive points," as such places came to be called, the logic of fixed costs drove railroads to cut rates to the bare minimum – below the actual cost of transportation, if necessary – in order to keep traffic from switching to other roads. An opposite logic applied to towns with only one railroad. Having no alternative, shippers and passengers at these "non-competitive points" paid not only their full cost of transportation but often a surcharge to help make up for a road's competitive losses elsewhere.'

Or, speaking of the pattern of traffic along a line, we might say that a 'non-competitive point' became simply a 'way-station.' A decade or so before the time Cronon describes, the competitive points along the waterways to the Atlantic were obvious. The foot of Lake Erie (to emphasize the proximity of Port Colborne and Buffalo) is the most obvious, and until the completion of the railways on both sides of the border the only real competition to either waterway east of Lake Erie was the branch of the Erie Canal at Oswego, New York. West of the Niagara Peninsula,

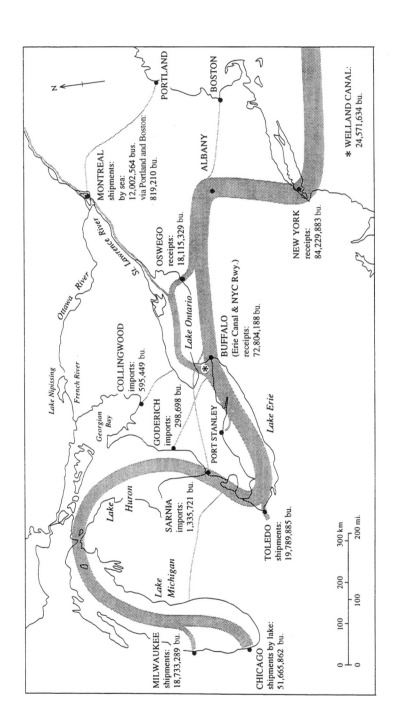

Figure 3.1
Course and comparative magnitude of the principal channels of the grain trade of the Lakes region, 1862

while Milwaukee, Toledo, and Cleveland were major ports, the history of their relative decline shows that the only competitive point was Chicago. Cronon's whole section on the 'Logic of Capital' is a demonstration of how 'the geographical orientation of physical networks' – primarily the interplay at that place of rail and water – made Chicago the major competitive point for the entire midcontinent. And while Port Stanley, in contrast (and at the other end of the scale), could not be even a minor competitive point, its harbour, plank road, and eventually its railway affect in other ways the Delivery of the produce of, for example, Biddulph Township. Harold Innis used Port Stanley as the example for his discussion of the weakness of the competitive position of Canadian canals and railways in attracting traffic. Innis quotes the legislature's *Sessional Papers* to the effect that by 1853 Port Stanley was considered 'one of the most important ports in the western part of the province.' He suggests that 'the ambitions of numerous ports, which had flourished with the dominance of transport by water, to take advantage of the possibilities of transport by rail, and of inland centres, anxious to link up with new territory and the waterways, were realized in the construction of feeders.'

Port Stanley attempted in precisely this way to connect with London, its inland centre. London merchants had found the Great Western Railway monopoly intolerable, and in October 1856 the twenty-four-mile London and Port Stanley Railway was opened as a feeder to supplement the plank road, to link up with the Huron Tract and to function as a main artery of trade between Canada and the states across the lake. Return cargoes could be expected: 'The lake fleets were in their hey-day; it was reasonable to expect a certain amount of off-water traffic for such a railway.' But despite the investment of the Board of Works, the early excitement at the long line of wagons bringing grain for shipment and the opening of the railway, by 1856 these plans were already short-sighted. The grain traffic to the lake failed to grow as hoped, and Port Stanley was destined to serve only for excursion and coal traffic. In the 1870s the London and Port Stanley Railway was amalgamated with the Great Western and subjected to its priorities, and when the Grand Trunk took over the Great Western in the early 1880s there was, as we see below, a general tightening up of operations, which drove the casual lake traffic from Port Stanley to other outports.

And yet the railway connection between London and Port Stanley had briefly made London a 'competitive point' for grain delivery. Its opening in 1856 'has caused a reduction of the freights on farm produce and merchandise of fully fifty percent,' thus 'answering the purpose for which the road was constructed,' as the Trouts point out, 'the general advantage and improvement of the country.' The Board of Agriculture's report for 1858 on Huron County suggested that 'the list of roads contemplated to be gravelled, and for which a by-law is at present published, will bring the whole county within three or four hours teaming of some depot on the railroad,' and another, somewhat boosterish commentator noted that 'by the end of 1858 London had rail connections to the west at Windsor and Sarnia and to the east or northeast at Stratford and Hamilton (thus with Toronto, Montreal, and Portland), Suspension Bridge (thus with New York and Boston) and to the south at Port Stanley.'

But these developments had some ill-effects and were symptomatic of major changes in the economics of the region. In 1858, the Grand Trunk had built a line to connect London to its main line, which had just reached St Marys on its way to Sarnia. This junction or branch down to London from what Talman called 'the east or northeast' was a pointed intrusion into the territory of the Great Western, designed to redirect grain and other traffic from Chicago to the Grand Trunk's route to Montreal and Portland and away from the Great Western's connections at Niagara. At this moment, London became so competitive a point that a Port Stanley transportation option became insignificant. In the fight between the Grand Trunk and the Great Western regional Delivery, which had initiated Port Stanley's plank road and railway and the expansion of its harbour, was subsumed into (and so marginalized by) the Through Passage of grain by both water and rail from Chicago and the American 'Great West' (Illinois, Michigan, Wisconsin, Iowa, and, in the early days, Minnesota and the Dakotas). Thomas Odle, who has studied it in the most detail, argues that in these years the grain trade of the Great Lakes was largely American. The degree to which this was so in the 1860s and 1870s, and the degree to which the export of the wheat of Canada West/Ontario was thus made superfluous to continental grain export, is indicated in the broad swoops of Figure 3.1.[18]

Railways and Through Passage

As we can see, we may read the first three decades of Port Stanley's history for how the capitalist development of the Delivery of southwestern Ontario's surplus produce was overtaken by the grander capitalist interest and investment in Through Passage. By the 1860s what was important to the controlling centres of transportation and other investment capital was the bulk of produce channelled through Chicago from the Great West and the necessity to transport that bulk to the East unbroken; the name for this set of priorities, axioms, technologies, and geographical and political locations and routes was the American Grain Trade. As I mentioned above, this was initially a waterborne trade, which is why the railway joined the waterway at Port Stanley. I want to keep that designation, American Grain Trade, to label for our purposes that system to the south and to turn now to the history of the northern, Canadian railway response. Since it was also Through Passage, this development too had little direct impact on southwestern Ontario as a region, beyond the maintenance of roadbeds and way-stations and other such services. Indirectly, of course, despite the Grand Trunk's 1873 lease to Bernard Stanley of land in Lucan to build a grain warehouse, the development of the railways defined Biddulph Township's Access and Circulation, and its Delivery of exports and imports, as marginal to the Canadian and North American economy. We can read these larger meanings in the more local changes; just as the history of Port Stanley allows us to trace relations in the 1850s and 1860s, so the history of London's railways allows us to follow the later relations of Through Passage.[19]

While the London and Port Stanley Railway was, in James J. Talman's words, 'the first railway built in Southwestern Ontario with a view to developing the region rather than providing a short cut across the peninsula,' much earlier the Great Western Railway had been planned for that same regional benefit. The Great Western originated practically in a public meeting in London in 1832, which petitioned the legislative assembly for a railway to transport produce from London to the headwaters of Lake Ontario, through the Escarpment and bypassing Niagara Falls, to Dundas, on Burlington Bay, which in those years was developing into the main Lake Ontario port for the southwestern part of the province. A committee of the legislature then studied the transportation needs of London, as well as the inland parts of the Huron Tract and the Western District, and recommended that a company be formed to construct that 'reproduction in iron of Governor Simcoe's road of the last century' (adding the fond hope that soon railways would be built from Goderich and the foot of Lake Huron to London), and in 1834 the London and Gore Railroad Company was incorporated. James Talman notes that the list of promoters of the London and Gore read like 'a Who's Who in London': among them were Edward Allen Talbot, Allan MacNab (eventually president of the Great Western), and the prospering London merchant who would not use Port Stanley, George Jervis Goodhue. As Thomas Keefer remarked in his *Philosophy of Railroads* in 1849, 'It is admitted upon all hands that the Great Western route is the best unoccupied one for a Railway in America.' The route was surveyed as far west as Chatham, but there were difficulties raising capital in England, and the Rebellion at the end of the decade intervened.

After the Act of Union, in 1845, the London and Gore changed its name to the Great Western Rail Road and was authorized to build to a point on the Niagara River, as well as from Chatham to Windsor and from London to Sarnia. G.R. Stevens describes, in summary, three circumstances that by the mid-1840s had driven the promoters of the Great Western to this further action: 'The local traffic was no longer restricted to Hamilton and London townships and the eighty miles of territory between them; to the north and south of this zone other towns and villages clamoured for rail connections. In Canada East and the Maritimes ... the Main Line was beginning to take shape; it therefore was urgently necessary for the London and Gore to stake out its claim in Canada West. Finally, United States traffic between the Atlantic seaboard and the Middle West had outgrown the existing services and Americans were eyeing the shorter route across Canada.' Thus, as another historian comments: 'Instead of being a local road connecting the interior of what is now called Western Ontario with navigation on Lake Ontario, it would be a through route between Detroit and Niagara frontiers.'[20]

From Delivery, in other words, to Through Passage, without laying a rail. The financing was arranged, and in 1849 the Great Western was able to take advantage of the Guarantee Act, by which the Canadian government guaranteed the interest on half the cost of any railway line over seventy miles long. By November 1853, the Great Western's track was opened from Hamilton to the new Suspension Bridge connecting with the New York Central at Niagara Falls. The (originary) line to London opened a month later, and the line from London to Windsor, connecting by ferry with the Michigan Central Railway, opened in January 1854. The Great Western, as Glazebrook says, 'was cast for a triple rôle: for the traffic of the peninsula; as part of a Canadian trunk line; and as part of an American Trunk Line.' Meanwhile, in 1851, the Main Trunk Line of Railway Act had declared that the Great Western's new line to Windsor would be recognized as the westernmost extension of 'a main line running from east to west of Canada, and connecting on the one extreme with winter ports and on the other with middle-western American railways.' But in 1853 that interprovincial line, the Grand Trunk, had also acquired the charter of the unbuilt Toronto and Guelph Railway, which was authorized to link those two places but also and more importantly to build beyond Guelph to Sarnia. As Stevens says: 'Whoever built to Guelph would build on to Sarnia, and so to Chicago.' Indeed, on a map of the Huron District compiled by the surveyor Donald McDonald in 1846 there is a signpost at Stratford pointing 'To Guelph direct 39 1/4 miles,' 'To Hamilton, 56 miles,' and to various other places, the most distant of which is 'Port Sarnia, 76 1/4 miles' (as we know, Donald McDonald would have land interests in that direction).

The Great Western management, wary of the Grand Trunk's intentions, immediately responded by planning a branch line from Hamilton to Toronto, which would both connect with the Grand Trunk and discourage that railway from building a competing line to the Michigan frontier. Whether or not this branch was an invasion of Grand Trunk territory, the prospectus of the newly reorganized Grand Trunk in 1853 revoked its commitment to making the Great Western its branch line to Windsor and declared Sarnia to be the terminus of its independent line through southwestern Ontario. And so by 1856 – when the London and Port Stanley Railway was opened, 'with a view to developing the region' – the similar plans of the original London and Hamilton investors for a regional line delivering produce to a Lake Ontario port had been radically altered by events. Not only had the Great Western become a through line supplementing the American Grain Trade by connecting Chicago with the American east, but it was wholly caught up in what were to be the continuing contradictions in these plans – the American connections and competition, the conflict with the Grand Trunk, and the desire to monopolize the region. As the American consul to Canada reported in 1851: 'The commercial position of Canada West as a "portage" or "stepping-stone" between the manufacturing and commercial States on the Atlantic and the agricultural and mineral ones of the northwest, is illustrated by the Welland Canal, the Great Western, and the Ontario and Huron railways.'[21]

The development of the railways across southwestern Ontario, the details of finance and entrepreneurship, the choice of routes and termini, the actual construction of the rail lines, and their relations with railways outside Canada form a complex, intricate history; we have already glanced at some niceties of the Grand Trunk's march across Biddulph Township. Here, in my attempt to display the characteristics and effects of this phase of Through Passage, I mean to limit my discussion to its large functions in the third quarter of the nineteenth century – the competition over the ground of southwestern Ontario for the trade of Chicago and the Great West and then in the late 1870s the very material anticipation of the Canadian National Grain Route, the transportation of Manitoba and western wheat across northern Canada to Montreal and the east coast. While a series of agreements and accommodations was made between the Great Western and the Grand Trunk through the 1860s and 1870s, there was inevitably strong competition. The Great Western also had its arrangements (enabled by the age-old bonding privilege) with Vanderbilt's aggressive New York Central, and in 1866 the Great Western provided a third rail (called by some the 'annexation rail') for the American narrow-gauge trains, allowing the first all-rail grain shipments from Chicago to New York.

As I have mentioned, in 1858 the Grand Trunk constructed a junction line between St Marys and London, giving Chicago shippers the option to continue their shipments by rail (and broad gauge) to tidewater at Montreal and Portland, instead of taking the Great Western route to the New York Central at Niagara Falls. This line connected the Grand Trunk with the trade to and from Chicago not only via Windsor, but also, from 1858, via the Great Western's branch line from Komoka, to Sarnia. James Talman was to remark in 1953: 'Interestingly enough the most important line of the C.N.R. through Southwestern Ontario is the old G.W.R. right-of-way, the Komoka to Sarnia branch, being the important link.' By the late 1870s, the bulk of the Grand Trunk traffic with Chicago went through London rather than over its own original line to Sarnia.

Passing through Biddulph from Chicago

As we have seen, that Grand Trunk line through Biddulph to Sarnia had produced, practically *ex nihilo*, the village of Lucan. The meaning of its decline as a main route, however, is not so direct and immediate: Lucan and Biddulph were made marginal by these later railway decisions but were made marginal most notably by the long-term purposes and chosen locations of transportation capital, of which that one rail line was but a tentacle. Lucan, called into being by the Grand Trunk right-of-way crossing the London–Goderich Road, slipped into inevitable decline in contrast to, for example, St Marys, a classic illustration of Marx's generalization in his chapter on 'Circulation Time': 'A place of production which possessed a particularly advantageous position through being situated on a main road or canal now finds itself on a single railway branch line that operates only at relatively long intervals, while another point, which previously lay completely off the major traffic routes, now lies at the intersection of several lines.' An 1898 U.S. transportation report recalling the change at this time to 'scientific rate making' demonstrates the logic of this process most succinctly. In the early days of the railways, freight charges showed very little differentiation from one locale, or one cargo, to another; rates were charged according to an inflexible, uniform schedule: 'The decisive change in rate making came when it was recognized that it may be profitable to establish a rate which will result in a net gain, however small, above the expenses arising strictly from the mere handling and moving of freight and such incidental expenses as are properly applicable to it. In other words, it is not always to be insisted upon that any given traffic must bear its full share of the total expenses of the road. The question is, rather, Will this traffic form a profitable auxiliary of the existing traffic?'

Here, the knowledge, plans, and objectives of the entire railway corporation, of that particular sector of Capital, dictate what shall be the rates in any specific locale or shipment, and such 'science' dictated as well the fate of the line through Biddulph. Figure 3.2 shows Biddulph's location in the pattern of railways, yet the curve down to London of the Grand Trunk junction line, which doomed the track through Biddulph to Sarnia, and the complementary slight curve by which the London, Huron and Bruce shuns Biddulph on its way up to Wingham, both perhaps overdramatize the point I am trying to make. It is not simply that Lucan had lost its chance to be a railway intersection, perhaps a competitive point; rather, it is that the changing geography of capitalist wheat production in North America and the logic of the transportation capital that served it were starting to marginalize not only Lucan and Biddulph but southwestern Ontario as a whole. In the emerging relations of capitalist agriculture, neither the line of wagons down to Port Stanley nor Bernard Stanley's 1873 grain warehouse in Lucan would count for much. The grain trade was becoming either 'American' or 'National.'

In the 1870s, the Grand Trunk competed ever more single-mindedly for the Chicago and western carrying trade, replacing its iron rails with steel in 1870 – an event 'of transcendant importance,' allowing heavier locomotives and more heavily loaded cars. In 1869 the Grand Trunk devised a way to change the gauge of cars by shifting the wheels on the axles, and cars fitted in this way were used to haul freight between Chicago and Boston without the need for a transfer at Sarnia and Montreal (or at London). The Grand Trunk switched from wood to the longer-burning coal in 1872 and finally narrowed its track to the American gauge in 1872–4. These actions are all responses to the axioms of transportation economics discussed above. 'At that time,' says William Wilgus, 'it was evident that the Grand Trunk had no aspirations to serve the

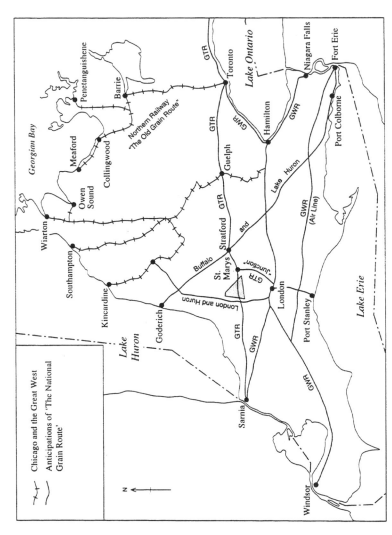

Figure 3.2

The pattern of 'Through Passage': main lines and principal affiliates, 1854–62

West, except as was made possible through its connections made in 1881 at Chicago with American lines reaching in a host of directions to the Ohio and Mississippi and beyond.' The Great Western tried breathlessly to keep pace, with both railways demonstrating the belief that was to dominate transportation policy for a century – 'namely, that by building trunk roads, canals and railroads, Canada could become the carrier of United States goods.' In 1873, finally taking advantage of the short-cut from Windsor to Niagara Falls south of the Great Western's main track, the Michigan Central, a New York Central affiliate, opened the Canada Southern Railway. According to the *London Advertiser* five years later, for a time it was thought that the Canada Southern might run through London, making it a powerfully competitive point, but the city lost its opportunity. The Great Western matched the Southern, in the same year and in roughly the same space, with its Air Line, from Fort Erie to Glencoe, continuing on its main track west of London; in the nineteenth century, 'air line' signified 'as the crow flies' – the most direct Through Passage.[22]

There are other details that indicate the effects, both specific and diffuse, on southwestern Ontario of the Grand Trunk's drive to Chicago in the 1860s and 1870s, overdetermined by the Great Western's competition and attempts by the New York Central to deny it a secure right-of-way through Michigan. The competition was not always over the grain trade. Throughout the 1870s, the minutes of the Grand Trunk's executive committee record a series of decisions related to the 'dressed meat' (as opposed to the 'livestock') traffic from Chicago to the east coast. In January 1876, the executive thought it necessary to fit up more refrigerator cars. By 23 November, nineteen cars were so fitted up, 'for the conveyance of fresh meat from Toronto to Portland for shipment to Europe on the principle of Week's Patent,' and in February 1877 an agreement was discussed for the use of 'Week's Patent Refrigerator as applied to Freight Cars.' The minutes note many such decisions – in 1879, to keep a stock (300 tons) of ice at Kingston; in 1881, to rent 120 more refrigerator cars and to erect an ice-house at Sarnia – as well as the larger decisions regulating competition, as in the proposal made by the American railways in Boston in August 1878 to divide the dressed-meat traffic from Chicago: 63 per cent to New York Central Railroad and 37 per cent to the Grand Trunk and the Central Vermont lines. Cronon's history of Chicago shows how these matters affecting the Grand Trunk Railway in Canada were the result of developments in the Chicago beef trade and the New York Central's desire to monopolize eastbound traffic.

As late as 1871, 96 per cent of the beef passing through Chicago to eastern cities was shipped live, in cattle cars. In the mid-1870s, Gustavus Swift, the Chicago meatpacker, commissioned new railway cars, refrigerated by ice harvested in Wisconsin, to transport dressed rather than live beef. Cronon writes: 'The refrigerated railway car, like the grain elevator, was a simple piece of technology with extraordinarily far-reaching implications. The most obvious was the steep growth in Chicago beef packing that began in the mid-1870s.' Cronon's account of the rise of the Chicago industry is detailed and fascinating, and it impinges importantly on the matter of rail transport through southwestern Ontario. The American railways had immense investments in stockyards for live cattle in Chicago, as well as in the railway cars to transport live cattle to eastern wholesale butchers. 'Faced with protecting their investment, and with their classic problem of fixed capital costs in a competitive economic environment, the roads tried to support livestock shippers who could guarantee them a large and reliable volume of freight traffic,' and they responded to dressed beef by 'passive resistance': 'They refused to provide capital equipment in the form of refrigerator cars and icing stations. They were reluctant to guarantee a steady volume of traffic or the rapid handling that was essential to iced shipments. They set rates that put dressed beef at a disadvantage against live shipments ... Although they could not forbid dressed beef shipments entirely, they did what they could to make them inconvenient and unprofitable.'

Fortunately for Swift, Cronon adds, there was a railway going east that did not significantly engage in the cattle traffic – the Grand Trunk:

Because its line was so much more circuitous than those of its competitors, and because cattle required constant feeding and watering while they traveled, the Grand Trunk had never succeeded as a livestock carrier. Locked out of the highly profitable American meat trade, its managers were delighted when Swift approached them about carrying dressed beef. Travel distance mattered little for chilled meat so long as ice was available along the way – and on that score the Grand Trunk's colder northern route was a positive advantage. The railroad quickly became the leading carrier of Chicago dressed beef. By 1885, the Grand Trunk was hauling 292 million pounds of the commodity, over 60 percent of the city's output.

From the early 1880s, there were fierce rate wars over dressed beef (the discussion in 1878 noted above was but a truce), and eventually there was a radical change in the structure of American meat marketing. But I am interested in this history only for what it reveals of the ways in which the Grand Trunk's increasing preoccupation with through traffic from Chicago in the 1870s displaced the regional services that it and the Great Western had, thirty years earlier, offered to southwestern Ontario, marginalizing that community, those communities, to the interests of North American Capital, which had originally enabled the delivery of their surpluses.

To complete this pattern, the geography of Through Passage through southwestern Ontario, I want now to return and look at how, from the 1870s, other Ontario railways began to think less of Chicago and to anticipate what came to be called the 'National Grain Route,' the second of the two large functions of Through Passage in the third quarter of the nineteenth century – transporting Manitoba and western wheat across northern Ontario to Montreal and the east coast from the 1880s on.[23]

Passing by Biddulph: The National Grain Route

The American Grain Trade, waterborne from Chicago to the foot of Lake Erie, was oddly instrumental in establishing Canada's National Grain Route. R.L. Jones records that by the early 1860s steamers were carrying grain from Lake Michigan ports to Sarnia or Collingwood. The Lake Huron ports actively competed for the Chicago trade, as of course did Buffalo, and in 1858 the Buffalo and Lake Huron Railway was opened from Fort Erie to Goderich, both to 'render tributary to [Buffalo] the rich peninsula of Canada West' and to divert rail traffic from the Suspension Bridge. In 1863, Thomas Keefer was to describe this line as simply a portage in the lake route, but his comments, his inevitable oversights and silences at this historical moment, marvellously intimate what was to come within the decade: 'Virtually connecting Lake Huron with Lake Erie, [the Buffalo and Lake Huron] can have, on this route, no through traffic – because this could only be supplied during the season of navigation when there is slack water of unlimited capacity between its termini, with which it is impossible it can compete.' Keefer is clearly assuming that the western terminus of this route must be Chicago, a natural assumption in 1863, during the heyday of the American Grain Trade. He continues: 'The great want of this road is a terminus on Lake Ontario, in which case it would become available for the grain traffic from Chicago and Milwaukee, or Cleveland and Toledo, to Oswego, Ogdensburgh, New York, or Montréal.' Keefer here tries (too early) to imagine a grain route that would not be American, would not originate in Chicago, and would not place Montreal last on its list of termini. Ironically, this route was in the process of being built (though not with clear foresight) along several lines in Ontario a few miles to the east, even as its point of origin was being established in agriculture and transportation in the Canadian northwest.

As we have seen, there had been for millennia two routes from the St Lawrence to the west, the one progressing up the successive Great Lakes, the other bypassing the lower Lakes and southwestern Ontario, whether via the Ottawa River and Lake Nipissing or from Toronto to Lake Simcoe and thence to Georgian Bay, by canoe or, later, the planked Yonge Street. As Harold Innis remarked, 'The geographically strategic location of Toronto on a direct route from Lake Huron to Lake Ontario ... made it particularly susceptible to the prospects of traffic developed in the north-west,' and the Ontario, Simcoe and Huron Railway (Upper Canada's first railway, known after 1858 as the Northern Railway) was built in 1853 to connect Toronto with Collingwood on Georgian Bay. The Northern Railway, while initially serving the local lumber industry, at the same time was a portage route, linking sections of the American Grain Route by the new technology. As Glazebrook says: 'In essence the Northern railway combined two ideas: to open up the fertile country north of Toronto, and – the more ambitious purpose – to make a portage railway to Georgian Bay whence steamers could connect with the ports of Lakes Huron and Michigan, and so draw the trade of the west through to Lake Ontario.'

Collingwood, with a grain elevator in 1871, is thus the oldest of the Georgian Bay transfer ports, tapping the American Grain Trade through the Lakes from Chicago to establish in Canada what was known as the 'old grain route': Chicago to Collingwood by water ('a veritable procession of vessels,' say Middleton and Landon), to Toronto by rail, and then from Toronto either by lake and canal to Oswego or Ogdensburg, or on to Montreal. This is, I repeat, still an *American* trade route, dependent on Chicago and the grain of its neighbouring states. It depended also on the protocol of June 1875 (revoked in 1883) to the 1871 Treaty of Washington, which gave Canadian forwarding companies the right to carry grain from one U.S. port to another, so long as part of the route was over Canadian soil. As yet (i.e., from the 1850s through the 1870s), the Northern Railway was simply an alternative route, an adjunct to the water route that I have already mapped and discussed – 'expressive,' as Wilgus says, 'of the extent to which the international boundary was ignored by both countries in the search for preferable ways of joining the eastern states with the region bounding the waters of the Upper Lakes.' While its significance for us at this point is that its route purposefully bypasses southwestern Ontario on its through passage from Chicago, it is equally significant that its sources, markets, and outlets were American, as Odle says, generally separate from the Canadian trade. But it was soon to separate more decisively from that American trade; in the meantime, a rail line was in place running south from Georgian Bay to meet the Grand Trunk at Toronto, with, from 1871, a grain elevator at Collingwood.[24]

Also in those same years of the mid-century, a linked set of discoveries had made possible the massive development of wheat-growing in the American northwest and on the Canadian prairies. The first was the increased awareness of the hardiness and bread-making qualities of a spring-wheat variety known as 'Red Fife.' Introduced in Wisconsin, Minnesota, and the Dakotas in the 1860s, Red Fife was the chief variety in Ontario by the early 1870s, when spring wheat made up about 60 per cent of the total crop. Cultivated in Manitoba (as 'Manitoba #1 Hard') during these same years, it 'began to attract attention in 1876' and made up the bulk of the first shipment to Britain from the Lakehead in 1883 (it is, incidentally, the male parent of 'Marquis,' the hybrid that, with its varieties, has been the Canadian standard ever since). But the introduction of Red Fife was itself made possible by the revolution in flour-milling that occurred in the 1870s; Red Fife flour, while an excellent bread flour, had a poor colour because the older milling methods were unable to remove the red bran. A 'New Process' in milling and a 'Middlings Purifier' developed at the Washburn B. Mill in Minneapolis produced a 'Patent' flour that was an immediate commercial success, encouraging the increased production of Red Fife and the opening of the Canadian prairies to grain production. These developments, with the new Canadian Pacific line to Fort William at the Lakehead, where the Canadian Pacific built the first of several grain elevators, made possible the new 'Canadian Grain Route.' Porritt suggests that we might also acknowledge the 'far-seeing men in the grain and forwarding business at Montreal and Toronto,' but it seems unlikely that there were many, if any, as far-seeing as the engineer-philosopher T.C. Keefer, and even he was unable in 1863 to anticipate the highly complex possibilities – railways on Lake Superior and Georgian Bay, a hardy spring wheat, a new milling process, and thus a geographical shift – that would produce the Canadian route.

For there are conditions for possibility of a Canadian route that could be recognized only later, by comparing its (historical) geography to that of the American route. As Tunell points out, from about 1868 the various eastern railways (including, I presume, the Grand Trunk and Great Western), with increasing success and contrary to Keefer's prediction, had competed with the water carriers for the American grain trade out of Chicago. But the continued westward and, most important, the *northward* movement of wheat-growing areas from the early 1870s decisively influenced the choice of transport. As the major wheat-growing areas moved behind and above Lake Superior, Chicago and its railways lost their geographical advantage. The Lakes carriers, now taking their cargoes from ports at the head of Lake Superior, were no longer handicapped by 'an excessively circuitous route,' though Tunell (in 1896–7) notes that in the future the Canadian Pacific would provide an even shorter line to Montreal. But by the early 1880s, the shortest, coolest grain route to tidewater was by steamer across Lake Superior, through Sault Ste Marie, to ports on northern Lake Huron and Georgian Bay, and thence by rail to Montreal and further east. The 1875 protocol to which I referred above encouraged for a time even Minnesota and Dakota wheat to be transported from Duluth to Ogdensburg by Canadian boats and the railway line from Collingwood to Toronto. And in the early 1880s it was taken for granted that all grain from Fort William and Port Arthur would go east by water during the Lakes navigation season to Georgian Bay ports in steamers too large for the Welland and St Lawrence Canals (see Figure 3.3).

How did this shift affect Ontario (not to be more precise)? As we have seen, the Northern Railway was in place by 1855, with its elevator at Collingwood in 1871, attempting to tap into the southern, American Grain Trade. This became the ambition of other Georgian Bay and Lake Huron ports, as they established branches of the main-line Ontario railways. The Great Western, encouraged by its connections with the New York Central to cultivate the American Grain Trade, sent branches in 1874 to Kincardine and Southampton (the hatched lines to the west on Figure 3.2), and the London, Huron and Bruce, from London to the intersection at Wingham in 1876 (the unhatched line running along the west boundary of Biddulph on the map). All these routes, while initially intended to connect with the grain trade out of Chicago (like 'the old grain route' through Collingwood to Lake Ontario), are to become links in the Canadian National Grain Route when, in 1882, the Grand Trunk swallows the Great Western group of railways.

But the future was clear (to even short-seeing men in the grain and forwarding business) as early as 1873, when the Toronto, Grey and Bruce

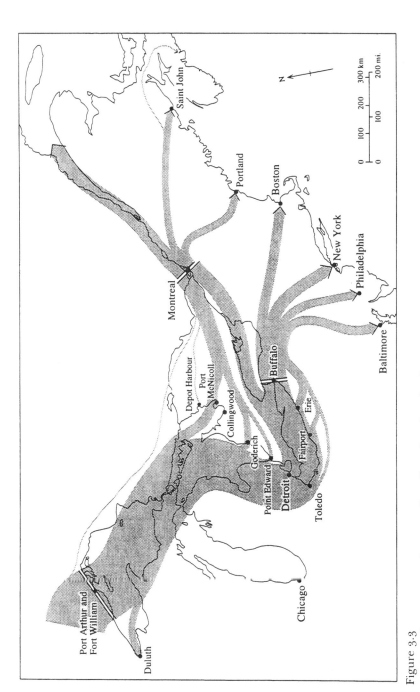

Figure 3.3
Eastbound movement of western Canadian wheat in calendar year 1913

Railway, affiliated to the Canadian Pacific, built a line connecting Owen Sound on Georgian Bay with Toronto, specifically as a through line for traffic from Lake Superior, with the Canadian Pacific adding a grain elevator in Owen Sound in 1885. The immediate future was to lie in the National Grain Route, taking western Canadian wheat by water to Lake Huron and Georgian Bay ports, for transfer to railways angling down to the east for connection with Montreal. This future did not include Biddulph Township or southwestern Ontario. As grain transport achieved ever more efficient Through Passage to Montreal and Quebec, by 1887 Toronto too lost its place: while still a market for grain, it was no longer on the grain route. This economic marginalization is the new pattern of transportation capital's shaping of community in southwestern Ontario, overdetermined by the geography and survey, the processes of settlement, the political institutions, and the practices of agriculture. These are the determinate circumstances of the Biddulph grain trade – not only, as we see below, of the business of such Lucan grain forwarders as Stanley, Dight and Co., but of the form of agricultural production and the kinds of produce out on the farms of the township, as with the farms on the Roman Line, the Donnellys' among them.[25]

4

The Trace of the Wheat Staple

I want now to look more closely at the cargo of those wagons, schooners, barges, and railway cars, to examine aspects of the agricultural history of southwestern Ontario. Like settlement and transportation, agriculture is at first glance an intractable topic, apparently static and ahistorical, like the glacier, or even 'timeless,' like the forest encountered by the first settlers. But as second nature, the agricultural history of nineteenth-century Ontario may be traced, first of all, by simple, empirical chronologies: the succession of harvests, the varying prices for produce, and the stages of its export history, marked by successive tariffs here and there, bonding agreements, periodic free trade with the United States, and so on. Just as there was constant glacial movement amid successive terminal pauses, so these events are merely symptoms of the historical development of Upper Canadian agriculture, as from its inception it developed a wheat staple with distinctive practices and linkages, which by the last third of the nineteenth century was transformed into mixed farming, whose practices and linkages, of course, were very different. This chapter is mainly devoted to tracing practices and linkages, but I realize that in choosing to focus on the wheat staple in this manner I am adopting a position, or at least an alignment, and I need at least to resituate the staples question as I direct my attention to Biddulph Township. I have been circling about that particular place and the places of which it is made up, delineating successive structures that together constituted its social formation in the mid-nineteenth century. In this chapter I address the fact that Biddulph Township's main crop was wheat; what did that mean, in that place and in those decades? And then, how does that fact interact with the geography, settlement, and kinds of movement discussed above?

In *The Fur Trade in Canada*, describing how eventually the canoe disappeared as the dominant form of transport for the fur traders, Harold Innis famously remarked: 'Dependence on the York boat rather than the canoe was symbolic of the increasing importance of capitalism,' and my discussion in the previous chapter of the construction of Port Stanley's harbour, plank road, and railway might seem to imply the same historical conclusion about the later trade, as synonymous with or symbolizing the increasing importance of capital in southwestern Ontario farming. But to emphasize the figurative relation is to play down the material historical relation. Innis, it seems to me, is content with a rhetorical flourish – 'symbolic of,' 'synonymous with.' I would want, possibly flirting with 'determinism,' to be more precisely materialist. Rhetorically speaking, the development of Port Stanley is a metonymy for the capitalist transformation of Delivery in southwestern Ontario – that is, it embodies representative material components of that transition, representing it while also in part constituting it. As we have seen, the harbour, road, and railway were, for a moment, important parts of the actual developing structure of capitalist transportation on Lake Erie. Innis's terms 'symbol' and 'synonym' evade that metonymic assertion of historical determinacy, but I want strongly to assert it in its full complexity. However small and short-lived their impact, Port Stanley and its road are metonyms for developing capitalist transportation relations, what we have called the American Grain Trade.

For the American Grain Trade, the stream of wheat flowing from Chicago's grain elevators to those in Buffalo and then onward, was by mid-century already capitalist. The wheat staple in mid-nineteenth-century Upper Canada, in contrast, was not capitalist (as is the modern western Canadian wheat staple, which exhibits capitalism's characteristic features: capitalization, mechanization, and exploitation of wage labour), but rather mercantilist. Thus agriculture in nineteenth-century Upper Canada existed as a contradictory structure: all agricultural production in the province was overdetermined by the wheat staple; that is what a staple is (originally, 'a town or place ... in which was a body of merchants having the exclusive right of purchase of certain goods destined for export'; *OED*). But the Upper Canadian staple, while itself mercantilist, was but a subsector of the developing North Atlantic capitalist economy. My assertions here – that an Upper Canadian wheat staple existed, that it was mercantilist, and that it had some relation to North American capitalist agriculture – engage the two main recent controversies in Canada over the wheat staple: on the one hand, the debate between staples historians and the neoclassical, cliometric economic historians, and on the other hand, the debate with a certain kind of marxism. I attempt to deal with both of these debates more or less at once, countering the cliometric denials that there was a wheat staple at all by means of a marxist analysis that both uses and rejects ultra-leftist criticisms of the staples historians. And then, of course, I point out the relevance of all this to the Huron Tract.[1]

Upper Canada's Wheat Staple

What is at issue in these debates is not that there was a great deal of wheat grown in Upper Canada in the middle third of the nineteenth century. In 1851, it was the impression of Israel D. Andrews, the American consul for Canada, that 'there is probably no country where there is so much wheat grown, in proportion to the population and the area under cultivation, as in that part of Canada west of Kingston.' This was not wholly impressionistic, for Andrews's report to the U.S. Senate included precise data on the number of acres under wheat and their produce in bushels. Even those contemporary Canadian historians who most consistently oppose the notion of an Upper Canadian wheat staple acknowledge that in Upper Canada 'wheat was the preeminent marketable commodity' and that 'it would be silly even to suggest that Canada did not have a wheat boom in the 1850s.' As Jones puts it, 'wheat was by no means the only crop grown by the wheat farmer; it was simply the one which he sold.' The issue is rather whether there was a staple in wheat or simply an 'unhealthy dependence on wheat monoculture,' raising the further historical (and theoretical) issue of the later transition to something else. Its supporters suggest that the staples thesis provides a framework for research, 'a point of view, a perspective, a way of *seeing* the data,' and I would agree, wanting at the same time to say some things about that perspective. Traditionally seen as 'a unifying theme of diffuse application rather than an analytic tool,' the staples thesis provides a 'powerfully wide-angled account' of the economic growth of Canada – 'a description of specific empirical matters and a statement about the origins and trajectories of resource-intensive exports and their linkages within "new" countries.' As W.T. Easterbrook put it (and this is why I believe that it is ultimately the most useful framework for my own inquiry), 'The staple ... may be viewed as a tool of analysis which enables study of total situations in terms of resources, technology and markets, and the institutions, economic, political and social, in which these are embedded.'

The Upper Canadian wheat staple was from its beginning embedded in a structured *colonial* relation. The structure is, first of all, one of dependence, the main significance of the term 'mercantile.' And that colonial relation is constituted by what Mel Watkins calls its various linkages: 'forward linkages,' such as further processing or manufacturing, as in the milling of wheat; 'backward linkages,' such as 'capital goods linkages' with the manufacture of agricultural machinery for wheat production; 'infrastructure linkages,' as in the construction of Port Stanley, its road and railway, and the Welland and St Lawrence Canals; and lastly, 'final demand linkages,' or the disposition of the income generated. The staples thesis thus attributes a complex dependence to the Upper Canadian social formation as a whole in its mercantilist colonial relation, which I want to explore in some detail.

While anti-marxist, Harold Innis took a stance critical of the capitalist system, which he called in a characteristically generalized way 'the price system,' and his categories imply a focus on relations of distribution rather than production of staples. As Drache points out, Innis described the Canadian economy as distinctively soft capitalism: 'The staple mode of development is defined by its commercial orientation.' In this it has affinities with the influential work of Innis's colleague Donald Creighton on the commercial empire of the St Lawrence. Over his entire career, Creighton argued against reading Canadian historical development through the lens of Turner's frontier theory, insisting that Canada's history was distinguished by 'the maintainance of her vital connection with Europe.' 'Frontier,' as we saw above, meant something different in Canada, and as William Cronon says, 'Canadians have always had a rather different way of thinking about national unity and connectedness.' As a Canadian economic historian points out, the frontiers of settlement 'were curbed and controlled in the interests of a unity threatened by United States penetration.' Or, in Creighton's words: 'The story of the frontier was the story of a metropolis insinuating its economic, social, and political influence into virtually every aspect of life on the continent, albeit with regional resistance to metropolitan effects on the basis of cultural and historical differences.' As distinct from the United States, Canada placed itself on an economic axis that was, he wrote, 'a great competitive east–west trading system, founded on the St Lawrence River and the Great Lakes, one end of which lay in the metropolitan centres of western Europe and the other in the hinterland of North America.'

The staples thesis in its widest historical reach thus sees at the beginning of the period we are discussing a Canadian trading system located

specifically on the St Lawrence, in Montreal, and on the shores of the
lower Great Lakes and linked by its mercantilist colonial origins to the
British imperial system. As Fowke summarized it: 'The commercial and
financial groups on the St Lawrence pinned their first hopes for prosperity on the possibility of continued expansion of staple-producing agriculture'; moreover, as he put it elsewhere, 'the merchants in Canada regarded the St Lawrence as the "natural" trade route for the agricultural
commerce of the continental interior.' The period of this development
that concerns us – that of the Upper Canadian wheat staple – began in
the early 1800s and was to end by the 1880s.[2]

Debating the Wheat Staple

The theoretical argument over the nineteenth-century wheat staple is
especially important for helping to clarify what was significant in the
history of Upper Canadian/Ontario wheat production and its place as
well in the social history of the communities of Biddulph Township,
overdetermining, with the other conditions we have examined, the events
of 1879–80 on the Roman Line. In examining the critique of the staples
thesis mounted since the 1970s by the Canadian cliometricians (the
'new economic' or 'market' historians), I concentrate on the work of
R.M. McInnis, mainly his omnibus article, 'Perspectives on Ontario Agriculture 1815–1930,' and in particular its first chapter, 'The Early Ontario
Wheat Staple Reconsidered' (1990). The market historians brought to
bear on the staples thesis what Donald McCloskey, a frequent apologist
for the new economic history, calls 'the economist's elaborate tools of
reasoning,' and McInnis takes as his thesis that in the early nineteenth
century 'there was no established staple export for wheat but that Upper
Canada successfully specialized in wheat farming.' He writes: 'Ontario
specialized in the production of wheat, and thereby did quite well economically. It did not have a wheat staple.' He enforces this conclusion by
examining the requisites for a staple, the 'staples framework,' using
McCloskey's 'economist's box of tools.'
   McInnis considers several features of the staples thesis, beginning with
its 'special or selective nature,' that it applies specifically to 'overseas
areas of European settlement' (what the staples theorists themselves would
further specify as 'new economies,' an important difference). He questions as well the focus on 'the exploitation of natural resources' because
'all parts of the world, settled and unsettled, have land of some sort'; we
have above looked enough at the particular sort of land in southwestern

Ontario not to linger on this point. Not surprisingly, McInnis finds the most salient feature of the staples framework to be its emphasis on export markets; again, these are specified historically only as being 'in the long-established economies of Europe.' And he further abstracts or reduces secondary effects of a staple economy, the linkages forward and back and so on, as neoclassical 'inputs' but then points to the larger institutional preoccupations of staples theorists – the influence of a staple economy on local markets, property holding, and the distribution of wealth. The final feature that he mentions is 'a strong commodity determinism,' what McCalla and George too called Harold Innis's 'staples determinism,' or C.B. Schedvin, 'a mild form of geographical and technological determinism.' I hope to examine specific linkages, to distinguish their determinacy while avoiding determinism.[3]

My comments on the points of McInnis's analysis of the staples thesis are not intended as sniping but rather as marking in each instance his retreat from that framework and the historical specificity with which its adherents endow it towards the inappropriate abstractions of a neoclassical economist's toolbox. For example, mentioning the high cost of transport over which Upper Canadian farmers and merchants had no control, McInnis speaks simply of 'transport costs' or 'transatlantic freights.' But these categories ignore too much in their abstraction as simple costs – or as 'a particular example of an investment process, which need not require a special approach through staples theory' – losing the concretenesses that we saw addressed by the very logic of capital, such matters as the geographical location of ocean ports, their climate, and their differing potential as entrepôts. These concrete elements constitute what Easterbrook called the staple's 'total situation;' what is gained by their evasion is simply 'the toolbox.' The tools of economic theory – cost-benefit analysis, productivity measurement, regression analysis, 'a consistent model of the cyclical determination of national income' (no determinism here!) – all were fashioned, McCloskey writes, 'to be used together in the economists['] work, to meet in a coordinated fashion one or another requirement of the description and analysis of economic events.' Or, as he put it elsewhere: 'Not counting but economic theory, especially the theory of price, is the defining skill of cliometricians, as of other economists.' The system in question being neoclassical economic theory, the conclusions, he acknowledges, have often been variations on the theme 'The Market, God Bless It, Works.' The reductions or abstractions that I have pointed to in McInnis's 'Perspectives' all point to this problematic. Indeed, the central plank in his argument against the existence of an Ontario wheat staple is that if Canada in the early nineteenth century had had an established staples market for wheat exports in Britain, then the price of wheat in Canada would have been dictated by its price on the British market: 'At some representative location in Upper Canada, say Dundas at the head of Lake Ontario, the price of wheat would be simply the British price less the tariff less costs of transport from Dundas to Liverpool.' The staples thesis thus presumes (and this he sees as its crucial failing) that 'the Montreal price was in fact the British offer price'; this was 'the price nexus,' 'the interconnection of markets supposed by the staples interpretation,' but he shows that it seldom obtained between 1817 and 1850. We examine below the meanings of 'price' in the townships of the Huron Tract.[4]

I can best focus my critique of this neoclassical criticism of the staples thesis, and clarify my own alignment, by contrasting briefly a left-marxist criticism of Harold Innis's work. In 1981, David McNally criticized the staples thesis in detail as 'commodity fetishism.' I want not to produce my own analysis of this controversial article and its sequel on 'technological determinism' but simply to point out that the questions McNally raises, in particular the issue of commodity fetishism, while misguided in their particular application to Innis and the staples thesis, are none the less useful in countering the attack of the new economic historians. McNally bases his charge of commodity fetishism first on his assumption that staples theorists identify capitalism with trade and exchange and hence fetishize the sphere of commodity circulation. The result, he says, is 'a conception of capitalist production as constituted by relations between *things* and culminating in the production of *things*,' attributing creative powers in the historical process to 'the staple commodity as a natural and technical object,' 'the primary commodity itself.' I have suggested that this reading is misguided: it certainly does not accord with my understanding of Marx's category 'commodity fetishism' in the first chapter of *Capital*. Marx is not talking there about a simple fascination with a 'thing,' the 'primary commodity itself,' or even about 'relations between things.' Rather, in characteristic fashion, he specifies the need to read the relations between commodities 'symptomatically' (to use Althusser's term), as standing fetishistically for the real historical relations, 'the *definite social relation between men themselves* which assumes here, for them, the *fantastic form* of a relation between things' (emphasis added).

Harold Innis, I would argue, was simply an empiricist, as Drache almost says: 'With the minimum of theory, he developed a practical approach to the larger issue of how frontier economies evolved in the international system.' He did not fetishize but merely attributed, in the empiricist's way, raw explanatory power (not a 'fantastic form') to certain facts of early Canadian economic history, the definite social relations of trade and exchange between 'men' themselves, which he saw none the less correctly as historically determinate. Again Drache makes the point: 'Trade and not production had been the cutting edge of change in the international economy since the sixteenth century.' Innis's conclusions were the result of historical research and generalization, attributing no mystical or fetishistic quality to any of the elements, but his conclusions were empiricist because untheorized.

Marx's comments in the third volume of *Capital* are pertinent here: 'The first theoretical treatment of the modern mode of production – mercantilism – necessarily proceeded from the superficial phenomena of the circulation process, as these acquire autonomy in the movement of commercial capital. Hence it only grasped the semblance of things. This was partly because commercial capital is the first independent mode of existence of capital in general. And partly on account of the overwhelming influence commercial capital exercised in the period ... of the rise of modern production.' Innis's staples thesis grasps only the semblance of things because it does not analyse theoretically mercantilism, the movement of commercial capital that it so clearly sees. The staples thesis usefully organizes and generalizes the phenomena of the circulation process in early Canadian history; the theorizing that is its necessary adjunct has been done by some of Innis's successors, drawing on marxist theories of political economy, seeing the elements of the staple not as fetishes, 'sensuous things which are at the same time supra-sensible or social,' but as dialectically related, overdetermining the historical social formation.[5]

The theoretical concern that McNally's critique raises is illuminating when it is applied to the market historians, who clearly do indeed, in the classic sense, fetishize selected empirical data, 'the semblance of objectivity possessed by the social characteristics of labour' – 'God Bless Them,' they might say. These historians make the mistake, as Marx would see it, of treating the value-form of commodities, the 'equivalent form' or price, as 'the eternal natural form of social production,' that is, as a fetish. Thus McCloskey argues that the theory of price is especially the defining skill of cliometricians, and this priority directs the research, for example, of his Canadian colleagues McCalla and George, when they write on Upper Canada. After measurement, they say, the main area of importance is prices: 'So vital are these to a grasp of real change over time that many kinds of long-term analysis would be impossible without suitable price data.' Hence also McInnis's argument based on the price of wheat at Dundas, or his quick jump of abstraction to the price of wheat when discussing the 'mini "wheat boom" that occurred in Canada in the 1870s,' or his interest in whether farm products are valued at local markets or at the farm gate. The method used here is hardly theoretical at all, being instead a process of abstraction and generalization from the empirical, arriving then at a 'theoretical' fetish.

Thus the categories chosen by the new economic historians to 'look at agriculture in the most comprehensive way and at the same time to examine the structure of agricultural production in a systematic fashion' (as that formulation itself demonstrates) never escape but merely fetishize the simply empirical, exhibiting what Marx labelled 'the fetishism peculiar to bourgeois economics,' 'which transforms the social, economic character that things are stamped with in the process of social production into a natural character arising from the material nature of these things.' 'Output' rather than 'linkage'; 'commercialization' rather than 'staple'; 'self-sufficiency' rather than 'use-value'; used as fetishes, all of these do indeed enforce the comprehensive ideological structure of the 'neo-classical line of attack,' as McCalla and George call it, or 'the power,' as Watkins calls it from another perspective, 'of the neo-classical paradigm to kill' all other lines of attack. For unlike Innis they, by fetishizing the superficial phenomena of the circulation process, forestall a theoretical understanding of these phenomena themselves, and an understanding of their historical significance.[6]

The Wheat Staple as Mercantilist

Vernon Fowke distinguishes two stages in the history of Canadian wheat export: first, the general provisions trade, from the French régime through the early nineteenth century in Upper Canada, and second, the later wheat exports from the Prairie provinces. The latter exports 'were not thought of as constituting part of the provisions trade; they had come to constitute an export staple.' Thus, at some time in the interval between the early nineteenth century and the establishment of wheat in the Prairies, wheat exported from Canada had passed from the status of a provision to that of a staple. While Fowke looks for the distinction between provision and staple in the relative importance of wheat in the export cargo, I think that the historical explanation lies elsewhere.

I can begin my theorizing on the Upper Canadian wheat staple as a coherent feature within the larger development of wheat production in mid-nineteenth-century North America by again adducing the comparison to the situation of the Wilberforce settlement, which, as we saw above, derived not only from the American colonization societies but more generally from mercantilist ideologies in the Colonial Office that were to be supplanted in the 1830s and 1840s by Wakefield's philosophical radicalism. As we saw, mercantilist colonialization before Wakefield was the attempt to use colonies to alleviate Britain's social problems, and, like the practices of the colonies of freed American Blacks, it encouraged dependence. Mercantilism itself is an ideology of much broader political economic relations, but it always encouraged those economic activities in the colonies that supplemented the resources of the mother country and prohibited activities that competed with the mother country.

In his influential textbook, Innis selected documents that show the mercantilist orientation of British North America through its more usual economic effects. Britain promoted an assumed mutual interest, as the Committee of Merchants in London wrote to the merchants of Quebec in 1776, 'by supplying the Colonies with her manufactures, by encouraging them to raise and receiving from them all raw materials, and by granting the largest Extension to every Branch of their Trade not interfering with her own.' Mercantilism was a set of mutual economic practices with a bias (I find R.T. Naylor's 'salient characteristics' of British mercantilism – the edification of state power, a strong paternalistic state, and policies adopted to stimulate industrial development by tariffs and subsidies – too general to be useful here). These practices were structured in law by the British Acts of Trade and Navigation for 'the increase of our merchant-shipping' and 'the vending of our manufactures' but equally enforced by loyalty, as the *Montreal Gazette* loyally proclaimed in 1815: 'This power belongs to Great Britain, and we would be the last to question anything that is established by law.'

Thus, as an effect of mercantilism, a staple may be regarded most generally as a system of control, or better, of direction, both direction by and direction to. It is a label for a material reality, like 'hegemony,' 'class,' or indeed 'capitalism,' which is strangely imperceptible as aggregation. And it is just this sort of complex structure (or 'total situation'), an ideology and its practices, rather than a 'price nexus' or a quantity of exports, that shaped Upper Canadian wheat production as staple production. The wheat staple was, in the first instance, wheat exported on mercantilist terms, according to the procedures and practices of the British colonial system.[7]

'As a theoretical concept,' Drache writes, 'the staple is usually thought of as a kind of shorthand for describing the social and economic relations of production, settlement, and commerce,' and its logic is thus geographical ('town or place,' or 'regional,' as Kenneth Buckley put it), limited from the start, as we have seen, by the disposition of the Canadian Shield and the climate and the waterways of eastern Canada. The logic of the staple is also historical, constrained by the resources (furs, cod) available in Quebec in the late eighteenth century, by the mercantilist colonial relation, and by the socio-political structures (the *seigneuries*) of Quebec and then, as we see below, by the economic structures and technologies of Upper Canada. It was these constraints that made the staple directional – that is, directed by its linkages to Montreal and beyond, and directed by the commercial empire of the St Lawrence and its far-flung agents, the grain merchants of, for example, Biddulph Township, Upper Canada. With the end of the Montreal fur staple in 1820 and the repeal of the Corn Laws and the Navigation Acts, these structures were overdetermined by the practices ('free trade') of North Atlantic capitalism. For a brief time then, the period on which we are concentrating, the logic of the Upper Canadian wheat staple is thus the contradictory logic of a structured petty-capitalist, mercantilist social form of production, emancipated but structurally dependent on, imbricated in, surrounded by, and gendered like North American capitalist agricultural production, and 'where commercial capital predominates,' as Marx wrote, 'obsolete conditions obtain.' The total situation that 'wheat staple' designates is therefore not simply European and/or American markets, or Liverpool or North American prices, but the structured east–west interplay of the geography, institutions, and technology, the Lakes and canals, boundaries and treaties, railways and elevators, within this contradictory logic: a mercantilist, dependent, and protected (indeed, obsolete) social form (a staple), within an emerging American capitalist mode of production – the American Grain Trade – which is itself driven by its own dynamic of competition and accumulation. Again, in a word (a pun), direction.[8]

After the Corn Laws

By the first half of the nineteenth century, as Innis and Lower point out, mercantilist ideology was already declining in Canada. A passage from the *Quebec Gazette*, 9 August 1821, catches the tensions of the decline, the peculiar contradictions between mercantilist loyalty and the submission that it demands, between the ebbing mercantilist ideology and the residual institutions of 'direction' that structured the staple:

These [British] Statutes restrain us from trying to obtain a market, and making our purchases all over the world; they restrain foreignors from coming here to purchase or sell, should they be so inclined; they oblige us to have our goods carried solely in British ships – in short, they establish a monopoly of our trade in favour of Great Britain; they oblige us to buy and sell there, and then, by the operation of the Corn Laws, they enact, in effect, that we shall not buy or sell at all. It is not the monopoly to which we object; we adhere to the doctrine and language of the Act of Parliament which declares that 'the power of regulating the trade of the Colonies is essential to the general welfare of the British Empire.' It is the partial interdiction of all the trade, by the operation of the Corn Laws, of which we complain.

Easterbrook and Aitken characterize the decline as a series of 'compromises with mercantilism' such as the Canadian–U.S. reciprocity agreement of 1830, not only political agreements but compromised practices, naturalized as 'diversified outlets' or what is called 'convenience trade.' These are dictated primarily by ease of transport, since the structuration about which I am talking is directed – that is, it is enforced – by such material institutions and practices as the St Lawrence–Great Lakes waterway and the route of the Grand Trunk, as well as by more precise structurations in the Biddulph grain trade, which I examine below. 'Convenience' should be seen to be simply a local, ad hoc escape from the constraints of some of these structures.

The process of decline began as early as 1787, when Lord Dorchester, the governor of Quebec, chose to exempt inland trade with the newly independent United States from the restrictions of the imperial trade laws, opening trade with Vermont via Lake Champlain and the Richelieu River. This was followed a year later by similarly local Canadian regulation of the import and export of specified articles with the United States. Jones quotes T.C. Keefer as declaring that 'the sympathy of every river and lake town is more with their trade across the St Lawrence to the United States, than with that to Montreal.' By the turn of the century, O.J. McDiarmid says, the Great Lakes were great free-trading centres, with the balance of trade generally favouring Upper Canada, and by the end of the Napoleonic Wars, the export trade of British North America combined a 'spasmodic, but sometimes flourishing, inland trade with the United States' with an expanding British market for staples, fur, timber, and wheat. In 1822 the mercantilist triangular trade with the West Indies was ended by Britain's Canada Trade Act. But the chief effort of the 1820s was winning from Britain a real preference for Canadian wheat, culminating in the new corn law of 1842. The overall shift can be traced as that from imperial 'prohibition' to 'preference.'

The first, political victory of free-trade policies followed Britain's Reform Act in 1833. 'The destruction of the shelters which protected the vested interests of the staple trades,' wrote Harold Innis, 'compelled realignments in the St Lawrence essential to the lowering of transportation costs to offset the loss of protection.' The residual mercantilist policies were further compromised in 1843 when the Canadian legislature imposed countervailing agricultural duties on the United States, over Britain's objection that this might interfere with its U.S. trade, and by the American drawback laws of 1845 and 1846, which allowed Canadian imports to pass in bond to and from U.S. ports, further weakening the direct east–west, mercantilist St Lawrence connection.

When Britain repealed its Corn Laws in 1846, the 'distinctly colonial or dependent phase' of Canadian history (at least, the *mercantilist* colonial phase) drew to a close. In 1847, the *Western Globe* of London, Ontario, rejoiced that Americans were buying large quantities of wheat at Port Stanley, 'FOR SHIPMENT TO BUFFALO, *not in bond*, BUT FOR HOME CONSUMPTION.' Trade in agricultural produce during the period of the Reciprocity Treaty with the United States (1854–66) was, as Jones points out, one of convenience, establishing it on a firmer basis than might otherwise have been possible and contributing to the further shifting of the Upper Canadian grain trade away from the St Lawrence route to the Erie Canal. One of the effects as well of the treaty was to discourage wheat production and to encourage farmers to produce coarse grains and livestock for the American market, but 'in spite of this incentive to diversification, and in spite of every hindrance, wheat continued to be regarded as the staple of central and western Upper Canada during the eighteen-fifties.' Moreover, as Marjorie Cohen points out, 'the highly specialized nature of staple production did not generate diversified use of communication networks. These networks were originated to serve the export sector and tended to have a rather lagged effect on integrating the domestic economy.'

Thus, whatever the attractions of convenience, the material structures of the mercantilist phase were to retain their influence on the Upper Canadian social formation for several decades, not only in the continued effort to make the Great Lakes–St Lawrence waterway competitive with the American transportation networks, but as we see below, in the persistence of the apparatuses and practices of the wheat staple in Upper Canadian agriculture. Having been, in Harriet Friedmann's terms, also a 'juridical' formation, the staple remains a 'commercial' formation. While the staple is ideological, because it is ideological, it inheres in particular commercial apparatuses and practices. The Canadian state, writes Peter Baskerville, 'acted as a bridge between the [mercantilist colonial] values, attitudes, and behaviours of commercial Upper Canada – typified by its resident entrepreneurs – and the demands of the industrial capitalist world with which Upper Canada was becoming increasingly intertwined.' But 'bridge' and 'intertwine' are not the first metaphors that I would choose. The wheat staple after 1850 is better seen as primarily the trace of the mercantile colonial relation in Upper Canadian agriculture. The contradictory, emergent capitalist agriculture tended to follow, in Innis's words, 'the more rigid channels of surviving commercialism,' tracing the mercantilist ideology in the residual practices and channels of direction. 'Trace,' in the sense in which I am using it here, means both 'a vestige, an indication,' and 'the track made by the passage of any person or thing, whether beaten by feet or indicated in any other way' (*OED*). After locating this trace in the actual apparatuses and practices of Biddulph Township and its neighbourhood, I describe in this chapter its eventual, contradictory insertion into the capitalist American Grain Trade and, in the next chapter, the social effects of that circumstance.[9]

Tracing Biddulph's Wheat Staple

While the Board of Agriculture reported that Biddulph had produced 6,000 bushels of wheat in 1856 and 20,849 bushels in 1851, these figures alone do not indicate that wheat was or was not a staple crop (though one meaning of 'staple' has been 'the principal product' or 'commodity chiefly dealt in'; *OED*). Rather, the influence of the staple on the Biddulph economy can best be read from the kinds and disposition, or orientation, of the technology of wheat production and delivery, how it was used (its apparatuses and practices), conceived 'in difference'; the staple (as direction) first of all signifies the trace of these determinations. At mid-century, the apparatuses and practices of wheat production and delivery in Biddulph and its surrounding townships were the still mercantilist social forms of the residual wheat staple. Thus the ultimate destination of Biddulph's wheat, for example, whether Liverpool or the West Indies or even Oswego, again provides only one minor indication of the way in which the market shaped wheat as an export commodity. For 'the market' is partly the effect of how Biddulph wheat actually was marketed, taken to market. In 1881, the Ontario Agricultural Commission surveyed the progress and condition of husbandry in the province, and to the question, 'What are your market facilities?' 'Biddulph Township' replied: 'Convenient. Granton, Lucan, Clandeboye all intersected by railroads' ('Clandeboye' meant 'Lucan Crossing,' where the London, Huron and Bruce crossed the Grand Trunk, about which more below). It might be argued that the very simplicity of that reply betokens a pre-capitalist, mercantilist mentality, but the role historically of these sorts of market in the construction of 'the market' should be explored further.[10]

Well into the 1870s, the newspapers of the Huron Tract listed the slightly varying prices of wheat at the farmers' markets in the surrounding countryside. 'Market' here seems simply to imply a railway station or siding, whether in a village or not, a 'place' rather than a 'process,' to use Allan Kulikoff's distinction. In the late 1860s, Seaforth's *Huron Expositor* regularly published the prices at the way-stations along the Buffalo and Lake Huron railway, which paralleled the Huron Road – Carronbrook (now Dublin), Seaforth, Clinton, and Goderich – printing in January 1869 a letter from 'Grain Dealer' arguing the advantages of the Seaforth market over farm-gate sales. In the 1870s, the *Exeter Times* listed prices in Lucan, Granton, and St Marys along the Grand Trunk and at Exeter's own market on the London and Bruce line. The Donnellys' grain, for example, might have been sold at any of these. In the same years, the *St Marys Argus* gave the prices in its own market and at Ingersoll (also on the Grand Trunk), as well as those at three junctions, or competitive points – London, Stratford, and Woodstock.

Other way-stations called themselves markets in the 1860s and 1870s. When the London, Huron and Bruce Railway was constructed up from London through Exeter to Clinton in 1876, it was made to cross the Grand Trunk at 'Lucan Crossing' in McGillivary Township, near 'Ireland' (which promptly changed its name to 'Clandeboye'), because Biddulph had refused to pay the fee for which the railway promoters had asked. While produce could be loaded at Lucan Crossing, only its flour mill and, by 1882, two grist mills (its forward linkages) are mentioned in the business directories of the time; even in the broad definition I am exploring, it was a market only minimally and intermittently.

Another example, Centralia, originally a mere postal village along the London–Goderich Road in Stephen Township at the northwest corner of Biddulph, rapidly grew with the arrival of the London, Huron and Bruce. While Centralia hardly appears in the business directories, its prices and shipments were reported weekly in its own 'Centralia' column in the *Exeter Times*. In January 1874, for instance, the *Times* announced that a wheat market had been established at Centralia. Nineteen months later, 'seven enterprising farmers have resolved to build a grain warehouse, 86 x 60 feet and 24 feet high,' and two months later Centralia boasted of having shipped in September 3,200 bushels of wheat bound for Montreal and 200 bushels for Glasgow, with 3,000 bushels more for Glasgow in the first six days of October; 'considerable shipments are made,' wrote the *Times*'s Centralia correspondent in 1876, 'on every freight train bound south.' These markets scattered about the countryside in the 1860s and 1870s, with their slightly differing prices quoted in the local weekly newspapers, are symptomatic of the pre-capitalist, petty-producer character of the Upper Canadian wheat staple. If price convergence is a measure of the degree of a developed, integrated market, there was no such market here. There was no simple price for wheat, 'Liverpool,' 'Dundas,' or otherwise: there were different prices, and, as Harriet Friedmann has pointed out, 'the existence of several prices indicates several separate markets. Even where commerce exists among structures with different prices, the lack of a uniform price indicates the lack of institutionalized relations among producers and consumers. Such commerce, therefore, has the form of a commercial formation instead of a market.' In this instance, the commercial formation is the trace of the mercantilist staple.[11]

But these railway way-stations are still markets of a sort, not only because of their access to the railway but because one or more grain dealers were in attendance, if only occasionally. For instance, on 6 October 1878, Messrs Hutchins and Atkinson, grain buyers, bought grain in Centralia. William Hutchins, from Lucan, listed himself as a 'grain merchant' in the 1871 *Lovell's Directory*, and in 1882, he and W.H. Hutchins appeared as 'produce dealers.' The pattern of such appellations again is perhaps historically significant. In 1864, besides its seven 'general merchants,' Lucan, newly a station on the Grand Trunk's Sarnia line, had listed in Mitchell's Directory three 'produce and commission merchants.' William Porte reported in 1863: 'There are at present four grain stores, capable of holding 60,000 bushels, and four more are about being erected by Messrs. H.M. Atkinson, Hodgins & Co., Jas. Laird and Wm. Frank – these will give a total capacity of 120,000 bushels. Situated in the centre of an exceedingly fertile country, Lucan promises ere long to become one of the finest wheat markets in the province.' In the same *Mitchell's Directory*, St Marys had no commission merchants listed, nor had Exeter, though Exeter had two flour and grist mills and nine general merchants – the London, Huron and Bruce had not yet arrived. In 1864 Port

Stanley had three 'forwarding and commission merchants'; Holcombe and Henderson had advertised to purchase 50,000 bushels of wheat in 1853. But in 1864 Edward Ermatinger of St Thomas, on the road between London and Port Stanley, was still listed only as an 'insurance and bank agent, postmaster and general merchant,' though he had been shipping cargoes of wheat from Port Stanley since 1843, soon after the harbour was built. The 1869 *Anderson's Province of Ontario Gazetteer and Directory* showed Lucan as having five commission merchants, a grain merchant, and a general merchant and agent, several of these connected with 'Stanley, Dight & Co. – general merchants and proprietors, flouring mill.' In the same year, St Marys had a grain dealer, a grain merchant, and a commission and forwarding merchant, and in St Thomas, F.E. Ermatinger & Co, as well as M.A. Gilbert & Co, had emerged as commission and forwarding merchants. I have more to say of the larger development that these announcements seem to record, but I want first to comment on the practices implied by these and by the newspaper accounts.[12]

In the 1860s and 1870s, the directories comment again and again on grain production and export in general in the Huron Tract communities; in *Mitchell's Directory* in 1864–5, 'St Marys is unsurpassed in the western part of the province as a grain market'; in *Anderson's Directory* in 1869, Lucan's 'principal business is the exportation of grain, produce and timber.' In *Lovell's Directory* for 1871, 'grain and cattle are shipped from this place [Lucan] very largely,' and 'wheat is shipped largely' from Granton, six miles east along the Grand Trunk. Even allowing for the vagaries of self-description, local pride, and publishers' styles, all the grain dealing, commissioning, forwarding, and shipping of wheat is clearly the nearest extension of Montreal and other merchant capital. These functionaries are themselves merchants or the agents of merchant capital (of the staple), indicating that while the production of wheat in the southern Huron Tract is being neither more directly capitalized nor encouraged by investment in machinery or attempts at economies of scale, it is being directed by the agents of merchant capital.

The farmers are petty commodity producers: a writer to the *Exeter Times* (29 April 1875, 2) complains that 'while the farmers around Lucan demand cash for their produce, they also demand credit from merchants.' While this practice is no doubt partly a measure of the 'hard times' during the 1870s, it is equally an indication of the wheat farmers' independence in the production process. Another such signal is the method of loading grain. The twenty-four-foot-high warehouse built by the enterprising farmers of Centralia in 1875 (or the warehouse that Bernard

Stanley built in Lucan in 1873) was what is known as a 'flat' warehouse, 'which provided covered storage bins at trackside but which lacked any machinery for elevation. Usually the floor of the flat warehouse was level with the floor of the boxcars into which bagged grain was placed by hand or bulk grain shovelled.' The most pointed indicator of the obsolete mercantilist structure (to recall Marx's epithet) of the Upper Canadian wheat staple in the 1870s is that it was loaded and transported from these loading platforms either packed in sacks or, if in bulk, shovelled into the railway car. Jones describes the 300,000 bushels of grain shipped annually, in sacks, from Port Stanley in 1850, and the *St Marys Argus* mentioned in 1871 that there still the wheat was traded in sacks; indeed, nowhere in southwestern Ontario in the 1870s could it have been handled in any other way. Marx's comment on 'the childish world of antiquity' is perhaps applicable to the not-at-all-childish but equally pre-capitalist world of nineteenth-century Ontario: pre-capitalist economic formations are characterized by a preoccupation with 'closed shapes, forms, and given limits,' taking 'satisfaction from a limited standpoint.' The sack of wheat, more than a package or simple means of conveyance, was such a symptomatic closed shape, which needed to be 'torn down' to achieve Capital's 'entirely external end.'[13]

Practices of the American Grain Trade

These are the apparatuses and practices (or linkages) that structured the residual Upper Canadian wheat staple: farm production marketed at village way-stations in sacks to grain dealers and commission merchants who directed it, except where convenient, into the ancient channels. The first encounter with the capitalist practices that had for some time been organizing the larger North American wheat market would be, for those merchant-dealers along the Grand Trunk line, Kingston, and for those along the two railways that followed the Huron Tract's two colonization roads – the London, Huron and Bruce and the Buffalo and Lake Huron – the convenience of Buffalo, where the world's first grain elevator had been erected in 1842. My point is that Kingston or Buffalo (or Port Stanley, to which I return below) would be the first place at which Huron wheat would be handled by a grain elevator. That technology – the grain elevator and its associated practices – is as significant as Harold Innis's 'York boat' or Cronon's 'refrigerated railway car': like those technologies in their fields, the grain elevator marks the coming of fully capitalist grain marketing, an instance of what Marx calls 'belated production processes that are inserted into the circulation process.' William Cronon analyses in detail the massive changes in grain handling that had taken place in Chicago and its tributaries in the 1850s, transforming grain in sacks, 'the product of a particular tract of land and a particular farmer's labour,' into 'a golden stream,' disrupting the link between grain as physical object and grain as saleable commodity. The invention crucial to this transformation was the steam-powered grain elevator: 'Structurally, the elevator was a multistoried warehouse divided into numbered vertical bins containing different lots of grain ... Grain entered the structure on an endless steam-powered conveyor belt to which large scoops or buckets were attached. After riding the buckets to the top of the building, the grain was weighed on a set of scales ... Grain dropped out of the scale into a rotating chute mechanism, which elevator operators could direct into any of the numbered bins inside the warehouse. Once it was inside the bins, workers could deliver grain to a waiting chute or railroad car simply by opening a chute at the bottom of the building and letting gravity do the rest of the work.'[14]

By the end of the 1850s, 'Chicagoans had refined their elevator system beyond that of any other city, leading the way toward a transformation of grain marketing world-wide.' The elevator changed the scale and efficiency of handling by doing away not only with sacks but with what could be called their logic: 'Only then could corn or wheat cease to act like solid objects and begin to behave more like liquids: golden streams that flowed like water.' For if breaking bulk was the greatest abomination in the logic of transportation capital, this, the possibility of continuous bulk, would be the greatest virtue. By 1863, grain elevators had transformed wheat into a golden stream. 'Already a mighty stream,' rhapsodizes one commentator (*mirabile dictu*, a statistician glossing our Figure 3.1):

it issues from the Ports of Chicago and Milwaukee. Flowing past Green Bay and Sheboygan, not without receiving important accessions, it leaves Lake Michigan for Lake Huron ... Here it gives off what is now a rill, but what may hereafter widen beyond our present conception; 595 bushels found their way last year by Collingwood to Lake Ontario. Another stream of 298,698 bushels diverged at Goderich and one of 1,335,721 bushels at Sarnia. The main current, continuing its majestic flow, receives the chief contribution of Michigan at Detroit, and of Indiana and parts of other states at Toledo, and in Lake Erie reaches its grandest development, representing, according to the most careful calculations, no less than 107,691,145 bushels ... An important bifurcation occurs near the foot of the Lake, the principal portion, viz, 72,804,188 bushels passing over the Welland peninsula to Lake Ontario ... Of the Buffalo branch, by far the greater portion, viz, 55,696,362 bushels goes Eastward by the Erie Canal ... , and of the Welland branch the greater portion seeks the same outlet, *via* Oswego, whence 18,155,927 bushels were forwarded towards Syracuse.

This flow was achieved by the technology of the elevator and certain other techniques. The traditional sack, as Cronon points out, separated one farmer's wheat from his neighbour's, maintaining the bond of ownership between that shipper and the grain being shipped. Realizing the potential of the elevator, the Chicago Board of Trade altered this relation in two stages: first, by changing in 1854 the standard unit of measure from a volume- to a weight-based bushel, and second, two years later, by initiating a momentous change, the standardized grading of wheat. First designating three categories, white winter wheat, red winter wheat, and spring wheat, the board then established inspection, with uniform grades of each: 'Club Spring,' 'No. 1 Spring,' 'No. 2 Spring,' and 'Rejected.' This practice allowed elevators to sever ownership rights from physical grain and to substitute an elevator receipt for a certain weight of a certain kind and grade of wheat, to be delivered when wanted from the appropriate bin in any grain elevator world-wide. This system 'provides the basis upon which organized marketing with future sales and hedging alone become possible.' Thus 'trade shapes the products into commodities,' as Marx says, in this case literally and specifically into petty-commodity sacks full of wheat, or alternatively into a capitalist-graded stream of 'Club Spring,' 'No. 1 Spring,' and so on, according to the dominant mode of production.[15]

While this system was in place in Chicago and in the American Grain Trade generally by the end of the 1850s, these apparatuses and practices, which were again the very structure of the capitalist grain trade, were never in place as a system in Upper Canada. Moreover, a world wheat market had emerged by 1873, and this capitalist system for handling wheat arrived full-grown in the Prairies in the 1880s along with the Winnipeg Grain Exchange, the western railways, the country elevators, and the harbour facilities and terminal elevators at Fort William and Port Arthur. Whereas a few discrete features of the American methods might appear in southwestern Ontario, there was no sign of the system, no intimation that there the grain trade was driven by the same logic of capital. There was discussion of installing a public weigh-scale at Lucan in October 1872, but no mention of changing the individual bushel from a volume- to a weight-based measure; the issue seems to be one merely of gross volume, or of village pride and general convenience to individual producers: 'The quantity of stock and farm produce sold here is many times as much as that at Exeter,' and 'Lucan will afford them the same facilities as London.' In 1877 Granton too planned to have a market scale. The *Farmer's Advocate* suggested in 1871 that there should be a public weigh-scale in every country town or railway station and that 'a record should be kept of the weight of each load and the price paid for it; that the weight master should each week ascertain the total amount of grain weighed and the cost of it, and strike an average,' and 'that he should transmit these returns to Ottawa, and that they should be ... published in each issue of the *Canada Gazette*.' These proposals again address only petty-commodity producers' concerns (or the future concerns of cliometricians) and are bizarrely beside the point in a rapidly changing historical situation. For while the newspapers and farmers' journals named categories of wheat when they listed prices – the *Farmer's Monthly Advocate* specified 'White Wheat,' 'Red Fall Wheat,' and 'Spring Wheat' – they display no consistency and do not mention grades of wheat; these seem merely generally descriptive labels.

In fact, it was not until the dominion General Inspection Act, 1874, that grading (as at Chicago, three grades and 'Rejected' for Spring wheat and Red and White Winter) and inspectors were established in Canada, with Boards of Examiners in Saint John, Quebec, Montreal, Ottawa, Kingston, Toronto, Hamilton, and London. Jones describes how ineffective an 1863 Grain Inspection Act had been, noting that 'there is some evidence that grading was of more importance by 1880.' Significantly, there was no institution established with the regulatory authority of the Chicago Board of Trade.[16]

The only 'country' (that is, inland) grain elevators that I can locate in southwestern Ontario before 1890 are one along the Huron and Buffalo line at St Marys by 1885; C. Sheppard's grain warehouse in St Thomas, shown on the 1882 Fire Insurance Plan to have a seven-horsepower engine attached; and W.J. Bissett's elevator in Exeter by 1890. Earlier elevators were located only at the Lakes ports and were devoted to the through passage of American or, later, western Canadian grain. *Currie's County of Huron Directory* records that, at Goderich in 1876, 'the Grand Trunk Railway has a large elevator at the dock, as also have Messrs Ogilvies & Hutchinson, the latter elevator being a splendid, capacious and well-furnished structure, having in connection with it the Huron mills. A large amount of grain is consequently transhipped here for eastern points.'

By 1857, there was the Richardson elevator in Kingston, sixty-nine feet high and capable of storing 80,000 bushels of grain, transshipping annually 'about 600,000 bushels, a great proportion of which is sent to England'; much of it, whether Canadian or American grain, must also have gone conveniently elsewhere to, for example, Oswego. In Montreal, of course, by 1875 there were seven elevators for transferring grain from vessels and four from railway cars. In addition, the Montreal Railway Company had eleven floating elevators, and the St Lawrence Grain Company had one. In March 1863, an elevator with a capacity of 220,000 bushels went up in Toronto – 'certainly a great boon to the commercial interests of the western portion of the Province,' said the *Canadian Agriculturist*. By 1865, Toronto was the leading grain market of Canada West, its prices tending to influence those in the smaller ports, but Toronto's commercial interests and railway connections were in the American west. Like so many cities, Toronto, as McCalla says, 'wanted to be an entrepôt in the trade of the American west and hoped to place itself astride the most economic route from Chicago to Montreal and New York, with both ports open to its merchants.'

Other places had the same sort of hopes. A grain elevator 115 feet high was built in Point Edward, at Sarnia, in 1859, and the Buffalo and Lake Huron Railway erected one at Goderich in 1866; as with the Northern Railway's elevator at Collingwood, these were built the more efficiently to portage American grain from Chicago and, eventually, western Canadian grain. Similarly, the elevator in Owen Sound was constructed to serve the early Canadian Grain Route from the west. West of Toronto, only the elevator at Port Stanley, built in 1869, was for loading vessels with presumably Ontario grain, 'to Buffalo, Toledo, Cleveland, Montreal and ports on the Welland Canal,' a collocation that clearly indicates a convenience peripheral to the main capitalist grain trade. *Might's Directory* indicates that there was an elevator operated by R.S. Hodgins in Lucan in 1892, but I cannot find out what produce it would have handled there in the 1890s. By then, the main North American grain trade, whether from Chicago or from the Canadian west, had long since passed by the Upper Canadian wheat growers. The railways, the grain elevators, and the infrastructure of North American grain production were built to serve a grain trade that was already simply elsewhere. The history of agriculture in Biddulph Township in the 1870s is thus a history not of its direct, evolutionary transformation to capitalist (i.e., modern) agriculture, from self-sufficiency to commercial agriculture, but rather of a much more disruptive, contradictory transformation out of the obsolete mercantilist petty-commodity production of a wheat staple and into inevitably domestic and dependent mixed agriculture. I want now to look at this strangely disjunctive transition as close to the ground of southwestern Ontario as I can get.[17]

The Social Composition of Lucan's Grain Trade

My point is of course that the engulfing or, more precisely, the bypassing of the residual staple structures and procedures of wheat production in Ontario by the capitalist apparatuses of the American Grain Trade and the new Canadian Grain Route inevitably produced wide-ranging economic dislocation and social disruption, and we must now examine its effects and, first, the subjects of those effects. I want to return to those merchants who were the agents (the directors) of Biddulph's grain trade in the 1870s, examining the society of which they were a part in the 1870s and suggesting the structuration of that society.

The 1871 Census of Canada for District 8 of North Middlesex, the first census after Confederation and hence a serious matter, comprehensively surveyed the adult male population of the three electoral divisions of Biddulph Township. The patriarchal assumptions of the census cut women short, as it were, generally giving only their names, age, places of origin, and religion, though occasionally indicating them as 'weavers,' 'carders,' or 'servants.' Exceptionally, Bridgit Dimond, in division 3, is a 'grocer,' and Mary Maguire, in division 2, is expressly a 'tailoress.' I discuss specific gender determinations arising from the census information in the next chapter, but here I want simply to mention the more general point, that the relations of the grain trade are always gendered as masculine, a point on which I expand as we deal with other Biddulph social groupings.

Across Biddulph, in both the Protestant western concessions and the Catholic central ones, the predominant occupation of the male citizens was of course farming. The next largest occupational grouping, again not surprisingly, was craftspeople: all manner of carpenters, smiths, weavers, wagon makers, barn framers, saddlers, harness makers, shoemakers, coopers, and machinists. It is equally to be expected that among these craftspeople, almost all of them immigrants from the British Isles or their offspring, while there was also a good number of Catholics and Anglicans, there was yet the largest proportion of the traditional 'Nonconformist' religious groups: Baptists, Presbyterians, Bible Christians, and Wesleyan, Primitive, and New Connection Methodists As for the merchants and tradespeople, hotel- and tavern-keepers, storekeepers and grocers, we find that this wider group, the petty bourgeoisie of Biddulph Township, is made up of fifteen Anglicans, six Presbyterians, six Methodists, and five Roman Catholics; except for Matthew Murphy, a miller, the Catholics are all general merchants. Thus, in the extended petty-bourgeois class of Biddulph, that 'transitional class in which the interests of two classes meet and become blurred,' twenty-seven of the thirty-two are

Protestant. Among those functionaries who primarily serve this bourgeoisie, one of the three telegraph operators is Catholic, and the postmaster
and the bailiff are Anglican. The watchmaker/jeweller and the photogra-
pher list themselves in the census, resoundingly nonspecifically, as 'Protestant.' This assertion of identity, at the lower edge of the petty bourgeoisie, of not so much a religious as a social allegiance, indicates most
clearly the appropriateness of such class designations as 'petty bourgeois.'
Far from meaning to emphasize sectarian differences as such, I am concerned with locating the nascent class differences in Biddulph; these
occupationally isolated, dependent purveyors specifically to bourgeois
tastes declare most sharply where lies the higher social status and their
own social aspirations. Moreover, within the petty bourgeoisie we may
discern a class fragment, the millers and grain merchants who make up
the grain trade of the township, which is even more completely Protestant. There are six millers listed in the 1871 census of Biddulph; Matthew Murphy, in division 3, is, as mentioned above, a Roman Catholic,
and the rest are Protestant. Donald Swainson notes that of the Ontario
merchants who were members of the second dominion Parliament (elected 1872), 'many men were in more than one field [wholesale, dry goods,
and so on]; most men however were grain or general merchants or both.'
Among the Lucan merchants enumerated in the census, there are four
whom the directories specify as *grain* merchants. These join the one
grain merchant enumerated in the census itself, the three 'produce dealers' or 'dealers in produce,' and three 'grain dealers.' These ten also
join, or are incorporated with, several partnerships, again 'grain' or 'commission' merchants: Cavanaugh & Armitage, McRoberts & Armitage, and
Stanley, Dight & Co. These three firms, with the ten affiliated or independent grain merchants and dealers and the six independent millers
(Stanley, Dight & Co. also ran a steam flouring mill in 1869), comprise
the grain trade of Biddulph Township, the dominant industry in the
township, structured residually, as we have seen, as a staple trade peripheral to capitalist North American grain production. With the exception
that we have noted of the one Catholic miller, the entire group is Protestant: eight Anglicans, four Methodists, and three Presbyterians.[18]

The structuration of Biddulph's (mercantilist, staple) wheat merchants
as a class fragment is indicated, first, by these religious connections.
Church affiliations and ethnic communities were 'at the core of personal
identity and social life in nineteenth-century Ontario,' and what Bruce
Elliott calls the cultural homogeneity of the Biddulph settlements was
overdetermined by family and other connections throughout the town-

ship. Biddulph's businesses were, of course, family firms, such as James D. and Thomas D. Stanley of Granton, general merchants ('Stanley Brothers'), registered in 1871, and James D. and Donald J. McCosh, dry goods merchants ('McCosh Brothers'), registered in 1875, built on relations of consanguinity (specifically fraternity), marriage, and friendship that often went back to the original chain migration. Stanley, Dight & Co. of Lucan, for example, was a registered partnership involving the brothers Bernard and William Stanley, Thomas Dight, and Robert H. O'Neill, a barn framer who became a grain merchant in the 1860s and who was married to the Stanleys' sister, Eleanor (these relations to Bernard Stanley were duly noted by R.G. Dun's credit assessor).

As partners, Dight and William Stanley occupied themselves primarily with the milling business, while Bernard Stanley and O'Neill supervised the export trade. Anglicans all, these men had been in business together since 1866. In 1870, they registered their partnership, as 'Stanley, Dight & Co.' and 'R.H. O'Neill & Co.,' under the new Registration of Co-Partnership Act (1869). In the 1871 census, Stanley, Dight & Co. declared a 'Fixed Capital Invested' of $10,000, a 'Floating Capital Employed' of a further $10,000, and an 'Aggregate Amount of Yearly Wages' of $1,240 paid to four male employees over sixteen years old (I return to these figures in discussing the social formation in the next chapter; here I want merely to describe the firm in the conventional terms of the time). In the 1870s Bernard and William Stanley, Thomas Dight, and Robert O'Neill were certainly 'securely propertied' ('those who owned two or more houses, or one warehouse, store, shop or other commercial property'); Bernard Stanley, in the 1851 census a twenty-six-year-old tavern-keeper, by 1871 owned three warehouses on four town lots, and William Stanley and O'Neill each listed a servant in their town houses.

The record of Bernard Stanley's business practices supports my contention that, whatever the attractions of convenience from time to time, the Ontario wheat trade followed the trace of the staple. In 1860, in the middle of the period of reciprocity with the United States, Stanley 'buys grain for shipment on the GTRR,' wrote the R.G. Dun & Co. assessor. Stanley purchased wheat on commission for a Montreal firm '& has a first rate trade in consequence.' In 1875, Dun & Co. was asked about Stanley's fitness to act as an agent for a Montreal shipping company, and the assessor replied: 'If he gives the matter his attention will be a fit, reliable agent.' While these Lucan merchants were all 'men of character,' commercial credit was a complicated matter. In his analysis of credit ratings in mid-nineteenth-century Brantford, David Burley writes: 'The meaning of the middle rank [of credit] remained constant throughout this period. It indicated one of two things: either a man's business was respectable but modest in scale and he was entitled to only "reasonable" credit, or he was experiencing difficulties which could be resolved with the careful forbearance of others.'

Lacking the actual business records, I cannot choose between these meanings, but we can see fairly clearly the situation of Stanley, Dight & Co. as grain merchants within the Ontario wheat staple in the 1870s. 'Pecuniary Strength' (the term used by R.G. Dun & Co.) marked a shift in the criteria for credit evaluation after the collapse of the commercial economy in 1857, away from individual, personal criteria to more strictly financial ones. This was accompanied in the 1860s and 1870s by the necessity generally for all of a man's assets to be in play and at risk for a firm to advance. By 1880, 'land was increasingly another form of business capital rather than a repository for business profits,' as clearly it had been for George Jervis Goodhue in the 1850s: 'In consequence, land, a mark of social respectability a short decade or so before, was rendered merely another commodity to be figured into the calculation of economic collateral.' By 1880, Burley estimated, in Brantford 'nearly half of the self-employed property owners who grew wealthier fell deeper in debt.' The mortgage was 'the major device for using land as security,' yet it is difficult, in the absence of other information, to infer the purposes, beyond the obvious, of the land transactions around Lots 157 and 158 on the north side of the London–Goderich Road ('Main Street') in Lucan from 1868 to 1871, among Bernard Stanley, Thomas Dight, and John O'Donohue (proprietor of the Queen's Hotel). But O'Donohue's discharge of his mortgage with Bernard Stanley on 17 September 1868 might well indicate Stanley's mobilizing of his business capital in the way Burley describes. Dight, in 1862, was said by R.G. Dun to own 'a valuable farm in McGillivray'; three months later, the assessor reported that whereas Dight 'owned a farm, [I] believe he sold it & put proceeds into this bus.' By 1876, Robert O'Neill had sold out his grain interests to his partners and, with his son, had set up as a private banker in Lucan.[19]

Writing in 1936, G.N. Tucker said of 'the commercial class of the colony' from 1846 to 1850: 'Their numbers were small, yet in the province they formed the bulk of that middle class which in a complete social democracy of the British colonial type is always extremely powerful, and better able to make its wants known than any other economic group.' With the qualifications, to say the very least, that sixty years have taught us, we certainly might agree with Tucker. All these men – the two Stanleys,

Dight, and O'Neill – were variously and from time to time reeves, village councillors, and justices of the peace (JPs). William Butt, for instance, identifies Bernard Stanley and Thomas Dight as the 'anti-Donnelly merchant magistrates' who initiated the attempts to arrest the Donnelly brothers that provoked the brawl during the Ryder wedding at the Fitzhenry Hotel in Lucan in February 1876, and Ray Fazakas names Bernard and William Stanley as the JPs who would have bound over James Donnelly, Jr, when he was arrested at that time. I mention these details here simply as examples of the extremely powerful commercial class fraction in Lucan by the 1870s, the same group that represented the wheat staple in the township. What I want to emphasize is that it is the grain trade of Biddulph – the millers, grain dealers, and commission merchants (all men), whose fixed capital investments or credit ratings would place them at the top of the township's social pyramid – that is, linked in these subtle ways into the most recognizable class fraction. What the extrapolations from the census and business directories, and the striking interplay of capitalized occupation and religion, would show is that the precise insertion, or embodiment, or institutionalization of the mercantilist wheat staple in Biddulph Township in the late 1860s and early 1870s (an empirical historical, 'Innisian' category) comprised a distinct, cohesive class fraction within the Biddulph social formation (a category in marxist historical analysis). The agents of the staple (a class in itself) constituted a distinct, concrete masculine social force (a class for itself) in the life of the township. But most important, this was the case at the very time, as we have seen, that the Upper Canadian wheat staple, of which they were among the directors, was rapidly becoming superfluous within the North American grain trade.

The Contradiction in the Ontario Wheat Staple

'From the opinion that wheat has had its day in this country,' wrote the *Farmer's Advocate* in 1877, 'we wholly dissent': 'Let us by no means give up sowing wheat, fearing that it has had its day, but let it not be our sole reliance ... In a word, let our farming be diversified. Seasons differ – demand for products and prices vary. Be prepared for the demand whatever it may be.' But whatever decisions about diversification might be made on the level of the individual farm, the material legacy, the direction, of the mercantilist structure persisted through the 1870s. And in 1880 Middlesex and Huron counties were still the leading producers of fall wheat. Jones says: 'Fundamentally, the decline and passing of wheat as a staple in Ontario was made inevitable by the expansion of the railways which opened the prairies of the American West and later of the Canadian Northwest. These distant regions now had the cheap lands and the agricultural machinery requisite for successful extensive farming ... The result was that when the high-quality grain of the West poured into the European market, the Ontario farmers turned to more profitable branches of agriculture than wheat-growing – to barley-growing, stock-rearing, dairying, or mixed farming.'

But this decline and passing formed not a simple evolutionary transition from wheat to cheese, any more than, in the cities of Upper Canada, the concurrent industrial revolution was a straightforward, direct technological development. The transition is not only a matter of the increasing depletion of the soil or the scourges of wheat rust and the wheat midge, nor are abstract 'competitive disadvantages' in the marketplace (falling prices) as against western wheats adequate descriptions of the political-social economy of Biddulph. I am suggesting instead that we can perceive the shape of a general social crisis in Biddulph at the end of the 1860s, overdetermined by all of these factors and also by the legacy of the staple. Biddulph Township presents a particular, local instance of the central structural crisis in Ontario agriculture. The critical position of the residual wheat staple embodied in the mercantilist direction of Biddulph's wheat production, displaced by the combined strength of the capitalist American Grain Trade and the capitalist western Canadian grain trade, is the result as much of its obsolete, staple structure as of the economics of sheer scale. The effects of this displacement would be felt differently by wheat farmers and grain merchants. Whether or not the unreliability of wheat prices finally outweighed its advantages as a cash crop, many Canadian farmers would, with the rise of the cheese-factory system after 1864, diversify into capitalist dairying (whether after 1880 or 'by an earlier date than usually recognized'*). Others would become suppliers to the developing capitalist dressed-meat industry pioneered by Gustavus Swift. But grain merchants, in contrast, had a different and more complicated transition to make. Robert O'Neill, as we have seen, sold his grain interest to his partners and left the grain trade altogether, moving in classic fashion into finance capital. But the Stanley brothers and William Dight remained grain merchants in the rapidly changing circumstances. As Allan Kulikoff points out, 'Capitalist transformation is not an automatic process but one fraught with conflict and violence,'

---

* 'The two dates are not necessarily in conflict,' says Wayne D. Rasmussen, 'Discussion,' *Journal of Economic History* 42 (1982), 216.

and we are approaching, I hope, a fresh understanding of some of the violent particulars of that transformation in the history of Biddulph Township.

I am arguing that the particulars of Biddulph's history indicate not only the emerging contradiction for the Lucan grain merchants, but an increasing, contradictory transition in agricultural production for the Donnellys and the other farmers on the Roman Line. This double contradiction, one part in the affairs of the class fraction conducting the grain trade, the other among the direct producers of Biddulph's wheat staple, is a major determinant of the Biddulph social formation in the 1870s. The merchants were unable to comprehend, explain, or escape the historical destruction of their direction of the Upper Canadian wheat staple, yet needing to act to save themselves; the farmers were driven (or not) into capitalist forms of farm organization; and each group sought to understand the causes of its difficulties and the ways to solve them, and each group was gendered to solve its problems in masculinist forms. I want now to examine how the Donnelly murders in 1880 were a solution dictated by the imaginary representations of these real conditions.[20]

5

Biddulph Township in the 1870s: Social Formation and Conjuncture

'Social relations are always spatial,' David Harvey writes, 'and exist within a certain produced framework of spatialities. Put another way, social relations are, in all respects, mappings of some sort, be they symbolic, figurative, or material.' It would not be enough, that is to say, for us to focus on Biddulph Township in the 1870s as some sort of straightforward 'place'; the word 'place' carries 'a surfeit of meanings.' Harvey quotes another theorist to the effect that 'space is a practised place,' and I have been attempting to map the framework of determinate practices that produced Biddulph Township as a particular historical space. In a similar way, it is not useful to think of Biddulph (or Lucan or the Roman Line) as a generalized, indeterminate 'society.' What I want to define, or locate, in that space are the social relations that constitute or determine a social formation: a particular articulation of its economic, political, and ideological levels, an overlapping of geography, modes of production, technology, culture. And so Biddulph, not Lucan or the Roman Line, is the particular space that I have chosen, finally, to examine as a social formation. Not only was the limit of the township the main Canadian way of constructing political space in the nineteenth century, not only does Biddulph physically encompass those other spaces, but it places them within other relations, locating them historically.[1]

In chapters 1–4 I tried to trace the historical processes that produced Biddulph, as well as Lucan and the Roman Line, in space and time. To recapitulate: on the land created by the glacier's pause and by the millennia of forest, Biddulph Township was created by a series of political decisions and arrangements, and a particular double-front survey that made the Roman Line possible as a distinctive space. Then the township was settled according to a particular sequence of colonial ideologies –

colonization, and then two distinct market ideologies – attracting first the settlers of Wilberforce, then Irish Protestants, and then Irish Catholics. Bounded by a main colonization road, Biddulph, uniquely in the Huron Tract, was also crossed by that road, which in time was itself traversed by the Grand Trunk Railway, ending Wilberforce and generating Lucan. And so these different spaces – Lucan, the two sectors of the township, and the Roman Line itself, all 'practised' places – are not simply located in, but interrelate so as to determine, Biddulph Township as a social formation. There are further levels of determination: not only the presence of the Grand Trunk but Biddulph's proximity to and its distance from the Great Western Railway and the absence (or Biddulph's dismissal) of the London, Huron and Bruce Railway. Also factors are the roads, lakes, ports, and canals, their geographical and political determinations, the soil and the historical experience that made the cultivation of wheat possible, traditional patriarchal social structures, the organization until 1846 of wheat production as a staple, and its residual trace in Upper Canadian wheat export, within a very different North American grain economy. These are other levels of the inevitably contradictory practices that determine Biddulph Township as a space.

We can begin to see in this set of historical determinations Biddulph's social geography, in the instant before the capitalization of its agriculture, as 'a constitutive moment within (as opposed to something derivatively constructed by) the dynamics of capital accumulation and class struggle.' Here, in this final chapter, while referring to, or constantly assuming, these other determinations, I want to concentrate on the major contradictory relationship on the socio-political and ideological levels – the articulation or overlapping of Upper Canada's residual wheat staple in the 1870s with the capitalist American Grain Trade. I want to explore Biddulph as both social formation and conjuncture, as the logic of North American capital produces '*a geographical landscape* (of space relations, of territorial organization, and of systems of places linked in a "global" division of labour and of functions) appropriate to its own dynamic of accumulation *at a particular moment of its history*, only to have to destroy and rebuild that geographical landscape to accommodate accumulation at a later date' (emphasis added). My purpose is, of course, to examine the social consequences or the accompaniments of that production, destruction, and rebuilding, and these as the workings of the logic of capital in the 1870s, as specific relations within certain sectors of that rural, pre-capitalist social formation and between them.[2]

Biddulph Township as a Social Formation

The Biddulph economy, as we have seen, was pre-capitalist, or mercantilist, one whose infrastructure was made up of practices left over from the wheat staple. Marx's analysis of pre-capitalist economic formations in the *Grundrisse* is pertinent here; it could almost be read as a gloss on the economics of the grain merchants in Lucan in relation to economic development on the Roman Line, my representative rural community out on the concession lines. Addressing the prehistory of the bourgeois economy, Marx speaks of 'the development of exchange and of exchange value, which is everywhere mediated through trade, or whose mediation may be termed trade, through which money achieves an independent existence in the merchant estate, as does circulation in trade.' Marx's comment might describe the coming of grain forwarding to Lucan, even the career of Robert O'Neill, barn framer, grain merchant, and merchant banker. Marx goes on as if to describe the related history of the Roman Line: 'The dissolution of *labour's relations of property in its* conditions of existence, in one respect, and at the same time the dissolution of *labour* which is itself *classed as one of the objective conditions of production*; all these are relations which express a predominance of use value and of production towards use value, as well as of a real community which is itself still distinctly present as a presupposition of production.' This comment may seem more difficult to apply to Biddulph, but I see in it the change in relations on the farms and the violence in the township; I explain this in detail. But my point again is that the overall historical process alluded to is far more complex than a simple switch from wheat to cheese. More is going on than is allowed by the assertion that, from 1880 and perhaps earlier to 1915, 'some Ontario farmers were willing to trade a larger expected income from wheat in order to obtain a smaller but more stable income from the dairy.' The transition to capitalist agriculture, far from being a direct, continuous development or evolution, was instead contradictory. That is to say, whether we examine Biddulph in the 1870s – the decade leading to the Donnelly murders – as a space or as a conjuncture, a moment in time, we are examining interconnected contradictions.

In this chapter I want to analyse this tissue of contradictions, Biddulph Township as a social formation and events in the 1870s as responses to contradiction. To begin I want briefly to re-examine Stanley, Dight & Co., the major Lucan grain merchants. This time I am interested in the partnership not in and for itself but dialectically, for its defining (contradictory) relations as merchant capital, both its defining internal relations and its relations to the farmers on the Roman Line. A fuller description would include, for instance, the tradespeople and the other small merchants mentioned in chapter 4, but I want now to follow out that main contradiction.[3]

Stanley, Dight & Co. as Merchant Capital

How may we understand Stanley, Dight & Co. as merchant capital, then and there? The credit ratings from the 1860s undertaken by R.G. Dun & Co. present a certain limited public understanding of the economic (and hence social) place of Stanley, Dight & Co. in Lucan. Until January 1868, Bernard Stanley's business had been listed as a 'General Store' and William Stanley's as 'Lumber, &c' (in Lucan in the 1860s, 'lumber forms the principal article imported'). After 1868 Bernard Stanley is listed as owning a 'General Store & Mill' (William keeping his original designation), and Stanley, Dight & Co. makes its appearance as 'Millers.' In that year, 1868, Bernard, William, and the partnership itself are each judged to have a Pecuniary Strength of from $10,000 to $25,000, for a rating of '3,' and a 'Fair' Credit Standing, the upper grade of 'Fair' ('2'). Then, as the 1870s unfold, changes occur in how their fortunes are recorded: after 1869, William Stanley is no longer listed separately. Robert O'Neill, the other partner but listed separately as 'Wheat,' had been rated since 1865 as having a Pecuniary Strength of only $2,000–$5,000 ('4'), varying thereafter between '4' and '3' until, becoming a 'Broker' ('3 ½') in 1877, he becomes a 'Banker' in 1878, with a Pecuniary Strength by 1880 of $25,000–$50,000 ('2 ½'). Throughout the 1870s, O'Neill's Credit Standing was always in the upper half of 'Good' ('2').

But the advancement of William Stanley and O'Neill also illuminates by contrast the progress over the decade of Bernard Stanley and the partnership, Stanley, Dight & Co. In the first place, until 1874 Bernard Stanley's own personal Pecuniary Strength and Credit Rating were always, in each category, one grade higher than that of either his brother or Robert O'Neill. His Credit Standing from 1864 through 1876 was always in the higher rank of 'Good' ('2'). Perhaps more significant, from July 1873 until January 1880, both the Pecuniary Strength and the Credit Standing of Bernard Stanley and the firm, Stanley, Dight, were identical, moving through the decade in tandem. As the 1870s progressed, the assessments improved, from a Pecuniary Strength of $25,000–$50,000 ('E') in 1877 to $50,000–$100,000 ('D'), with a similar shift from July

1876 in Bernard's Credit Rating: from 'Good' ('2') to 'High,' ('1 ½'). We see below why such an improvement was likely, but I want to conclude this discussion of the public perception of 'worth' and 'credit worthiness' – a 'repute' that has an important place in this chapter – by noting that while Stanley, Dight & Co.'s Credit Rating was always (except in 1869–71 – early days) the highest ranking in Lucan, by July 1876, along with Bernard Stanley's, it had moved up one level, capital worth and credit both being ranked two steps above those of any individual or firm in Lucan. We can now speculate on why these evaluations of the firm, our primary interest, should have been made.[4]

These Dun ratings, like all essentialisms, aimed at specificity and fixity, enacting those conventions of assessment that are reassuring to investors and creditors. It is more useful for us historically to view the internal workings of a business enterprise dialectically, that is, in their distinctive mobilization of its means of production. Using information from the 'Schedule of Industrial Establishments' in the 1871 census, we can attempt such a relational view of the 'organic composition' of Stanley, Dight's capital, both in itself, which invites certain conclusions, and as compared to the capitals of contemporary Lucan businesses, both grain merchant/millers and others. These comparisons invite other conclusions. We can thus attempt to estimate the relative condition or health of Stanley, Dight & Co. (and other Lucan merchants) historically, within a problematic different from that of R.G. Dun & Co.

The organic composition of a capital indicates a relation, a ratio, between what Marx calls its 'constant' and its 'variable' parts (or functions). The constant capital in an enterprise is the value of all the means of production brought to bear – that is, the fixed constant capital (buildings, machines, tools, draught animals, and so on) and the capital constantly circulating through each production period, in the form of raw materials, and so on. These two forms of constant capital are distinguished from the variable capital of a firm, 'the value of the social labour-power applied in this branch of production, i.e. the sum of the wages paid for it.' The ratio between constant and variable capital, Marx points out, 'varies considerably with the extent to which machinery has already penetrated, or is engaged in penetrating, those trades.' This is exactly the sort of knowledge about the Lucan grain merchants that we are seeking, since, in Ernest Mandel's words, 'the more advanced an enterprise, a branch of industry or a country is, the higher is the organic composition of capital, i.e. the bigger is the share of total capital which is spent on buying machinery and raw material.' This would take us beyond merely noting the 'worth' of a firm or its credit standing, or indeed the absence of grain elevators as the trace of the staple economy in Biddulph's history.[5]

In the census of 1871, as we saw in chapter 4, Stanley, Dight declared a 'Fixed Capital Invested' of $10,000 and a 'Floating Capital Employed' of another $10,000. I assume that these figures were accurately reported, and, since I am aiming for only a generalized ratio, I assume that 'Fixed' and 'Floating' in the census make up the 'Constant' capital of Stanley, Dight: $10,000 for mill, warehouses, and so on, and $10,000 for 'constantly' (over the year) buying $48,000 ('Aggregate Value') worth of grain, so as to produce $53,000 worth of flour or exported grain. The 'Aggregate Amount of Yearly Wages' for Stanley, Dight's four employees was $1,240, and so, with those assumptions, the organic composition of Stanley, Dight's capital in 1871 was roughly 20,000/1,240, or 16.

Unfortunately, the schedules appended to the 1881 census do not survive, so that we are not able to follow any change in the capital composition of Stanley, Dight through the 1870s. But we can compare it to other industrial establishments in Biddulph in 1871. The grist mill of the Catholic miller, Matthew Murphy, for example, did 'nothing but custom work,' as Murphy declared to the census-taker: 'Myself could not state the amt. of profit.' Be that as it may, his 'Fixed Capital' of $1,500, put to use by his one employee, who was paid $300, produced for the year $1,950 worth of flour out of $1,500 worth of grain. Whatever the profit, the organic composition of Murphy's capital was 3,000 divided by 300, or 10, a considerably lower ratio than Stanley, Dight's, indicating a less advanced capitalist enterprise (i.e., a 'custom' mill), mobilizing its capital and labour less productively, and less fruitfully exploiting over the long haul the logic of capital.

We can make a further comparison with two of the foundry/machine shops in Biddulph. In September 1871, according to R.G. Dun & Co., Galloway and Mason, 'Iron Foundry and Agricultural Implements,' was 'a small house, doing business with a small capital.' Galloway and Mason's Constant capital was $6,000 – $2,000 Fixed and $4,000 Floating – and they paid their five employees $2,000. The organic composition of their small capital was thus 3, a measure, compared to the millers, of the difficulty in mechanizing implement manufacture in Biddulph at that time. There was in Lucan another, larger iron foundry and machine shop, run by John Jackson. In 1871, Jackson declared that the shop had 'made 100 combines, reapers & mowers last year,' with an aggregate value of $20,000. But there seems to be more to be deduced from other

details of the firm's history, as recorded in the census and in R.G. Dun &
Co.'s credit ratings. 'Jackson & Rogers'/'John Jackson & Co'/'Jackson,
Diamond & Co' had never achieved more than a '3' (Fair) Credit Rating, and its Pecuniary Strength was never more than '4' ($2,000–$5,000).
Jackson, trained as a wheelwright, and while 'of good character and
industrious,' had little capital; as R.G. Dun's credit assessor put it, 'available means sm. will be able to pay if they succeed.' 'Vy economical in
their bus.,' Jackson's foundry could only 'pay up as they go' and was
reliant on 'friends who are indulgent with them.' In 1868, though the
firm was listed, it was none the less assigned no Pecuniary Strength and
given no Credit Rating, and by 1871 its Pecuniary Strength had dropped
to 'K,' less than $2,000. In September 1871, the year of the hundred
combines, reapers, and mowers, those persons planning to do business
with Jackson were carefully advised: 'One of the firm (or per written
order) call at the [R.G. Dun] office,' presumably to receive particular,
private information. In that very year, 1871, Jackson had declared to the
census a Fixed Capital of $15,000 and a Floating Capital of $16,400, a
larger total ('Constant') capital than Stanley, Dight in the same year. But
Jackson paid twenty workers $7,000 (contrasted to Stanley, Dight's four
employees at $1,240), for an organic composition of 4.5, not surprisingly
not much higher than the other foundry but far lower than Stanley,
Dight's 16.

Again we can see quite clearly the relative degree of capitalist organization of these firms. Jackson's foundry was not 'moving with the times,'
despite its claimed capital turnover and the number of farm implements
produced, and would be bankrupt by 1879, with Bernard Stanley the
creditor. For Stanley, Dight & Co., again by way of comparison, had
organized its production so as to maximize long-term profits, despite its
mercantilist relation with its clients (Stanley, Dight told the census-taker:
'It would be about impossible to tell the exact amt ground as we exchange considerable wheat with farmers for flour.')[6]

In the midst of the Biddulph grain economy, still handled as a staple
economy, Stanley, Dight & Co. was working its capital and its labour well,
according to the progressive capitalist logic. That the obsolete economy
of the township, and of rural southwestern Ontario, was itself enclosed
in, overruled or marginalized by the capitalist grain trade of North
America, made the particular, small insertion of Stanley, Dight & Co.
doubly contradictory. Again, this perhaps unsettles historically the conventionally assured finality of the R.G. Dun evaluations of the firm.
Whereas the immediate pecuniary strength was very high, as was its credit

rating, the long-term prospects for even a productive firm of grain traders in that place at that time were not favourable. It is impossible to know how much of this contradiction the firm's principals – the Stanley brothers, Dight, and O'Neill – perceived and how they explained it, its causes, and its solutions. But historically, in the 1870s, the respectable, creditworthy, profitable firm of grain merchants Stanley, Dight & Co. was caught in a destructive double contradiction. However the farmers out on the concessions might deal with Ontario's transition to capitalist agriculture, from wheat to cheese, the Lucan grain merchants, even with a capital investment composed appropriately to a progressive, capitalist grain trade, were in a different, less flexible predicament, and this in articulation with the other elements comprising the social formation, in particular those very farmers. It is that articulation with those farmers to which I now turn, having marked the contradictory predicament of the Lucan grain merchants.

The Form of Agriculture on the Roman Line

Bernard Stanley's remark to the census-taker – 'we exchange considerable wheat with farmers for flour' – gestures towards an economic relation that we have not noticed yet. It is only when we turn to the farms out on the concession lines – still focusing on the economic level – that we begin to see the complexity of the Biddulph social formation. When Marjorie Cohen, for example, describes the dual nature of the rural economy, she is alluding not to the contradiction that we have been examining between capitalist and mercantilist modes of production, but to another (gendered) relationship that overlaps it, that on the farm between market and extra-market production, between subsistence production, or self-sufficiency, and production for export, using 'subsistence,' as I do, not to signify a general historical form of farm production but rather to describe the immediate, particular exigencies of a specific farm, 'the *relative* significance of this form of production.' Cohen speaks more than once of an instability in Upper Canada's wheat economy that shaped rural society, forcing a particular type of organization on its labour force For while subsistence production – that is, production for consumption – serves more immediate functions, 'its primary importance for the capitalist sector [for Stanley, Dight & Co., and beyond] is in supplying and maintaining a labour force at prices which permit capital accumulation.' This is one reason for the willingness of Stanley, Dight to accommodate by bartering for wheat. Since agricultural production is seasonal, and its labour employed intermittently, it was necessary to find alternative support for farm workers during slack seasons or years. The 'underdeveloped domestic economy' and, as Cohen demonstrates, the sexual division of labour were the ways in which the labour force was maintained in rural Upper Canada. I return below to the sexual division of labour on the farms of Biddulph, but first I want to characterize the political economy of those farms. My analysis here adapts and adjusts Marx's description of the French peasantry in the last section of *The Eighteenth Brumaire* to Harriet Friedmann's recent analyses of 'the peasantry' in the transition to a capitalist agriculture in North America, all in the light of the historical commentary that I have been assembling thus far. Marx describes persuasively the socio-political situation of a peasantry, while Friedmann places it economically, showing why the term 'peasant' is imprecise and confusing, having no status in contemporary political economy.[7]

What Marx says of the social relations of small peasant proprietors in rural France seems applicable in several ways to relations generally among the farmers of Biddulph. He characterizes these in a well-known passage:

The small peasant proprietors form an immense mass, the members of which live in the same situation but do not enter into manifold relationships with each other. Their mode of operation isolates them instead of bringing them into mutual intercourse ... Their place of occupation, the smallholding, permits no division of labour in its cultivation, no application of science and therefore no diversity of development, variety of talent, or wealth of social relationships. Each individual peasant family is almost self-sufficient; it directly produces the greater part of its own consumption and therefore obtains its means of life more through exchange with nature than through intercourse with society. The smallholding, the peasant, and the family; next door, another smallholding, another peasant, and another family. A bunch of these makes up a village [or a 'line'], and a bunch of villages makes up a department. Thus the great mass of the French nation is formed by the simple addition of isomorphous magnitudes, much as potatoes in a sack form a sack of potatoes.

I take issue below with some of Marx's assertions, but here I want first to call attention to the isomorphous magnitudes stretched out along the Roman Line, connected, as Marx puts it, merely 'on a local basis.' Another point arises from Marx's analysis of the political tendencies within the French peasantry and their connection with the Bonaparte dynasty. There were clearly also 'parties' along the Roman Line, and I would suggest, trying to stand outside the conventional reading of these as traditional Irish factions, that, like the Bonapartists, the Lucan petty bourgeoisie, the merchants, was allied with 'the conservative, not the revolutionary peasant: the peasant who wants to consolidate the condition of his social existence, the smallholding, not the peasant who strikes out beyond it. It does not represent [i.e., is not 'allied with'] the country people who want to overthrow the old order by their own energies, ... but the precise opposite, those who are gloomily enclosed within this old order.'

I am not casting the Donnellys, for example, as revolutionary peasants; I want merely to recuperate, for the time being, Marx's particular distinction between what he calls 'the modern consciousness of the peasant' and the 'traditional consciousness' and the alliance of the latter, in France, with the bourgeois forces of order. Marx goes on to say that the bourgeoisie 'shares with the peasant the illusion that the cause of their [the peasants'] ruin is to be sought, not in the smallholding itself, but outside it, in the influence of secondary circumstances'; that perception, too, I wish to use. Finally I want to recall Marx's suggestion that in France, in the course of the nineteenth century, 'the urban usurer replaced the feudal lord'; 'the mortgage on the land replaced its feudal obligations'; and 'bourgeois capital replaced aristocratic landed property.' These conditions of the 'undeveloped smallholding' produced what, from different perspectives, could be called the contradictions of 'mortgage debt,' 'enslavement by capital,' or 'a progressive deterioration of agriculture and a progressive increase in peasant indebtedness.' Out of these analogies, I propose to build my description of the Roman Line as a particular sector of the Biddulph social formation, but first I must examine and update Marx's category 'peasant.'[8]

Our analysis of anything like the progressive deterioration of agriculture, whether on an individual farm or across Biddulph or southwestern Ontario, depends on our understanding the form of agricultural production in that place in the mid- and later nineteenth century. Several years ago, in a series of articles reviewing its theoretical history, Harriet Friedmann brought up to date the idea of the 'peasant,' the only concept available to Marx in *The Eighteenth Brumaire*. As we have seen, the mode of wheat production in Ontario was pre-capitalist and mercantilist; what we now must consider is its *form*: how we theorize or characterize the formal relation between the farms, the basic productive units, and Biddulph Township itself, the social formation that we have been examining. For it is the matrix of relations within the social formation, the township, that 'provides the context for reproduction of units of production [farms], and in combination with the internal structure of the unit, determines its conditions of reproduction, decomposition, or transformation.'

In earlier chapters we have noticed various specific social relations structuring Biddulph: mortgages, often exorbitant, with the insurance companies, merchants, and bankers of London; barter arrangements for milling at Stanley, Dight; and the farmers' insistence on immediate cash payment for produce from merchants from whom they may at another juncture demand extended credit. These details suggest a particular development of market relations, a form of agriculture, for which 'peasant' is an inadequate term. In current historical and sociological theory, Friedmann says, '"peasant" is not a concept'; 'peasant' farms are not 'isomorphous magnitudes,' having the same or similar forms, like potatoes in a sack. Pre-capitalist agriculture invites more precise differentiation, and she posits a new concept, 'independent household production,' distinguished both from 'simple commodity production' and from 'capitalist production,' and capturing, I believe, the historical differentiations in Biddulph agriculture in the 1870s.[9]

The capitalist farm, as we have seen, is characterized by elements – a high organic composition, wage labour, and so on – that were not present in Biddulph Township in the 1870s, though they were perhaps present elsewhere in Canadian agriculture and certainly existed south of the border. Thus what we are looking at here are forms of pre-capitalist household farm. Friedmann shows how the degree and kinds of intrusion of capitalist practices shape the different non-capitalist forms of household agriculture, 'in which the domestic group jointly provides labour, possesses at least part of the means of production, and may dispose of at least part of the product of its labour.'

Simple commodity production is that form of household production most assimilated to capitalist practice. In it, commodities circulate in both directions and market relations replace personal ties for the mobilization of land, labour, means of production, and credit. Production thus takes place under conditions of competition; there is competition among producers and the legal and social competition of a labour market: 'When household production is specialized and competitive, and means of production and subsistence must be purchased, it is *simple commodity production*.' While pre-capitalist, these again are clearly not the conditions of the peasant production that Marx described in *The Eighteenth Brumaire*, nor were they universally the conditions of agricultural production in

Biddulph, even in the 1870s. Households engaged in simple commodity production are well into the transition to fully capitalist, market conditions. This is precisely the transition for which we are searching on the Roman Line and in Biddulph generally, a formal change rather than a simple transition to another commodity, like cheese, but we have not yet found the characterization of the 'peasantry' that will allow us to chart it in the necessary historical detail.

For there is an earlier stage of household (peasant) agricultural production. To the extent that the aims of production are limited by the relations of production, as Harriet Friedmann says, 'all households aim for satisfaction of the consumption needs of the domestic group': 'The more "commercial" behaviour of simple commodity producers relative to peasants stems not from motivational differences, but from the individualisation of the household which accompanies commoditisation, and the resulting transformation of communal and particularistic relations, both horizontal and vertical, into competitive and universalistic ones.'[10] Friedmann's suggested complementary concept, independent household production, thus designates a form of household production that ante-dates simple commodity production and resists it, a conservative form fostering production for use, implying a relative absence of competition and, while a greater or lesser part of the product may be 'appropriated by merchant capital' (sold), the relative absence of market relations causes 'difficulty in measuring value and therefore surplus labour appropriated through exchange' (profit).

The labour and consumption of an independent peasant household were flexible: 'If the land was owned, there was no rent. In fact, the peasant household was even more flexible than the simple commodity producing household. The amount of labor of the household and the level of its personal consumption could be varied without external constraints, except rent and interest, to a greater degree than in the simple commodity producing household because it supplied most of its consumption and replacement fund directly. It was therefore more independent from the market: greater labor devoted to the production of means of personal and productive consumption would increase the total products available to the household for those purposes.' But there were other structural differences in this form of 'peasant' production: '[Independent] household production lacks a structural requirement for a surplus product. Personal consumption and the net product are structurally identical; the money that remains after renewal of means of production constitutes a single sum belonging to the household ... There are no separate groups to struggle over the division of the product into "wages" for personal consumption and "profit" for expansion.'

Independent household production is based on conditions antecedent to capitalist relations of production; its basic condition is 'the continued re-creation of the integrity of the household as unit of productive and personal consumption,' and 'the whole complex of institutions of "peasant" reproduction which resist commoditisation must decompose in order for capitalist (or simple commodity) production to emerge.' The ('revolutionary') historical transition, then, from independent household production to simple commodity production, and beyond, to capitalist agriculture, is the intrusion of market relations, the commoditization of household relations, the dissolution of that single sum belonging to the whole household and the division of the domestic unit, the family, into separate groups; perhaps here, to anticipate my argument, we can see a foreshadowing of the Donnelly farm in the 1870s. The transition was experienced as the separation of production from consumption as organized activities of members of the household: 'If family members seek employment outside of the household and pool their wages with the family consumption fund, units of production and consumption have begun to diverge': 'What began as a cash supplement to the household ends as a subsistence supplement to the wages of family members. Under this circumstance the family ceases to be an [independent household] productive unit.'[11]

Friedmann argues that the world market for wheat emerged after 1873 – 'after 1873 separate prices in different areas of wheat production converged,' being 'the historical conjuncture at a world level of effects of existing *forms of production* and of relevant costs for each form within all *social formations.*' (This conjuncture also coincided with the onset of the world-wide depression, a coincidence that would have to be explored elsewhere). In Biddulph at that time the emergence of the world market would begin to show in the interaction of the independent household and simple commodity producers on the Roman Line with the Biddulph social formation as a whole, in particular with the petty-bourgeois wheat merchants of Lucan, and especially with Stanley, Dight & Co. Economically, these two sectors of the social formation – the farms on the concessions and the grain merchants – were in transition in different ways, while in relation to each other. If the merchants of Lucan were caught in the contradictory practices of mercantilist and capitalist grain production, on the Roman Line the transition from independent household to simple-commodity or capitalist relations of production was experienced more or less disruptively, as a household's relative ability to sustain its independent production. There the process of transition was the undermining of subsistence, as each household's needs expanded beyond the farm's capacity to satisfy them, and as wage labour, whether hiring in or hiring out, became a necessity.[12]

The Farms on the Roman Line

Independent household production was thus the basic, originary form of the Roman Line 'peasant' farm, as through the last half of the nineteenth century it evolved towards simple-commodity and then fully capitalist agricultural production. Rather than renewing or reproducing their family-based techniques of production from one growing season to the next, year after year, households came increasingly to depend on various forms of commodity relations. And as it worked itself out in the real circumstances of the Roman Line, this was not a simple transition from one form of agricultural production to another. Here, among these circumstances, the *under*determination of *virtù* and *fortuna* (whether for separate groups or individuals) becomes most obvious. In 1860 the northern fifty acres of Lot 18, Concession VI, the Donnelly farm, is a case in point. As the census-taker noted in 1861, James Donnelly was at the time in the 'penatentiary' in Kingston (*virtù* or *fortuna?*), leaving the thirty-seven-year-old Johanna alone to supervise the farm and a family of seven boys, aged twenty, fifteen, fourteen, twelve, eleven, nine, and seven and Jenny, aged five.

The 1861 census information indicates clearly the burden of necessity borne by the family and the form of farm production within which the members met it. This is, first of all, a 'subsistence' farm, in the particular, relative sense that Marjorie Cohen gives to the term. The overwhelming constraint is the absence of a grown man's labour. Without it, the form of production necessarily differed from that of other fifty- (and one-hundred) acre farms along the Roman Line, signalling the need simply to keep the farm, and to feed that woman and those children, of those ages and with that distribution of sexes. All farm households, Harriet Friedmann points out, go through a demographic cycle; they start with a maximum of two people, and 'the situation of labour shortage must continue for at least 14 years, even under the best circumstance of the immediate birth of a male child.' For, as Marjorie Cohen has shown, those nineteenth-century Ontario farm households were characterized by a gendered division of labour.

Thus the particulars of age and sex on the Donnelly farm in 1860, as well as the absence of the father, set the contradictory form of its production and its general place in the agriculture of the township. On their twenty-one cultivated acres, three of them pasture, Johanna Donnelly and perhaps two sons – one of them, Will, was lame, and the eldest, James, was a wage-labourer elsewhere – farmed ten acres of spring wheat, producing a not very fruitful 140 bushels. They produced as well 100 bushels of potatoes. The two acres of peas, two acres of oats, and half-acre of turnips (had the crop not failed that year), the three acres of pasture, and (for the pigs) twenty-nine acres of uncleared wood would feed the two oxen, three steers/heifers, the cows, the three sheep, and the eight pigs. These in turn provided milk, eight pounds of wool for twenty yards of flannel, and 600 barrels of pork. Any surpluses might be bartered or sold.

The hybrid form of this family farm is signalled, first of all, by young James's wage labour, presumably for the cash to pay the mortgage. For not only is the household characterized by a meagre subsistence, but it is one that is divided – 'communal and particularistic relations' being transformed into 'competitive and universalistic ones' – by the (not-uncommon) mortgage debt but also by the necessity of James's wage labour. This is not an easeful, simple commodity production, yet the circumstances that we have recalled and the 'enslavement by capital' deny the household the form of independent production. The family is left not only in penury, but in a deeply contradictory situation from which to remedy that condition. There are no visible surpluses produced as commodities: no maple sugar, no fulled cloth, no butter. The absence of butter is perhaps especially significant: butter-making was a woman's task, but Johanna's labour was required elsewhere and there was no other working woman, and the milk was probably needed in the family diet.

My reading here of the simple commodity *form* of production on the Donnelly farm in 1860 becomes less speculative when we contrast it to the form of other fifty-acre (and 100-acre) farms and see the lineaments of their independent household production. On the southern half of the same lot, Michael Maher and his wife, with a thirteen- and an eleven-year-old daughter and five younger children, harvested 200 bushels of Spring wheat from eleven acres and produced 100 pounds of butter.

Also, the Donnellys' friend and neighbour John Dagg, on fifty acres of Lot 17, Concession V, produced with his wife (they had only a two-year-old child) 180 bushels of wheat on the eight acres sown, 100 pounds of butter, 200 pounds of maple sugar, eighteen yards of flannel, and five yards of fulled cloth, clearly allowing marketable surpluses. The larger farms, one hundred acres and over, were even more clearly independent household producers. Mitchell Haskett, Lot 23 on Concession IV, who had only two years earlier brought in his fugitive friend, James Donnelly, to face trial for murder, produced 260 bushels of wheat on fourteen acres (18 ½ bushels an acre), while Mary Ann, his wife, and their four daughters aged between ten and eighteen produced 100 pounds of maple sugar, 150 pounds of butter, and 1,000 pounds of barrelled pork.

The two Keefe farms on the Roman Line, Lots 13 and 14 of Concession VI, declared identical produce figures to the 1861 census, each farm producing 600 bushels of wheat from thirty acres, 100 pounds of butter, and ten yards of fulled cloth, while Robert, the younger brother, and his wife, Mary, added 100 pounds of maple sugar.

These neighbours' farms, of differing size and with families of differing composition, are all engaged in independent household production, the incursion of competitive markets occurring only in the bargaining, as surplus becomes commodity. Whatever else may be said, in 1860 the Donnelly farm is economically an anomaly, a contradictory insertion into the economic structure that connects the farmers of the Roman Line to the merchants of Lucan. At this point we can perhaps guardedly recall Marx's remark about 'revolutionary' and 'conservative' peasants in nineteenth-century France and their 'natural' alliances.[13]

James Donnelly returned from Kingston in 1865, and while, by the time of the 1871 census, the signs of driving poverty are no longer evident in the record of its produce, the picture of the Donnelly farm as an anomaly in the developing agriculture of the Roman Line is even more insistent. While the sons are now all old enough to work the farm, 'excess labour,' as Harriet Friedmann points out, 'is of no use in increasing the income of the enterprise,' especially, on this farm, excess male labour, and the farm continues to exhibit a historically contradictory form. The surrounding farms, too, have of course changed since 1861, moving more obviously into diversified independent household production, the transformation portrayed as so smooth by conventional agricultural histories. Michael Maher no longer farms the south fifty acres of Lot 18, but there John Cain, with his wife, and only a two-year-old daughter, is a successful independent household producer. By 1870, the one-acre pasture of 1861 has grown to fourteen acres, so as to feed, augmented by oats, hay, and peas, six cattle, six sheep, and eight pigs, all slaughtered for export. The two Cains added to this 100 pounds of butter, ninety bushels of barley, thirty pounds of wool, twenty-three yards of flannel, and twenty bushels of apples, as well as eighty bushels of Spring wheat from four acres. Nearby, on Concession V, John and Jane Dagg and their six children still under fourteen, produced a similar range of commodities from their forty improved acres, ten of them pasture: three cattle, three sheep, and four pigs butchered, 300 pounds of maple sugar, 140 pounds of butter, forty pounds of wool, and forty yards of flannel, and eighty bushels Spring and thirty bushels Fall wheat from the fourteen acres sown.

The Keefe brothers' farms show the same form – successful independent household production. James and Margaret, with two working sons and two working daughters on, now, 195 acres, own not only two houses, five wagons, and three ploughs, but, among other useful implements, a threshing machine. From their large farm and with the useful sex distribution of their children, they produced 400 bushels of barley, 120 bushels of Spring and fifty bushels of Fall wheat (on fifteen acres), twenty bushels of apples, four bushels of pears/plums, 600 pounds of butter, 200 pounds of maple sugar, and 100 pounds of wool, and they butchered three cattle, five sheep, and ten pigs. Robert Keefe and his wife, on the hundred acres next door, and with three daughters over fourteen years, slaughtered only pigs (fourteen) but also produced two hundred bushels of Spring wheat from twenty acres and proportionate amounts of a range of produce similar to his brother's, along with 300 pounds of butter and fruit from one acre of orchard.

The Donnelly Farm in the 1870s

In the midst of this economy, the Donnellys are indeed now able to farm their fifty acres more productively. With only half of Robert Keefe's wheat acreage, for example, the Donnelly farm produced the same amount, 200 bushels, of Spring wheat. And presumably Johanna, released from some of the field work and with the help of fourteen-year-old Jane, can now produce 200 pounds of butter, twenty pounds of maple sugar, fifty bushels of apples, forty pounds of wool, and fifty yards of flannel. Moreover, the farm produced for slaughter one steer, four sheep, and six pigs. But again the point is not simply to compare these figures to the others, but to try to infer the form of production on the Donnelly farm; there are again formal anomalies. There are four sons at home on the farm in 1870: Will (twenty-three), Michael (nineteen), Robert (eighteen), and Tom (sixteen) – young James is in exile in Michigan, John is in his brief marriage to Mary Johnson, and Patrick is listed as a blacksmith. Patrick's occupation, as a blacksmith while yet a member of his parents' household, is, again, I would suggest, a symptom of the sort of individualization of the household that accompanies commoditization that we saw above.

And there is another item in the 1871 census that seems similarly symptomatic, signalling the anomalous, contradictory form of the Donnelly farm as an economic unit. On the two other fifty-acre farms mentioned above (Dagg and Cain), the census records firewood produced: eight and eighteen cords, respectively. The hundred-acre Haskett farm produced fifteen cords, James Keefe, twenty cords, and Robert Keefe, twenty-five cords. Patrick Ryder, the Donnellys' enemy on Lot 16 across the road, produced thirty-eight cords on his 185 acres, and the Donnellys' friend, William McLaughlin, Lot 17, Concession VII, produced twenty cords from his 150 acres. The Donnellys, in contrast, produced from their fifty-acre lot 200 cords of firewood. There is no knowing where this cordwood was sold – as we know, the Grand Trunk would not switch to coal until 1872. There was clearly some market, at least a buyer, for cordwood in 1870, but it is not a commodity that figures in any of the records (except the census) that I have seen. In the 1870 Biddulph economy, chopping and selling cordwood, for any buyer, would have been the pettiest of petty-commodity production, not unlike 'living on capital.' But what this detail primarily signals is again the excess male labour and the contradictory economic form of the Donnelly farm; it is a sign of economic distress.[14]

With neither the independence nor the self-sufficiency as a household farm to 'consolidate the condition of [their] social existence' (Marx), or 'to recreate the household as a unit of productive and personal consumption' (Friedmann), nor yet the capacity of neighbouring farms to specialize and compete in simple commodity production, 'overthrowing the old order by their own energies,' the Donnelly farm is singular, exceptional. It is an anomaly in an agricultural order that is changing not only its products but the form (not to say the mode) of its production – a farm economy in close relation to a mercantile order that is itself increasingly needing to change – but the Donnelly farm is out of step. Whatever the conduct, imputed or known, of individual Donnelly sons, the family's ways of coping with the exigencies of lot size, their farming practices, and the labour available and its gendered division would inevitably have appeared eccentric, uneconomic, even disruptive of good order, viewed from Lucan and against the form prevailing on the other farms. Moreover, while the farms of Biddulph are productive, the 1870s in Ontario, as the local papers constantly point out, are 'hard times.' It is in this situation, I am suggesting, that some parties can become caught up in the illusion that Marx mentions, 'that the cause of their ruin is to be sought ... in the influence of secondary circumstances.'

The best-known episode in the Donnellys' struggle to supplement their household production by 'the more "commercial" behaviour of simple commodity producers' is that of the Donnelly stage-coach line between London, Lucan, Centralia, Crediton, Exeter, and, for a time, Clinton. In *The Donnelly Album*, Ray Fazakas traces the family's involvement in the carrying trade along the London–Goderich Road, all of the sons except Patrick working as drivers in the late 1860s and several, in different configurations, as proprietors from 1873 to 1878. In 1873, Will Donnelly was awarded the mail route from London to Centralia and invested in a stage, the family mortgaging the farm to provide him capital. Using local newspaper accounts, Fazakas describes well the often violent competition, on and off the road, with the other carriers, Hawkshaw and then Flanagan, Armitage, Walker, and Watson. He recounts the Donnellys' momentary partnership with Alexander Calder of London, the arson and mutilation of animals on all sides, and the final demise on that route of all profitable stage-coach carriage brought about by the arrival of the London, Huron and Bruce Railway in 1878.

What has not been considered (except implicitly in William Butt's pointing out Will's loan from his father) is the place of this extended entrepreneurial effort in the family's whole economic enterprise. Indeed, the term 'entrepreneurship' obscures what is going on. At different times over this ten-year period, different sons are no more than temporarily surplus members of a simple commodity-producing household, and the frantic competition and the violence on the road ultimately are driven by those sorts of contradiction within the farm's economic practice and within the larger agricultural economy of the Roman Line. In the absence of Stanley, Dight's records, I do not know how to discover the terms on which the Donnelly farm sold it its wheat; did Stanley, Dight, for instance, 'exchange considerable wheat for flour' with *the Donnellys?* In any case, Stanley, Dight's relative 'monopoly power in the market' would be reduced in its dealings with the Donnelly family by the existence of the Donnelly stage line. The competitiveness and violence are 'secondary' to, that is attendant on, these economic circumstances.

But while retaining my emphasis on the historical determinacy of the economic contradictions, both on the Roman Line and in the grain trade in Lucan, I want here to pick up on the general references to gender that I have been making, to point out the effects of gender as itself a historical structure. The lives of the Donnelly sons and their companions were gendered 'masculine.' Theirs was a clear instance of the 'rough culture' that Lynne Marks describes in *Revivals and Roller Rinks*: in general, social behaviour punctuated with public drinking, brawling, and heckling, perhaps flirtation and sexual harassment, and 'loafing' on the streets of Lucan. Marks's study, emphasizing 'the reality as well as the messiness of actual historical experience,' shows that the lines between the rough and the respectable were not always clear: some women in nineteenth-century Ontario drank in public, even brawled, and sometimes members of the respectable bourgeoisie or their sons engaged in rough behaviour. But so to emphasize the historical 'reality' and 'messiness' risks losing the distinction between 'sex' and 'gender,' as between the *male* and the ideology of *masculinity*.

From time to time I have been noting the male exclusivity of not only the Donnelly brothers and their fellows, but also the farmer-landowners, the Lucan grain merchants, and the stage-coach owner-drivers. For besides the disposition of tasks on a farm on the Roman Line, the gendering of actual historical experience was realized in an ideology of masculinity, of which the competitiveness and violence of the Donnelly sons and their opponents are only the most obvious symptom. By far the 'roughest' behaviour in Lucan in the late nineteenth century was the murder of the Donnellys, and an examination of rough behaviour as ideologically gendered must comprehend the murderous vigilantes and the political persons and jurors who shielded and exonerated them.

Masculinist ideology in Biddulph was not limited to violence on whatever side; violence is a symptom of power relations, whether it be the outburst of a person or group otherwise powerless or the quiet, inexorable exercise of power, whether legally or merely socially sanctioned. I return below to this matter of the socially sanctioned exercise of violent power, but here I want to emphasize that in Biddulph it was gendered ideologically as 'masculine.' My point about the ideological gendering of the Donnelly 'gang,' the Lucan merchant-magistrates, the Vigilance Society, the juries, and so on, is not that the inclusion somehow of innately gentle females would have softened the behaviour of any of these groups, but that the simple fact of the (gendered) limitation of membership enforced a circular, self-validating fetishism of the narrow male experience of, for example, strength, power, conquest. An unlikely example would make the point: had the vigilantes' discussion and planning been conducted in full public view, the breadth of human experience on call – social, religious, and, not least, of the law – would possibly have prevented the murderous outcome. My example is, of course, haunted by the Holocaust, but in nineteenth-century Biddulph, the presence in those councils of a wholly different female experience – perhaps of 'strength,' 'power,' 'conquest' – would perhaps have changed the gendered limitations of male experience universalized into masculinist ideology. I am emphasizing gender as a mode of structural limitation: masculinist ideology as a structure rather than merely individual male *virtù*. If the 'rough culture' of Biddulph Township was messy, it was overdetermined by a gendered and thus limited structure, masculinist as well as economically determined.

This is as near as I want to approach to the usual accounts of individual lives and motives, to the fetishizing of *virtù*; I am attempting to read Biddulph Township in the 1870s symptomatically, as a structured social formation, over- as well as underdetermined. The economic relations, again to insist on structural determinations, between the Donnelly farm and the grain merchants of Lucan would be intermittent and irregular, as the family farm pursued its awkward, opportunist productive path. In so far as we can imagine the Donnellys' place in the context of the merchants' relation to the surrounding conservative farms, we can perhaps begin to explain the influence of secondary circumstances. But I want now to turn to another sector of the ideological level of the Biddulph social formation, to examine how these economic and social contradictions were seen – that is, translated into less complicated explanations or 'representations of their real conditions of existence.'[15]

Fazakas and others, and William Butt rather more rigorously, have explored the social and political (as distinct from the economic) levels of the Biddulph social formation – sets of relations that inhere in the family and religious connections, the various kinds of lodges, the political structure of the township and village, and the local justice system within the rhythm of the assize courts. Each of these sectors generated its own explanation of the ills of Biddulph society, from the problems imagined in the dominion economy to the social disorders of the township itself. To these we must add the explanations assumed by the Vigilance Society inaugurated in St Patrick's Church by Father Connelly on Sunday, 15 June 1879. Parishioners were there asked to sign a pledge to be vigilant against crimes against property that had beset the township, and an offshoot of this society, with its own murderous explanation of cause, effect, and cure, began meeting in the autumn of 1879 in the Cedar Swamp Schoolhouse.

The social relations on this level of the Biddulph social formation and their particular, local ideologies are more or less well understood, but I want to look now at an event, or a series of related events, that, in the summer of 1878 could mobilize the contradictory economic positions we have been examining and place them in meaningful (and permissive) relation to those local social concerns and explanations. I am referring to the 'National Policy' election campaign that summer, which brought Sir John A. Macdonald's Liberal-Conservative party back into power in the dominion Parliament with a policy of protective tariffs. In Biddulph Township, I suggest, that campaign rearticulated, made meaningful as ideology, the violence of the contradictions in the social formation, while constructing a new social order, new practices and loyalties, in the township.

The 1878 Election as Conjuncture

The 1878 dominion election was a turning point, 'a watershed in Ontario's political allegiance' in national politics, as the province, a traditional stronghold of Reform (as the Liberals were then called), went Conservative by a majority of thirty-eight seats. Sir John A. Macdonald's Liberal-Conservatives (to give the Tory party its contemporary name) had built and amplified their National Policy since 1870 at least. It had three planks: a transcontinental railway, the opening of the west agriculturally, and a national system of protective tariffs – but by 1878, and argued for and against in various ways, protection was the dominant ideological element. The mature form of the Tory policy of protection in 1878 called for 'a judicious readjustment of the Tariff' in order 'to benefit the agricultural, the mining, the manufacturing and other interests, ... moving (as it ought to do) in the direction of a reciprocity of tariffs with our neighbours,' and this distillation of the National Policy became the major issue of the 1878 election.

The Conservatives were able to mobilize resentment against American tariffs on Canadian goods and produce and to attack, as well, the perceived 'slaughter' (in our terms, 'dumping') of American goods in Canada. Bringing agricultural products under the protectionist umbrella was crucial to the Conservative election strategy. The grain millers, closely allied with the Ontario manufacturers' group, were powerfully influential in this effort. J.B. Plumb, Conservative MP for Niagara, informed Parliament in 1876 of a petition from the millers of Ontario, and G.T. Orton, MP for Wellington Centre, read into Hansard a report of the Select Committee on the Agricultural Interest indicating that, of the number surveyed, more than twice as many millers, officials of agricultural societies, reeves of townships, and so on, supported protection of grain and flour as rejected it. The concerns of the grain forwarders of Toronto, Montreal, and Quebec (the business partners of such merchants as Stanley, Dight & Co.), always fearful of losing more of the U.S. grain trade bound for Europe, were to be met by allowing American grain intended for overseas to be shipped in bond. In 1876, the executive committee of the Grange in Canada attempted to survey its members' attitudes towards agricultural protection. The results of the controversial survey were not published, but 5,000 Grangers, about one-third of the membership, signed the petition, and it is believed that 'the majority of grangers went to the polls in 1878 and helped in the downfall of Mackenzie by voting for higher tariffs.'

Not only did the protectionist policy bring in a Liberal-Conservative government in Ottawa and carry Ontario, but even western Ontario, 'traditionally the home of Grittism,' went Tory. The Clear Grit party (the more radical wing of Reform) 'was antipathetic to middlemen and money-lenders, to land speculators, to forwarding interests,' and four years earlier, Reform had carried twenty of western Ontario's twenty-eight seats. But in 1878 the Conservatives won sixteen ridings in southwestern Ontario, holding their own seats and winning nine from the Reformers. Among the nine was North Middlesex, which included Biddulph Township.[16]

North Middlesex had been a Reform riding since before Confederation; Thomas Scatcherd of Exeter had held it through three elections, and on his death in 1876 it was won by his brother, Colin Scatcherd. Before 1878, Lucan and Biddulph as a whole had tended to vote Tory (Bernard Stanley was the leading Tory of North Middlesex), but the Catholic farmers, the Donnellys among them, had traditionally voted for the Scatcherds and Reform. The National Policy election changed all that: the issues and how they were presented in southwestern Ontario, and pre-eminently the selection of the Tory candidate in North Middlesex, produced a Conservative victory in the riding and, as I hope to prove, more.

During that campaign there was constructed in Biddulph a new set of cross-class, cross-sectarian allegiances; there was instituted, around the issues and through the conventions of electoral politics, not only a new political apparatus but a new general consensus, a texture, as always, of acquaintance and trust, promises and obligations, that persisted after the election. While the issues of the election engaged the class groupings in the township (gendered masculine in the way I have described) – the merchants and the farmers – in different ways, the electoral process as it progressed established distinct new social relations, which were to be crucial in the event of the Donnelly murders and in the subsequent defence not only of the murderers but of the township itself as a social formation. We can approach this shift both through a discussion of the issues of the election and their implications – for both grain merchants and grain farmers – and by an analysis of the processes of the election in the riding and the township, the nominations, the campaign, and the voting.

The Issues of the 1878 Electoral Campaign

The electoral battle over a dominion protective tariff in the 1870s had been, on the level of political ideology, a struggle between conflicting ideas of Canadian nationalism. Liberal and Reform nationalism was 'nationalism directed against the imperial powers of Great Britain, preoccupied as it was with enhancing the constitutional autonomy of the Dominion.' And by extension, after 1867, as Frank Underhill put it, the Grits 'were constantly in arms against any interference by Ottawa with matters of local Ontario concern' – interference in 'business,' for instance.

In the budget debate of early 1878, Charles Tupper, the Conservative finance critic, called attention to a phrase that Richard Cartwright, the Reform finance minister, had used in an earlier speech at Fergus, Ontario, which for Tupper captured the Reform government's 'policy of helpless inactivity' in economic matters. It would seem that Cartwright had said in Fergus, 'The country may stand or fall, may be prosperous or the reverse, we are as flies on the wheel, and those who say that the Government can advance the interests of the country know nothing of what they are talking about.' Tupper pounced on the image of 'flies on the wheel,' using it to condemn 'the fatal mistake which underlies all the honourable gentleman's blunders' – the belief that 'it is beyond the power of Parliament to do anything to help the industries of the country.' His Tory colleagues in Parliament echoed him, and Tupper himself used it again and again, as when he accused Cartwright of counselling 'no other thing to do but to continue the policy of masterly inactivity and to rest upon the wheel a contented fly as long as he was not disturbed from his position.' (Indeed, Cartwright's unfortunate image provided a mocking Tory refrain well into the 1880s).

Reform's laissez-faire development of anti-imperial nationalism was in sharp contrast to the nationalism of the Conservatives, which was 'essentially anti-American in character' and carried its own particular implications in 1878. Underhill points out that the national spirit in Canada was being 'canalized into economic rather than political channels.' 'Canalized' is a telling specification of the metaphor. Like the Conservative tariff of 1870, the protective tariff fostered the St Lawrence transportation route from Lake Erie to the ocean, indicating the Tories' attachment to the traditional political economy, what I have called the trace (or direction) of the wheat staple. In 1870, the Conservative government's policy, rather than simply bowing to Canadian manufacturers' demand for a protective tariff, had 'combined reciprocity and incidental protection with its support for the Laurentian trade route,' just as, eight years later, in 1878, the Conservatives 'hoped to divert economic ties from a north–south to an east–west axis.'

While the Montreal grain merchants had traditionally opposed any tariff that might divide their Canadian–American staple-producing hinterland, now they were mollified by the potential for drawbacks on American grain exported. Thus the 'prestige, national status, national dominion' that Macdonald preached in Parliament on 7 March 1878, when moving the National Policy amendment to the Reform budget, was not a disembodied ideal, mere glittering generalities, or, as Colin Scatcherd told his North Middlesex nominating convention, a 'mysterious something which they had it in their power to bring about.' Rather it was a policy grounded in the traditional economic practices and partnerships of the Great Lakes–St Lawrence trade connection. This was a material ideal that even, for example, a practical-minded Lucan grain merchant could envision. Indeed, for the grain forwarders and farmers of southwestern Ontario, whatever their usual loyalties, the issue of this election nationally was the traditional tension, writ new, between the trace of the staple and the attractions of 'convenience,' what the London *Free Press* labelled the Grits' 'tentative, empirical policy' of Free Trade. We must examine the 'writing anew' that took place from 1876 to 1878.[17]

Protection and Convenience

Nationally, the press and the politicians often cast the debate as between abstract free trade and abstract protection, supporting their arguments on the one side with Adam Smith and the main thrust of J.S. Mill's *Principles of Political Economy*, or, from the other side, 'hugging and nursing that little paragraph in Mill's Political Economy in which he says a word on behalf of *temporary* protecting duties in a new country.' But to the voters of North Middlesex, the debate was presented in more immediate, concrete, and familiar terms – an interplay of oppositions between not only general and particular but concrete variations on 'far' and 'near.' In earlier versions of the National Policy, the Conservatives had emphasized a tariff on manufactures, on building a home market for manufactured products. When they went into opposition in 1873 they had argued that farmers should see this as also building a home market for agricultural produce. This argument, not surprisingly, was not politically persuasive: 'The farmer claimed that his industry might reasonably expect protection also ... It would be only just and fair that agriculture, in like fashion, should receive a measure of protection.' As L.A. Wood has pointed out: 'Such a demand coming from the agricultural communities did not escape the observation of protectionists who foresaw that it might be used to their advantage; to wit, the *Monetary Times* suggested that a scheme of co-operation between manufacturers and agriculturalists on the tariff might be brought about in order to facilitate the propaganda for a National Policy.' And protection for agriculture obviously most involved the direction of foreign trade: 'John Granger,' a farmer (perhaps) writing in favour of protection to the *Farmer's Advocate* in 1876, asked: 'Are the farmers content with the home market for their crops? Do they not know that their best markets are abroad?' The *Advocate*'s readers could easily see that the debate was over which 'abroad' should be cultivated by Sir John's 'judicious readjustment of the Tariff' – the far (and traditional) 'abroad' or the near.[18]

These were, of course, ideological spaces, familiarly far and, traditionally, threateningly near, and as such lent themselves to the easy comprehension of the effects of a protective tariff on both imports and exports. In his speech in the budget debate in March 1878, Sir John A. Macdonald told Parliament: 'In the abstract, Free-trade is the liberty of buying in the cheapest market, and selling in the dearest. In the abstract, it is a proposition not to be disputed; but, when brought down to the concrete, when the needs of nations are considered, and the peculiar needs of Canada are considered, it is found impossible to carry it out.' As a gesture to the concrete, he told a homely little fable: 'I put a case in the Eastern Townships of a man upon the imaginary line which was between this country and the United States. Suppose a man has 100 acres on the Canadian side of the line and 100 acres of land on the American side of the line. Suppose he grows 1,000 bushels of barley on each of his farms. He takes his 1,000 American bushels to the American market and gets one dollar a bushel for it. He takes his 1,000 bushels of Canadian barley to the American market and gets but 85c. per bushel, because he has to pay 15 per cent duty for taking it across that imaginary line. How can it, in this case, be said that the consumer pays the duty? It comes out of the pockets of Canadian farmers.'

This story would seem to have been extremely effective rhetorically; at least it enraged the Reformers and provoked much rebuttal. For example, David Glass, Reform candidate for East Middlesex (and a lawyer who had in March unsuccessfully defended Robert Donnelly against charges of shooting at the Lucan constable), attacked the Tories as demagogues, telling them: 'This was no fly on the wheel, this was a mad bull on the wheel,' while admitting that 'Sir John is an exceptionally able politician and he tells the story about the two fields of barley with the charming tact which has led him successfully out of many a fight.' But Glass attempted to counter Macdonald's rhetoric by correcting his economics. Claiming that he had 'carefully studied this story, with no feeling of ill-will,' he undertook to 'prove it to be wholly wanting in merits.' He did so by relocating the farmer on the U.S. side of the border and by introducing some new suppositions, changing the lesson of the story to one of the abstract laws of supply and demand: 'If the 1,000 bushels of barley raised in the States are sold there for 85 cents per bushel, and that quantity is sufficient to supply their market they will not come to Canada for any, but if not sufficient they will come and will have to pay the 85 cents which the supply and demand fixes it at as well as 15 cents duty. That is, they will have to pay $1 per bushel for their Canadian barley, whereas, they got the American barley for 85 cents per bushel.' Glass's explanation is certainly less charming than Sir John's, and the loss of charm is primarily the result of the changes that I have mentioned, the preoccupation with the 'laws of supply and demand' instead of with place or locale. The difference in the stories can be taken as representative of the difference in the two parties' campaigns in southwestern Ontario, if not nationally. If, as Frank Underhill said, the national spirit was being 'canalized into economic channels,' that spirit was evoked by embedding it in a local and concrete, if imaginary, example, a farm straddling the Canadian–American frontier.[19]

Tactically (ideologically), the 'home–abroad' distinction could be and was made to work either way on behalf of the National Policy. The

Conservative *Exeter Times*, for example, enthusiastically supported protection of the home market in 1878: 'The sooner the Canadian farmer awakes to the necessity of being protected against the Americans, the better it will be for himself. How does he like the idea of having to send away grain which should be used at home? ... If the Canadian farmer cannot have a market established near home, he must pay the cost of forwarding the grain to a foreign market, and the more distant it is, the lower the price he will nett. This is exactly how he is placed by the Americans, whose grain coming into this country free, or sometimes at a merely nominal duty, displaces a large amount of Canadian grain, which is thus forced to be sold at a more distant market. It is against this injustice that Sir John purposes to move.' Robert Porter, the Tory candidate for Huron West, made this argument again and again in his campaign speeches, and when his Reform opponent, Thomas Greenway, voiced 'the worn-out assertion of free traders that Liverpool governs our grain market,' Porter simply responded: 'if the Government place a duty on that article so that the Canadian farmer will have no competition in the home market, Liverpool cannot control the price of wheat in Canada.'

What is important here is of course not the choice or correctness of either economic theory, but the forms and intensity of the struggle over protection in southwestern Ontario in 1878. For the argument was made just as intensely by other Tories that Canadian wheat sales abroad would benefit from Macdonald's proposed tariff. The Tory *London Free Press* wrote: 'There is no glut of products with us seeking a market and finding none because the United States is ungracious. If it can send its own surplus to the great European markets so can Canada, and the Canadian producers meet the Americans on equal terms on the wharves of Liverpool. Whether the States choose to tax our products as they cross the lines or not, they are powerless to take toll of them elsewhere, and it is that "elsewhere" which regulates the price of that which we have to sell, as well as that which the American agriculturalists have to dispose of.' Whether the farmers and grain merchants worried about the home market or the markets abroad, the Conservatives' National Policy might be made to seem to address their worries, doing that more directly and immediately, more simply, than Reform's advocacy of free trade and a revenue tariff. The Tories' promise of a home market effectively undermined even Reform's traditional emphasis on the convenience of an import trade with the Americans, making, for example, the Reform MP for York North, A.H. Dymond's, typical remarks in Parliament about coal imports seem merely plaintive. The effect of a duty on American coal, said Dymond, would be 'to thrust back the coal fields of America to a distance of 900 miles and to destroy those advantages which nature had placed at our command, advantages which were given to the central portion of the Dominion with respect to a foreign country ... Not only were the coal fields of the United States more favourably situated for the supply of our need, ... even if our Nova Scotia mines were situated much closer to us then they were, ... the topographical features of the country were such that [coal] was delivered almost without handling on board the vessel that bore it across the lake to its destination.'[20]

Whatever the economic virtues or faults of Macdonald's National Policy, the tuning to which the Liberal-Conservatives subjected it from 1870 to 1878, the 'glitter' given even to its generalities in Parliament, made it more immediately relevant to the grain merchants and farmers of North Middlesex. At a Reform meeting in Strathroy, Wilfrid Laurier, the Reform minister of inland revenue, 'laughed at the idea of constructing a protection policy which would suit the whole dominion': 'It would be as easy for Brigham Young to keep his twenty wives in one cottage as to construct a protection [sic] tariff that would suit all the Provinces.' 'Protection had to be sectional,' Laurier said, but his very word, 'sectional,' instead of embodying the near and familiar, as would even 'local' or 'provincial,' betrays the besetting abstraction of the Reform defence of free trade. Four days later, the Tory *Free Press* stated editorially that the issue before the country was 'whether Canada has good men or bad men, *statesmen or empirics*, at the helm' (emphasis added), a contrast that, while obviously loaded in favour of Tory 'statesmen,' nevertheless catches the weakness of the Reform arguments against protection in 1878. Ideologues were not (then) going to persuade Ontarians that their best interests lay in trusting to abstract laws of supply and demand and the accompanying practices of 'convenience,' rather than fostering traditional and familiar Canadian practices. The Reform government, writes David Lee, might have gained political support by bringing in a modified protective tariff, but it chose not to: 'This refusal ... was only too characteristic of the federal Liberal administration. They, of course, considered it a virtue to stick by their principles, right or wrong. But others regarded their inflexibility as mere arrogance.'

What the Liberal-Conservative's arguments in favour of a developed home market for manufactures and produce had in common with their apparently contradictory arguments against the convenience of free trade with the Americans (if the Americans could be persuaded to reciprocate) was precisely the emotional linking of the local self-interest of farmers and merchants to a national alliance with manufacturers, mobilizing traditional economic channels and practices. The Reformers, in contrast, sought to undermine precisely that generalizing unity, both in speeches such as Laurier's to the voters of Strathroy and in their tactics in the House. There, in the session leading up to the election, the Reform government tried to demonstrate 'the fallacy of the protectionist idea, and the impossibility of getting unity of action on such a question' by bringing forward a succession of bills, each offering a different set of products to be protected by tariffs. 'In every instance,' crowed the *London Advertiser*, 'these were voted down by large majorities – those in favor of "protecting" one interest showing that they were opposed to giving similar "protection" to any other interest.' Rather than merely showing the power of Reform's parliamentary majority, this tactic, said the *Advertiser*, showed the vacuity of the Conservatives' election manifesto: 'When stripped of its glittering generalities, and presented in plain form by specific mention of the particular articles requiring protection – the "National Policy" humbug crumbled to pieces before majorities ranging from 60 to 120.'[21]

The Election in North Middlesex

Flexible in the ways that we have seen, the National Policy provided the Conservatives in 1878 with a platform that they could present to southwestern Ontario's farmers and grain merchants alike, and the Tories of Biddulph quickly took the advantage. The election was eventually called for 17 September, but electioneering, or at least a certain pointed preparation, had begun by the time of the budget debate in Parliament in late winter. The Conservatives held mass meetings at Ingersoll, Preston, and Brantford in early March that endorsed the National Policy as Macdonald had spelled it out in Parliament. On 19 March the Liberal-Conservatives of the West Riding of Middlesex nominated N. Currie as their candidate and endorsed protection, and on 20 March the Conservatives of North Oxford met at Woodstock to endorse it also. On 22 March, the *Free Press* reported meetings in Arthur, Brucefield, and Barrie supporting the policy, and three days later, in a long editorial entitled 'The People Alive,' the *Free Press* excitedly announced 'premonitory symptoms of a political upheaval': 'There has been remarkable enthusiasm as well as a remarkable accord in the people's acceptance of what has been called the "National Policy."' On 1 April, the East Middlesex Liberal-Conservatives gave 'unqualified approval to the national policy.'

From the other side, the Reform *Advertiser* revealed in late April that the Tories of North Middlesex (which included Biddulph Township) were 'working a quiet game to retain the seat for the Local [member of the Ontario legislature] at the next general election.' Convinced that a Conservative candidate had 'not a ghost of a chance' for the dominion seat, the *Advertiser*'s correspondent mistakenly assumed that the Conservative aim must be somehow to influence the next provincial vote, at the same time misidentifying the suspected Tory candidate: 'The scheme is to run Mr. Daniel Cochrane, Reeve of Stephen, for the Commons, with a view to securing the Catholic vote in favour of McDougall at the Local [provincial] election.' In fact, Timothy Coughlin, reeve of Stephen, was to be the Irish Catholic farmer nominated by the Tories for the coming dominion election, the scheme being far more direct and ambitious, as we see below.[22]

The Conservative and Reform newspapers in London each insisted that its party was assured of victory in North Middlesex. The Grits had in their favour the Reform tradition in southwestern Ontario, the Scatcherd dynasty since 1861, the incumbency in North Middlesex, and an electoral majority of 177 in the 1876 by-election. The *Advertiser*'s 'Northern Sparks' correspondent wrote as late as 19 August that Colin Scatcherd's return for North Middlesex 'may be regarded as certain.' But, mistaken as he may have been in the details, and in Coughlin's name, the *Advertiser*'s correspondent in April had uncovered the major features of the Conservatives' careful plans to unseat Scatcherd in North Middlesex. The riding association chose its candidate at a well-attended meeting in Ailsa Craig on 11 May – the delegates, of course, were men. The Lucan delegates (Lucan being one of the riding's three incorporated villages) included Bernard and William Stanley and R.H. O'Neill, and among the Biddulph delegates were the Donnellys' neighbours, James Keefe and John Dagg, who had sat on the town council for several years, as well as Patrick Breen and Patrick Dewan, whom Fazakas identifies as among the Donnellys' murderers. The report of the nominations meeting in the *Free Press* is very matter-of-fact: all was straightforward, Coughlin was nominated in an open contest, and the proceedings closed with a vote of confidence in Macdonald and the National Policy.

The *Advertiser*, in contrast, Reform and suspicious, added details to suggest that, led by Bernard Stanley, the Tories' quiet game, all along, had been to nominate Coughlin, the Irish Catholic farmer from McGillivray. Eleven names were put in nomination. Several of these were polite, *pro forma* nominations: John Levi, president of the East Williams

Association and the defeated Conservative candidate in the two previous elections; the Hon. John Carling of London; and H. Gilchrest, president of the North Middlesex Association. Four of the eleven nominees were put forward by the Lucan and Biddulph delegations: Bernard Stanley, Robert H. O'Neill, Patrick Breen, and J. Fox, all nominated and seconded by Lucan and Biddulph delegates. Abel Steel of Lobo was nominated, and R.H. O'Neill nominated Coughlin. The remaining two nominees were proposed and seconded by the Parkhill delegation: A.A. McDonald of Parkhill, and J.H. Woods of North Oxford, nominated by W. Phippen, president of the Parkhill Association. When asked if they would stand, all declined except Coughlin and these last two (the *Free Press* correspondent says incorrectly that Woods also declined). According to the *Advertiser*, Woods 'went like a brick to the poll and succeeded in scoring ten votes'; he did so, it was understood (rightly or wrongly), 'with a view of letting the matter down easy on the defeated candidate. Misery loves company, etc.' But 'misery' seems not to have been the defeated candidate's predominant emotion, the circumstances of Coughlin's victory seeming to justify the *Advertiser*'s suspicion of a 'quiet game.'

In the *Advertiser*'s sceptical account, the Parkhill McDonald's candidacy had come as a surprise, 'as nothing was heard of his intentions previous to the Convention'; had it been otherwise, 'we cannot but think A.A. would have received a much larger vote.' As it was, McDonald announced that he was 'not prepared to-day to say definitely whether he would accept the nomination, but would work heartily for whoever was chosen by the Convention,' appearing to have wanted to play the convention as it had developed, so as to oppose the plans for Coughlin. In the voting McDonald was overwhelmed, receiving seventeen votes to Coughlin's sixty (and Woods's ten). The *Advertiser*'s Reform partisanship seems to have blinded it to the significance of the result of the 'game': 'Both Mr Coughlin and Mr McDonald are Catholics. The one, however, is Irish and the other Scotch. But we cannot see why that should make any difference.'

It is hard to know how much we can trust the *Advertiser*'s claim that 'there were five or more delegates inside who did not vote, and a few who had occasion to go outdoors,' but, alerted by the last-minute resistance offered, not only by McDonald but apparently by the whole Parkhill caucus, its reporter might have noticed the part played by the Lucan and Biddulph delegations and the strategy of directly courting the Irish Catholic Reform voters of that township. A few days later, the *Advertiser* saw it more clearly: the Tories' object in North Middlesex was to split the Irish Catholic vote, and Timothy Coughlin himself was to indicate the driving force behind that strategy in September, when, at the time when he officially filed his nomination papers in Ailsa Craig, he naively began his speech 'by denying that he was Mr Bernard Stanley's candidate; he had been regularly nominated by the Conservative Convention.'[23]

The Campaign in Biddulph Township

The Catholic vote in Biddulph immediately began to split. On 30 May, the *Exeter Times* reported in its 'Centralia' column: 'Mr Ryder, of the 6th or 7th concession of Biddulph, on going into his stable the other morning, found the tail of one of his best horses clean shaved, and on it tied a placard reading, vote for Coughlin.' The *Times*, while a Tory paper supporting Coughlin, was extreme in its condemnation of the outrage: 'To put a stop to such acts as this, the township council should offer a very handsome reward for the apprehension of the perpetrators of the act, and hand them over to the hands of justice, and if justice would not act properly by them by sending them to penitentiary for one thousand years, they should be handed to a vigilance committee, who would hang them to a telegraph pole, after torturing them for a few days. It is worse than treason that such scoundrels should go unpunished.'

Certainly the Ryders, and perhaps the *Exeter Times*, assumed that the culprits were the Donnelly boys, for the Donnellys, perhaps partly because of favours received from the Scatcherds, or their loyalty to David Glass (the Reform candidate in East Middlesex), again voted for Reform. James Reaney suggests that after their vote in the 1878 election the Donnellys' 'ability to hold their own on the Roman Line seems to weaken, ... partly because their opponents suddenly become well organized.' That organization, I am suggesting, began with the quiet game at the 1878 Liberal-Conservative convention. For in the ebb and flow of election excitement in Lucan reported in the press, the Tory election plan required a resolutely quiet, anti-sectarian coalition politics. On 22 May, the *Free Press*'s Lucan reporter acknowledged the uncertainty introduced by the Conservatives' campaign for Coughlin: 'It is admitted by all reasonable persons that the success or defeat of either party depends on the disposal of the Roman Catholic vote, and whether that body gives their entire support to their co-religionist or not remains to be seen.'

Clearly, just as election observers could not judge the *political* effect of the mutilation of Ryder's horse, so neither Tories nor Reformers could afford to overplay the ties either of religious or of traditional party loyalties. When Sir John A. Macdonald campaigned for Coughlin at a large Conservative rally at Parkhill in July, he of course 'did not ask that [Coughlin] should be either voted for or against because he was a Catholic,' and the opposition *Advertiser* thought that it could similarly indirectly influence voters by a simple geographical signal. When Scatcherd was 'busy among his constituents on the celebrated Roman Line,' 'several respectable farmers are openly advocating his return and that without any solicitation whatever as yet on the part of Mr S.' Before he was bundled off on a holiday trip to Ireland in August, the *Advertiser*'s 'Lucan Letter' mocked 'our Barney' [Stanley] in stage Irish for his reaction to a Reform attempt to link the Tories to Fenian threats. 'Barney' stepped out of his own Protestant connection to advise Biddulph voters: 'I tell yees, it's all done just to turn the Orange vote in their own favor. Now mind what I'm telling yees.'

And while no one could directly appeal to Catholics to vote for the Catholic, the partisan press could (as always) report as fact what it wanted to happen. 'In all their assertions,' wrote the *Free Press*, 'the Grits have acknowledged that whichever candidate receives the Roman Catholic vote will undoubtedly be elected, and as the main part of Mr. Coughlin's co-religionists have promised to support him in the coming election, his return is therefore considered certain beyond doubt.' The Grits' equally veiled attempts to resist veiled Tory appeals to Catholics to vote their religion reached an extreme of useless generality when a Reform meeting in Strathroy most emphatically rebuked the 'silly attempt by [Tory] Senator McPherson to make political capital against [Reform] amongst any portion of our race.' 'All this talk about the blending of the orange and the green is fast playing out,' wrote the *Advertiser*'s Lucan correspondent wishfully, 'and the voters are beginning to see through the fulsome flatteries of Barney Stanley and Deputy District Dagg, who boast they hold five hundred votes, both orange and green, under their thumb in Biddulph.' But the Lucan constable complained that the Conservative JPs refused to support his actions against Lucan's troublemakers (and the Donnelly boys would be mentioned first), 'fearing that by so doing the votes of a certain portion of the electors of Biddulph will be cast against the party from whom these Magistrates received their honorary distinction.'[24]

The day after the election, the *Free Press* was able triumphantly to announce: 'A constituency that used to carry a Grit majority of from 600 to 800 now ranks proudly with the Liberal Conservatives.' The Tory

victory in North Middlesex was a momentous one. Coughlin was to hold
the riding with an increasing majority through the next two elections (in
part because of his conduct during the Donnelly trials) until he retired
from politics in 1891. The results in Biddulph Township were equally
momentous. As we know, the Conservatives' muted effort to rewrite the
allegiances, political and religious, in Biddulph Township was successful,
with Coughlin capturing North Middlesex by seven votes. Coughlin's
victory was celebrated in Lucan a week after his election by what the *Free
Press* called a 'large company of Conservatives, and the Reformers who
assisted them [by voting for Coughlin] in securing the recent victory,'
and the inevitable triumphalism was tempered by that consciousness of
just how the triumph had been achieved. While John Carling of London
might assert his pride in being 'a humble individual who had assisted in
wrenching the seat from the Family Compact' (meaning twenty years of
Scatcherds), John O'Donohue of Lucan, who had worked for the Reform party for many years, spoke more quietly of how proud he was 'that
the two great parties to an election in this Riding had united in the
return of Mr Coughlin.' O'Donohue encouraged the Catholic voters of
Biddulph to turn out as willingly for the provincial election, and then, he
said, 'he was certain very many Reformers would be found in the ranks of
the Conservative Party.' It remained for Bernard Stanley, grain merchant
and politician, to place these local considerations in a national perspective: 'He hoped that the new government would prove loyal to the farmers who had placed them in power ... He had every confidence that Sir
John Macdonald would put in practice the policy he advocated while in
opposition.'

The Ideology of Loyalty in Biddulph

I am suggesting that 'loyalty,' in several ways, had emerged as an ideological theme, and an ideological outcome, of the 1878 national election
in Biddulph – the possibility, and in some cases perhaps the necessity, of
new patterns of acquaintance and even friendship, of obligation and
perhaps debt, which crossed those political, sectarian, and class boundaries that had traditionally structured the township's allegiances. What
had been perhaps a mere business relationship might now be transformed by the success of Bernard Stanley's Conservative election strategy: Timothy Coughlin, an Irish Catholic farmer, now held North
Middlesex for the Tories, and ancient loyalties had necessarily been re-
strained, abandoned, or otherwise transformed. I do not know how we

can know comprehensively who did what in the election in Biddulph, any more than we can know in a comprehensive way which individuals did what on the night of the Donnellys' murder. We can, however, infer the extent of the transformation induced in Biddulph by the 1878 election; the issues of the campaign; their complex impact on different parties, classes, and groups; the tactics; and, of course, the choice of candidate. And this ideological transformation of Biddulph's social formation, I am arguing further, was determinate in the events that took place eighteen months later. While we cannot trace the intricacies of *virtù*, as they left the Swamp Schoolhouse the men who killed the Donnellys were united in their mission by a confident loyalty, a set of social relations and allegiances, shaped by masculinist ideology and crossing all the boundaries that they had known before. Most important, they were united in the knowledge that they had claims on the loyalty of the Lucan and Biddulph power structure, Catholic and Protestant, Tory and Reform, and of the new MP for North Middlesex. This new texture of loyalty was a major factor in the Donnelly murders in February 1880. And if we cannot measure it directly in the murderous actions on the night of 4 February, we can see its effects very clearly in the struggle, following the murders, over the proposed venue of the trials – my final instance of the interplay of conjuncture and social formation, time and space.[25]

Law and Ideology in Upper Canada

The inquests and trials that followed the Donnelly murders can themselves be seen not as simply administering, successfully or not, the processes and procedures of Ontario criminal justice, but as articulating the features analysed above in the Biddulph (and Middlesex) social formations with the specific assumptions and practices of English law in Canada. As I have suggested, this is most clearly evident at the Middlesex Spring Assizes in April 1880 in the struggle over where in Ontario the accused murderers should be tried, whether in Middlesex or elsewhere. The decision of course was to hold the trial in London, and it might be argued that this was a foregone conclusion. Foregone or not, as with the identities of the murderers and their guilt, that finality is not important; the point again is how place and time are realized in a particular social formation and a particular historical conjuncture, and how these factors, on a level now shaped by the ideology of the law, determined the outcome of the struggle over venue. Far from showing a certain contempt of court, one hundred and some years later, I am trying again to show how, regardless of the actors, it could hardly, then and there, have been otherwise.

Upper Canadian legal ideology, the assumptions and practices of the law, while English in origin and deferential to English authority, underwent a transformation in Ontario in the course of the nineteenth century. Since there was no significant movement towards codification in the first half of the century, it has been suggested that 'no-one in power in Ontario seems to have been influenced by Jeremy Bentham.' Yet the transformation that I want to emphasize seems to have been considerably influenced by Benthamism, much as were the ideologies of colonization in the Huron Tract in the same period. As in England, in Canada most judges had at least a sympathy with the broad spirit of laissez-faire, with 'a view of the world in which the state and its law kept the civil peace, secured property for its owners and upheld bargains.' And as in the United States in the early nineteenth century, so in Canada, 'law was no longer conceived of as an eternal set of principles expressed in custom and derived from natural law. Nor was it regarded primarily as a body of rules designed to achieve justice only in the individual case. Instead, judges came to think of common law as equally responsible with legislation for governing society and promoting socially desirable conduct.' The greatest happiness, we might say, of the greatest number.

Canadian courts were less instrumentally innovative than the American courts at the time; indeed, the legal community in Canada, writes Richard Risk, was 'a legal colony, forbidden and eventually unwilling to consider its own legal destiny openly.' Risk is not arguing here that Upper Canada's law was a 'perfect reflection' of England's, 'a mere aping of the English judicial and legal scheme' (as has been charged against him). So much is indicated by his suggestion that Ontario was England's legal colony, leaving open the question of the real historical relation (decidedly not a reflection) between Ontario's judicial and legal scheme and that of the mother country. Moreover, by mid-century, the law in Ontario and the United States was similar in organization, in structure, and in most of the terms of doctrine, so that, in Morton Horwitz's words, 'Law, once conceived of as protective, regulative, paternalistic and, above all, a permanent expression of the moral sense of the community, had come to be thought of as facilitative of individual desires and as simply reflective of the existing organization of economic and political power.'[26]

Paul Romney has described the legal history of nineteenth-century Ontario as a progress from the rule of law to responsible government. This too was not a smooth, evolutionary progress; nor was it confined to only one level of government, or to one sector of Ontario society. The call for responsible government was a recurring pattern in the ideological formation of Upper Canada, and it was conjunctural, an 'instinctive' collective response from time to time to a familiar configuration of events (as in 'the Family Compact'). The original campaign for responsible government, Romney writes, 'set a pattern of Ontario politics that was to be repeated twice before the end of the 19th century: the mobilization of agrarian radicalism behind conservative Toronto leadership in a struggle against an external oppressor.'

For Romney, the pattern happens to be Toronto-centred: the first campaign aligned the radical vote behind the Baldwins, father and son, over 'the disenfranchisement of the colonial community as a whole by the orthodox, Blackstonean doctrine that denied colonial sovereignty.' We have seen this above, on the economic level, as 'mercantilism.' The second campaign, around the railway and led by George Brown, was against Montreal capital allied with British bankers; and the third, under the leadership of Oliver Mowat, upheld Ontario's sovereignty and territorial rights in the boundary controversy with Manitoba. But the Baldwins, Brown, and Mowat were not Conservatives. Their conservatism, however, appeared in the circumstances peculiar to each struggle; it was conjunctural. And if we recognize Romney's 'agrarian radicalism' as more accurately 'agrarian *populism*,' we can see the ideological configuration signified by 'responsible government' determining again, in a fourth instance, the struggle over the venue of the Donnelly murder trials.

For the transformation of the law in Upper Canada can be traced in the debates over the province's legal practice, in particular in the rise of a new attitude towards the jury. Romney traces through the middle of the century the increasing restrictions on access to trial by jury in civil and criminal law: 'The elimination of the jury from most civil litigation was consistent with the tendency of late nineteenth-century legal intellectuals to think of the law as an autonomous, internally coherent system of rules, which could be relied upon, if skilfully applied, to supply a just resolution for disputes.' The soft Benthamism, so to speak, of this doctrine of 'skillful application' ran directly counter to the practice of juries as it had developed in England. *Bushell's Case* (1670) had established 'the right of an English criminal jury to render a verdict according to conscience.' Moreover, whereas in England juries were selected from a class that habitually deferred to the local elite, in rural Upper Canada the class positions and habits were different, and in civil and criminal courts, as we might expect, 'most of those qualified for jury service were agrarian smallholders, a debtor class unsympathetic to the local elite and resentful of laws that offered little protection against oppressive creditors.' As a young Reform lawyer in the 1870s, Oliver Mowat had worked to limit trial by jury – to ensure a speedy trial – and when Mowat became premier and attorney general of Ontario in 1872, the legislature passed a bill that limited a plaintiff's right to a jury trial to the judge's discretion in all matters but a few that concerned persons rather than property. Again, I am interested in this particular history not for its direct application (if any) to the Donnelly trials, but rather for its display of the terms of the ideological climate in Ontario law at the time. For the shift in general, in Canada as in England, was away from a jury (if there were a jury) deciding cases out of its own collective knowledge and close to local sentiment, towards deciding on evidence given before it in court.

The larger transformation in Upper Canadian law was thus a battle between the skilful application of legal instruments and the common law tradition of jury independence, intensified by the particular class relations obtaining in Upper Canada and the recurring pattern identified by Paul Romney: 'At times of political turbulence, ... it was claimed that the jury's duty [i.e., to prevent unjust conviction and punishment] extended to considering whether the facts alleged in the indictment constituted a crime and, if so, whether they merited the punishment assigned to the crime by law. The most radical conception of the jury's duty gave it the power in theory – a power, which as a result of *Bushell's Case* it came to enjoy in practice – to nullify any law, even if the law were a criminal statute that defined specific actions in such a way as to leave no scope for discretion.' In England, indeed, the grand jury was traditionally a powerful weapon, with the right to speak for the community on matters of common interest. The source of this radical conception of the jury's role, says Romney, was a 'sense of unjust disenfranchisement.' In England, the injustice could be a particular set of property relations, but in the light of his discussion of the pattern of nineteenth-century Upper Canadian politics, there it could ground itself in the ideological structure that he identifies as rural populism under conservative leadership.

Romney sees the struggle for responsible government in Upper Canada as promoting a sort of communal conformism; he quotes another historian, S.F. Wise, on 'intense local patriotism' and 'Ontario sectionalism' and refers elsewhere to 'the world-view of the ordinary agrarian smallholder.' But while this populism was 'heir to an age-old localism (of which the doctrine of the censorial jury was only one expression),' it was, as I have suggested, conjuncturally activated, and the issues surrounding any important jury trial – the venue of the trial and, the right of the all-male jury to speak for the community – could easily arouse it. The struggle over the venue of the Donnelly trial (while we can acknowledge naked individual and group self-interest) can thus be seen historically as situated at the conjuncture of the embattled legal ideology of the right of juries to express the will of the community with the political ideology, recurrent in Ontario history, of responsible government, and this during the government of Oliver Mowat, a lawyer who had been associated with the gradual diminishing of jury power, but 'a canny politician with a shaky majority.' The hearings over the venue of the Donnelly trials, and aspects of the trials themselves, show the workings of this particular conjuncture.[27]

Ideology and Public Comment

'Trials expose local culture,' write Carolyn Strange and Tina Loo, because they 'raise uncomfortable questions about the limits of behaviour.' We can be more specific: in the case of the trials for the Donnelly murders, the struggle, legalistic but political, over what was to be the location or venue of those trials exposed precisely the limits of behaviour that shaped Biddulph and North Middlesex as the practised place that we have been analysing in this chapter. The decision not to move the venue from London not only made the verdicts a foregone conclusion but completed the reconstruction of the Biddulph social formation initiated by the 1878 dominion election (or by the transformation of farming on the Roman Line, or by the slow displacement of the Ontario wheat staple). At the Middlesex Assizes in London in mid-April 1880, and then again on appeal one month later, at the Courts of Common Pleas and Queen's Bench in Toronto, a legal decision had to be made whether a fair and impartial trial could be had either in Middlesex or outside Middlesex. The final decision in May, as William Butt has convincingly shown, was a narrowly partisan political one, driven mostly by Premier/

Attorney General Mowat's reading of the electoral implications of his Ontario Reform government's appearing to rule against Irish Catholic farmers. But that decision necessarily was presented in (overdetermined by) an inchoate Middlesex popular opinion, perceptible in gossip, in newspaper interviews and letters to the editor, in the editorial opinions of those newspapers, and of course in the affidavits presented at the venue hearings. And the competing efforts of counsel to generalize convincingly these materials are also informed by the British and Upper Canadian legal history that I have summarized.

The two parties to the battle over venue presented opposite views of opinion in Middlesex. The *Toronto Globe*'s reporter wrote that in the large crowd at the coroner's inquest in Lucan 'the feeling was all for the accused, and I overheard more than one man say he would not hang them if the evidence was ever so strong against them.' In contrast, John McDougall, the Conservative MPP for North Middlesex, affirmed in court that 'possibly with the exception of the immediate neighbourhood of the place where the crime was committed, where I have no doubt some members of the community have formed opinions in some cases for and in other cases against the prisoners, the general sentiment of the people of the county is that a searching investigation should be made.' Different newspapers presented different readings of popular opinion. On the day following the murders, the *St Marys Argus*, a Reform weekly in neighbouring Perth County, gave its opinion that 'while every person regrets that so foul a deed was perpetrated, no one regrets that the community is rid of most of a family who have made themselves a terror to the part of the country in which they resided ... And while we regret exceedingly that such an atrocious murder was committed in our neighbourhood, yet the people of the township of Biddulph will breathe the freer.' In Oxford County a week later, the correspondent for the weekly *Ingersoll Chronicle* reported a man saying to a friend, 'who seemed to agree with the remark, ... hundreds of people are glad in their own minds that the family has been reduced by five members' and commented ambiguously: 'Such an admission as this is horrible to contemplate, even though the murdered persons were the most desperate and wicked in the wide world.'

Many newspapers and their correspondents were prepared to think the worst of the Donnellys and to excuse their killers. The Tory *Toronto Mail*, two days after the event, knew that 'at least two of the victims had been guilty of heinous offenses and that the whole family were enemies of society.' After two weeks' reflection and closer to the scene, a Tory weekly, the *Strathroy Western Dispatch* ('Support Legitimate Home Manufactures and Enterprizes') was prepared, while admitting to a difficulty (and some very dubious 'Yankee' political theory), to justify the murders:

While the majesty of the law and the well-being of society require that the perpetrators should be sought out and punished, yet it is difficult to get rid of the feeling that the provocation called for the deed, heinous though it was. The murder is awful to contemplate, and yet the state of things which undoubtedly called it forth, is also awful to contemplate. When things have come to such a pass, ... severe measures are an absolute necessity ... We are far from advocating Lynch Law, but as sure as day follows the night, when the law fails to punish the lawless, people will take it into their own hands to right society and punish the wicked. All power is in the people, and when those to whom they delegate that power for the preservation of law and order, fail to execute it, the natural result will be that the people will resume the power and execute it themselves. The great difficulty is that ... the innocent are liable to suffer with the guilty.

And a month after the murders, the *London Free Press*, also Tory but a daily, commented with editorial gravity: 'There have been other instances of such irruptions of banditti [the "Donnelly gang"] into neighbourhoods similarly unprotected, followed by equally violent measures of self-redress on the part of the people.'

These editorial comments were often supplemented by 'interviews' and 'letters from readers' (I am indicating my caution here; as the *London Advertiser* pointed out, these demand to be read critically). The *Western Dispatch* on 11 February published an interview with an anonymous Lucanite that gave 'the anti-Donnelly view of the situation' – there was no complementary 'pro-Donnelly view' given. The 'Lucanite' was sure that the murderers were well known: 'There is no doubt in my mind that the Vigilance Committee is in the secret, but they will keep it. Moreover, the people of the neighbourhood are under a debt of gratitude to them for their action to rid the place of the Donnellys, and no one will testify against the Committee.' Asked if the murderers were not as bad as the Donnellys, the 'Lucanite' responded: 'No siree! If the truth were known it will be found that the murderers are the most respectable people in the township – good farmers and honest men. But they had to do it. There was no other way.' 'The Donnellys had to be killed,' he added; 'Perhaps it was a mistake that Bill was not killed, but that can't be helped.' 'Lucanite' goes on in this vein, in his own mind clearly winning the debate with his interviewer, but my purpose here is to call attention to the ideological work done by such an interview, one week after the murders.

What is being signalled across North Middlesex (not, as we see below, by this Strathroy paper alone) is not only an acceptable anti-Donnelly view but confidence, even masculine bravado – 'No Siree!' Reminded that the Donnellys' crimes do not excuse the legal liability of the murders, 'Lucanite' responds with a shrug, 'Well, perhaps not. But they ain't caught yet.' The *Toronto Mail* called it 'not merely sympathy ... but exultation,' and these published interviews, I suggest, are less a sounding of public opinion in Middlesex, still less a survey, than a signal, an assurance, or (as an ideological practice) a rehearsal of solidarity. Here the new social formation, local and conjunctural, reminds us, and – more important at that moment – the populace, of its existence. The *London Advertiser*, as I have mentioned, a Reform daily, implied as much in its inevitably partisan attacks on the attitude towards the murders practised by its 'esteemed contemporary,' the Tory *London Free Press*. In an editorial on 21 February, the *Advertiser* charged that the *Free Press* 'continues to rejoice, under the guise of a correspondent, that the Donnellys were butchered.' The *Advertiser* surmises that the *Free Press* sees a Conservative electoral advantage in that position and challenges the publisher of the *Free Press*: 'Until the editor of our very esteemed contemporary announces the name of the writer who defends the murder, people are justified in assuming that it is the opinion of Mr Josiah Blackburn [the publisher of the *Free Press*].' A month later, the *Advertiser* returned to the attack, charging that the *Free Press*, 'by correspondence and comment, has done much to influence sentiment against the Donnellys and to hold the murderers up in the light of great purifying agents.' There is no question that the columns of the *Free Press* in the weeks following the murders gave much support to this suspicion; I have quoted one editorial and, to indicate the sort of party-political slant that the *Advertiser*, itself not immune, criticizes, I might cite a letter on 21 February, from 'Fair Play': 'It is a sad and humiliating fact, that the great bulk of the Catholics of Biddulph were actually driven to the polls by the Donnelly gang under threats of the incendiary's torch, and the bullet of the assassin. And that in the interest of the late Colin Scatcherd.' Again there is no need here to establish the truth of these 'facts,' or the authorship of these 'letters from readers,' in order to recognize that the *Free Press*'s publishing these superficially various comments signals not only a widely held body of opinion and its acceptability (signalling thereby an ideological position), but its association with (I might say, its practice by) powerful institutions, the *London Free Press* and the Liberal-Conservative party of North Middlesex not least among them.

Ideology and the Struggle over Venue

But this is not to overemphasize, as do both the *Advertiser* and the *Free Press*, the party allegiances indicated here. As we have seen, these are more complexly at play in Biddulph and North Middlesex than either of these London newspapers can perhaps explain. I have noted the apparent political loyalties of these papers (signalled often, in 1880, by comments on the working of the National Policy) because there does seem to be in general a pattern in their response to 'the Biddulph Tragedy': the Conservative papers seem by and large at least to emphasize the crimes alleged against the Donnellys, with some going on to argue that the murders were justified; the Reform papers tend to focus on the horror of the murders and to call for swift, sure justice. But these positions, as I have tried to suggest by pointing to the kinds of signals being sent – confidence, even bravado, and a supporting line of argument – determine and are determined by the new complexity of the social formation in Biddulph, evading simple political or sectarian explanations.

More important, the newspapers attempted to influence the legal struggle over the venue for the trials, and the party political pattern seems generally though not invariably similar. Tory papers tended to support a trial in Middlesex; Reform papers tended to call for a trial elsewhere, but even this general pattern is subsumed by the other forces intent on influencing the decision. The *Toronto Globe*, so far as I have been able to learn, was the first paper publicly to demand a change in venue for the Donnelly murder trials, and thenceforth the demand was associated with the *Globe* and, soon, with Toronto. In an editorial on 6 March, after the coroner's inquest into the deaths, the *Globe* attempted to describe the state of feeling in Biddulph: 'The district is divided into two factions,' it claimed, 'the larger one hostile to the murdered family, the other to the prisoners.' The coroner's inquest, in the *Globe*'s estimation, demonstrated two things: that the coroner's jury was prepared to 'show a total disregard for the evidence adduced' and that 'the satisfaction with which the verdicts were received by many of the Biddulph people, and the sympathy shown at London for the prisoners by many inhabitants of the county, show that it will be difficult to get a jury in Middlesex which can be trusted.'

Here we have added to the opposing judgments of the crime and the latent party affiliations the very matters of legal practice – the independence of a jury and its relation to the local people – that were in the process of changing in British and Canadian (and American) law. The question of venue, as raised by the *Globe*, thus locates these issues histori-cally, in that place at that time. The *Globe* claimed that 'all the Ontario journals outside of London who have spoken on the subject' demanded that the trial's location be removed from London – some of these, such as the *St Marys Argus*, only reluctantly followed the lead of its fellow Reform journal. In London, the *Advertiser* took no position but mocked its Tory rival's 'wild howling' against a relocation: 'Our esteemed con-temporary should have sufficient faith in the judiciary of the Province to believe that they will do what is right and proper in the circumstances.' Indeed, throughout March 1880, the *Free Press* railed against the *Globe*'s position: 'The Toronto paper was never very favourable to London' and was casting 'a slur on Middlesex and London.' The *Free Press* argued that the open verdict of the coroner's jury – that the murders were commit-ted by 'persons unknown' – was not a nullification of the evidence but simply allowed a later, appropriate court to decide the guilty parties. When the Tory *Toronto Mail* – 'Not Local Purposes, Not Local Prejudices, Ought to Guide, But the General Good' was its motto – came out for a change of trial venue, 'howling with the *Globe*,' the *Free Press* pointed to the investigations already done by the London police into the Donnelly murders and asked, 'Are these not sufficient guarantees that the men of Middlesex and London know how to do their duty?' The *Mail* thought not: 'The people in the vicinity are evidently incapable of adjudicating on the matter calmly; indeed they appear for the time being to have lost all power of discriminating between right and wrong,' and 'a fair and just trial of the case at London is out of the question.'

But on 19 March, the *Free Press* published 'A Common-Sense Letter from Justitia,' which, after again telling the tale of the Donnellys' 'scoundrelisms,' tendentiously raised the issue that embodies those his-torical determinations to which I have pointed and which will dominate the venue hearings. Sharing the *Free Press*'s 'common sense,' 'Justitia' rebukes the *Globe*: 'The Toronto Thunderer forgets that none can better judge whether a homicide is justifiable than those who know the facts and circumstances.' Who can best know the facts and circumstances – *what* facts and *what* circumstances – was not only tactically the central legal issue in the venue hearings and in the trials themselves but, as we saw above, a question with a long history in jurisprudence.[28]

The Middlesex Spring Assizes sat in London on 13 April. 'Applying on behalf of the Crown, instructed only by the Crown,' Aemelius Irving ('in his day,' says Fazakas, 'one of the most dreaded of prosecutors') moved that the place of trial be changed from Middlesex to some other county.

He then presented in evidence the only two affidavits that he had been able to obtain, from Charles Hutchinson, crown attorney for Middlesex County, and W.T.T. Williams, chief constable of the City of London ('the clever police of London,' the *Exeter Times* called them). These men both testified that a fair and impartial trial could not be had in Middlesex, citing the 'remarkable' and 'unseemly' sympathy demonstrated for the accused at the inquest and the 'bad feeling' and 'prejudice' shown over the years towards the Donnellys. Hutchinson contrasted the Vigilance Society's searching the Donnelly farm for Thompson's cow the previous August to the reluctance of the society or any of its members to make any effort to discover the Donnelly murderers: 'No assistance need be expected from said association or its members.' Both officials tried to present a reading of the larger situation, of public opinion in the township and county, yet, strangers to Biddulph, and because no witnesses would come forward, they could speak only of 'bad feeling' and 'prejudice.' Hutchinson tried to show the texture of social relationships binding the township, the six accused 'being all either themselves persons of consideration in the said township or connected with such persons, and several have connections in the city of London and other parts of the county. They are well-known, and until now have occupied respectable positions and have been of good repute.' Though seriously hampered in his effort, Hutchinson is here, with his discourse of 'consideration,' 'connection,' and 'repute,' attempting to convey his perception of 'said township' not as a simple but as a 'practised' place, a social formation with certain practices of power and obligation, a society of interrelating social groups, loyalties, and pressures that at this time would preclude the extraction of a fair jury panel. This, Hutchinson's sixth and last point, might be taken as the crucial text of the assize hearing, as well as at the appeal.

Hugh MacMahon was counsel for the defence at the London hearing, and he was joined at the appeal hearing in Toronto a month later by W.R. Meredith. William Butt rightly stresses the tactical significance of this partnering of a Reform lawyer with the Conservative MPP for London and leader of the Opposition in the Ontario legislature. Based on the common law ideology of the importance of the local and societal in jury trials, the strategy for the defence was to emphasize every facet of 'outsiderness' in the prosecution's case for removal. The notion that the venue needed to be changed arose only, *could* arise only from 'the repeated demands made by *The Globe* and *Mail*, published in the City of Toronto, each having a very large circulation throughout this Province, that the trial should not take place in the county of Middlesex.' The affidavits of the Londoners Hutchinson and Williams contained 'meagre evidence' and 'very general statements'; aside from three facts, said Meredith, 'all they had to go upon was the opinion of Mr Hutchinson and the Chief of Police.' MacMahon pointed out that Williams had lived in Toronto until 1878, and after that he knew Middlesex only from London; he was clearly motivated by the reward alone, 'activated ... by a desire to see the prisoners convicted whether guilty or not.'

These tactics of the defence presented directly and by implication a wholly other reading of the situation in Biddulph Township and Middlesex. As distant as possible from inhabiting anything like a social formation, the citizens of Biddulph, even along the Roman Line, lived relatively isolated lives (as separate as potatoes in a sack), they had only a neighbourhood acquaintance, and even this was constructed only along the most attenuated connections of family and trade. MacMahon called Martin McLaughlin, one of the accused, to the stand and presented affidavits from the others to testify how few relatives they had in London and Middlesex. The father of James Ryder, one of the accused, testified that his son had always lived on the farm with him, 'and so far as he knows is almost unacquainted with people outside of the locality in which he lived.' Thomas Dight, wheat merchant of Lucan, testified that Lucan, not London or elsewhere in Middlesex, was 'the market to which the farmers of Biddulph brought the great bulk of their produce.' Surely, except for immediate neighbours, who might be expected to attend the inquest and express sympathy, there was potentially a large panel of fair and impartial jurors in Middlesex. And, while not partial, the jury at the Lucan inquest had demonstrated the role of the sort of local knowledge that Hutchinson and Williams so completely lacked: 'The jurors of said inquest,' argued MacMahon, 'knowing personally the character of the witnesses on behalf of the prosecution [Johnny O'Connor, Will Donnelly, Patrick Whelan, and so on], placed, as I am informed and believe, very little reliance on the evidence given by them.' Beyond family and trade relations, this unimpeachable combination of local knowledge and experience, and reputation, were the only social relations admitted in the defence of the accused murderers. MacMahon saved his most sardonically powerful arguments for the sixth point of Hutchinson's affidavit, which I have quoted, on the respectability and social connections of the accused, turning the prosecution's arguments on their head, dismissing them as 'general' and 'round' assertions and insisting again on the importance of local knowledge narrowly and very conventionally construed.

'All the people of the highest respectability,' said MacMahon, 'believe that the prisoners can obtain as fair a trial in the county of Middlesex as they could in any other in the Province.' To demonstrate this at the London hearings, MacMahon called as witnesses James Armstrong, reeve of Westminster and warden of Middlesex; Josiah Blackburn, managing director of the *London Free Press*; and Donald McKenzie of the Agricultural Society of London Township and Conservative candidate for East Middlesex in the last provincial election. As we have seen above, Thomas Dight, of Stanley, Dight & Co., would testify at the May hearings (as would his senior partner, Bernard Stanley, at the actual trials), and this 'phalanx of probity' (in William Butt's phrase) at both hearings embodied MacMahon and Meredith's rebuttal of Hutchinson's remarks on the legal status of 'repute.' In April, MacMahon argued that 'reputation,' far from giving some unfair advantage, was simply part of an individual's local capital, integral to his identity (as it was seen to be, for instance, by R.G. Dun & Co.): 'The point I desire to make is this, that the good repute of the prisoners in this locality is one of the strongest reasons why the place of trial should not be changed. If the prisoners are turned out of this locality they are going to where a prejudice has been created against them through the instrumentality of the newspapers, to a locality where their former lives and good repute will be of no avail to them whatever ... They do not ask for sympathy, but they ask that their former good characters in this country should be of some avail to them.' In May, Meredith made the same point, placing it in an argument about juries in the common law tradition. He ignored the larger social concerns that the prosecution had tried to raise and simply suggested that Hutchinson and Irving were expressing an unwarranted fear of jury intimidation. It seemed to him 'an extraordinary view' 'that the place of trial should be removed because these prisoners had been respectable members of the community in which they had lived. He thought that was rather a reason why their common law right to be tried in the county where the crime was committed should be sustained.' Moreover, he argued, if attempts had been made to intimidate the jury, Irving, instead of making the charge in general terms, should openly 'specify them, giving the names of the jurymen interfered with.'

Irving was not of course charging direct interference with the jury, nor did he view 'reputation' in this case as merely an individual's fixed social capital. In his rebuttal for the prosecution, he argued again, and somewhat tortuously, an understanding of social relations in the township that might acknowledge class differences other than repute or its lack, filiations of power in a social formation that the defence was at such pains to deny and conceal:

> With reference to the affidavits of prominent persons which have been filed, I think the affidavits from persons who are in the habit of receiving popular favour are not a class of affidavit which carry the same weight with them as those of persons who are in a less prominent position, because we know that they are subject to the solicitation of favours which it is not easy to deny ... My learned friend laid great stress on the point that removing these men for trial from this county to another county would deprive them in their defence of the benefit of the former good character which they had, but there is nothing of that kind that ought to weigh with any jury except the evidence of character brought before them and sworn to in the ordinary progress of the trial.

The makers of the defence's affidavits, he added 'were men more or less dependent upon popular favour and therefore could hardly be expected to give a perfectly independent opinion in a case of this kind.'

Here, while he recognizes the ordinary progress of a trial by jury, acknowledging the common law community basis for juries, Irving at the same time insists on another consideration, another reality outside that ordinary progress, indicated by 'popular favour' and the solicitation or bestowal of such favours. Outside the courtroom, especially in Biddulph, there are relations of interest and power (the new loyalties of which I have been speaking) that a trial in Middlesex cannot escape. These relations of social power have already affected the police investigation, the readiness of persons with special knowledge to come forward, and perhaps the testimony of those who did come forward. This is not, Irving implies, a simple matter of who knows or is related to whom in Middlesex, nor yet direct intimidation, but rather the existence of material social relations, relations of loyalty and class power such as I have sketched, that inhibit individual action and interfere with a just verdict.

As William Butt has shown, the matter of the venue of the Donnelly murder trials was in the end influenced more by the provincial political parties' attempts to court the rural Irish Catholic vote in Ontario than by the insights of Aemilius Irving, QC: 'In Toronto the case was, publicly, a racial and religious concern.' And so, finally, in April, Mr Justice Adam Wilson's judgment in the application for a change of venue ignored the sorts of consideration that Irving was trying to raise. Wilson reviewed the allegations of prejudice in the township against the Donnellys, saying that if he were simply to act on his own impression he would move the trial to prevent the 'slightest trait' of a suspicion of unfairness. But, emphasizing the common law tradition, he stated that the prisoners had 'the legal right to be tried in this place, and whatever that legal right may be worth, I have not the power to take it from them, unless I have the sanction of the law, and that sanction I do not think I have on this occasion.' Thus the prosecution's rudimentary analysis of the peculiar characteristics of the occasion (or conjuncture and social formation) was displaced in Wilson's judgment by arithmetic – the size of Middlesex, stated twice, and its population, also stated twice – and Irving's concern with the special social power represented by reputation in any social formation was rejected in favour of the defence's description of reputation as simple social capital. The affidavits on the prisoners' behalf, said Justice Wilson, 'are made by gentlemen of position, influence and respectability, who have long resided in the different parts of the county, ... and who have filled, and some of whom still fill, places of local trust and honour.' No mention of 'the habit of receiving popular favour,' the uses of influence, at that time in that place.

The Donnelly Murders and History

The decision to hold the trials for the Donnelly murders in London predetermined the verdict of those trials, as the accounts of Butt and Fazakas so clearly show. What I have tried further to demonstrate is the historical structure of the determinations of that outcome, not as the result merely of individual witnesses and individual jurors more or less freely choosing to speak and act in certain ways, but individuals whose more or less free actions were more precisely constrained than we usually admit. On 23 March 1880, the *Advertiser*'s 'Northern Sparks' correspondent communicated the following: 'Martin Collison is about as decent a man as lives either off or on the Roman Line. He did not sign the Vigilant book, neither was he a member of the Cedar Swamp Parliament. Everyone will admit that it wasn't the Donnellys burned his frame barns and woodsheds down last Tuesday night. Who was it then?' While that is the correct legal question, addressing the matter of personal guilt and striving for an answer that 'settles the matter,' it is not, in the sense that I have been trying to establish, the correct historical question. A historical question might be: 'Why were Martin Collison's barns burned?' While it is unlikely that either question will ever be answered, the argument that I have been making in this chapter suggests if not a precise answer to the second, the determinations of whatever the precise answer might be.

And the *Advertiser*'s note, mentioning the 'Vigilant book' and the 'Cedar Swamp Parliament,' gestures towards what other specific questions, given those determinations, might be asked: 'What was Martin Collison thought to have seen on the night of 4 February?' 'What was he thought to have heard since?' 'Was he talking of testifying?'

This interminable series of speculations does not need to be answered; it merely suggests how further to explore that determinate space and time, the social formation and conjuncture, Biddulph Township in 1880. That kind of thinking, I have been arguing, produces a more useful historical knowledge than the various identities and other precisions that are thought adequate in courtrooms and elsewhere. But if what I have been trying to do primarily is to demonstrate what I call 'overdetermination,' that complexity of historical causality is further complicated by 'underdetermination,' the effects of individual impulse and chance. These effects too have appeared in this book from its first pages: what could I say, for example, had ordained, several millennia ago, that over a very particular terrain north of what were to become the Great Lakes, and for a certain length of time, the rate of glacial melt would exactly cancel the movement of the Wisconsin glacier? That occurrence, as with innumerable other moments in this story, I willingly concede to chance. As for individual action, I would admit that the residents of Biddulph Township (such as, perhaps, Martin Collison) who knew the specifics of the events of 4 February 1880, and who yet decided not to come forward as witnesses, freely chose that course of action. But they made those choices *not* under circumstances that they themselves had chosen but (again, like Martin Collison) under given and inherited circumstances. Because of the land inherited from that glacier, because of the way in which it was settled, because of how it came to be traversed and to what end, because of the history of wheat production in Upper Canada in relation to elsewhere and a particular electoral history, a society was produced with a distinctive structure (a social formation) that in turn produced the material circumstances of the murder and its aftermath – circumstances, that is, that the Donnellys' murderers did not themselves freely choose.

Just as this book has little to do with individual actions and more to do with limestone, the Niagara Escarpment, and class, so it has little to say about guilt. That 'clever boy' Johnny O'Connor (so disparaged by the *Exeter Times*) and Will Donnelly (universally recognized as clever) saw what happened and who did it; I know of nothing to add to the story told by Ray Fazakas or William Butt. But the assigning of guilt (or in this case, jury nullification of evidence) is only the narrowest conclusion to the story and as such, a historically impoverished meaning to the whole episode. I have attempted to demonstrate that the meanings of the Donnelly murders, historically, are Ontario meanings, Canadian meanings, and not only, when placed in the history of railway construction or wheat production on this continent, eastern Canadian meanings. The meaning of the Donnelly murders is ultimately about how we have made our history, about the determinate circumstances (not of our own choosing) within which that history was made. For my part, I was given the usual, familiar histories of the Donnelly murders. While widely various, these have certain shared assumptions about the history of individuals and societies. It is against the grain of these narratives, very much not of my own choosing, that I have made this history of the 'Biddulph Tragedy.'[29]

Notes

1: Siting and Surveying

1 W.L. Morton, 'The Significance of Site in the Settlement of the American and Canadian Wests,' *Agricultural History* 25 (1951), 97. William Cronon, *Nature's Metropolis: Chicago and the Great West* (New York: W.W. Norton, 1991), 25. Donald F. Putnam and Robert G. Putnam, *Canada: A Regional Analysis* (Don Mills, Ont.: J.M. Dent, 1970), 2–5.

2 R.W. Packer, 'The Physical Geography of the Fifteen Counties of Southwestern Ontario,' *Western Ontario Historical Notes* 12 (1954), 53. L.J. Chapman and D.F. Putnam, *The Physiography of Southern Ontario* (Toronto: Ministry of Natural Resources, 1984), 119, xxi, 1–2, 9. J. Brian Bird, *The Natural Landscapes of Canada* (Toronto: Wiley, 1972), 7, 11–12. Jacob Spelt, 'Southern Ontario,' in John Warkentin, ed., *Canada: A Geographical Interpretation* (Toronto: Methuen, 1968), 336. Peter B. Clibbon and L.-E. Hamelin, 'Landforms,' in Warkentin, ed., *Canada*, 65–9. R.W. Packer, 'The Geographical Basis of the Regions of Southwestern Ontario,' *Canadian Historical Association: Report of Annual Meeting Held at London, June 4-6, 1953, with Historical Papers*, 45. 'Bedrock Geology' (map), *Ausable Valley Conservation Report* (Toronto: Conservation Branch, Department of Planning and Development, 1949), pt 1: 'General,' chap. 2, 4–5. J.M.S. Careless, *Careless at Work* (Toronto: Dundern Press, 1990), 256. William J. Wilgus, *The Railway Interrelations of the United States and Canada*, first pub. 1937 (New York: Russell & Russell, 1970), 5.

3 Chapman and Putnam, *Physiography*, 9–41, 127, 237, xxi. R. Cole Harris and Geoffrey J. Matthews, eds., *The Historical Atlas of Canada, vol. I, From the Beginning to 1800* (Toronto: University of Toronto Press, 1987), plate 1. A.S. Dyke and V.K. Prest, *Paleography of Northern North America, 18000–5000 Years*

Ago (Ottawa: Geological Survey of Canada, 1987), Map 1703A, 1:12500000, Sheet 1, accompanying Dyke and Prest, 'The Late Wisconsonian and Holocene History of the Laurentide Ice Sheet,' *Géographie physique et quaternaire* 41 (1987), 237–63. Frank B. Taylor, 'The Moraine Systems of Southwestern Ontario,' *Transactions: Royal Canadian Institute* 10 (1913), 58, 59. Bird, *Natural Landscapes*, 110. *Ausable Report*, 'Soils,' pt 3, 13.

4 D.F. Putnam and L.J. Chapman, 'The Climate of Southern Ontario,' *Scientific Agriculture* 18 (1935), 41. Packer, 'Geographical Basis,' 46. F.J. Monkhouse, *A Dictionary of Geography*, 2nd ed. (London: Edward Arnold, 1970), 71. Charles J. Krebs, *Ecology: The Experimental Analysis of Distribution and Abundance*, 2nd ed. (New York: Harper and Row, 1978), 429, 432, 442.

5 *Historical Atlas of Canada*, I, plates 3, 4. William Cronon, *Changes in the Land: Indians, Colonists, and the Ecology of New England* (New York: Hill and Wang, 1983), 11, 32. Eric A. Bourdo, Jr, 'The Forest the Settlers Saw,' in Susan L. Fader, ed., *The Great Lakes Forest: An Environmental and Social History* (Minneapolis: University of Minnesota Press, 1983), 5. R.J. Whittaker, 'Biogeography and Ecology,' in A. Rogers, H. Viles, and A. Goudie, eds., *The Student's Companion to Geography* (Oxford: Blackwell, 1992), 44. E. Lucy Braun, *Deciduous Forests of Eastern North America*, first pub. 1950 (New York: Hafner, 1967), 307–8.

6 *Historical Atlas of Canada*, I, plates 17, 17A. Putnam and Putnam, *Canada*, 36, 195, 38. Roland D. Craig, 'The Forest Resources of Canada,' *Economic Geography* 2 (1926), 401. *Ausable Report*, pt 3, 'Forestry,' chap. 1, 'The Forest,' 2. Putnam and Chapman, 'Climate,' 405. L.G. Reeds, 'The Environment,' *Ontario*, in R. Louis Gentilcore, ed., *Canada* (Toronto: University of Toronto Press, 1972), 6. 'Forest Ecology and Terminology,' in Braun, *Deciduous Forests*, 10–27.

7 *Soils of Middlesex County* (map) 1:50,000, Sheet 3, Ontario: Eastern Townships, Soil Survey Report No. 56 (Ottawa: Agriculture Canada, 1991). *Soil Capability for Agriculture* (map) 1:250,000, Kitchener Sheet 40P-O (Ottawa: Canada Department of Agriculture and ARDA, Canada Department of Forestry and Rural Development, 1968). *Soil Capability for Agriculture* (map) 1:50,000, Lucan West Half, Sheet 40P/3 (Toronto: Ontario Department of Agriculture and Food, Canada Land Inventory, ARDA section, 196?). Gwen Smith Harrison, ed., *Families and Farms of Huron Township with Its Hub, Ripley* (Owen Sound: Ripley-Huron Reunion 1985 Historical Committee, 1985), 133.

8 *Ausable Report*, 'Forestry,' 2, 3, 4. Putnam and Putnam, *Canada*, 25. R.L. Jones, *History of Agriculture in Ontario, 1613–1880* (Toronto: University of Toronto Press, 1946), 20. Thomas R. Cox, R.S. Maxwell, and P.D. Thomas, *This Well-Wooded Land: Americans and Their Forests from Colonial Times to the Present* (Lincoln: University of Nebraska Press, 1985), 10. G. Elmore

Reaman, *The Trail of the Black Walnut* (Toronto: McClelland and Stewart, 1957), 143. R. Louis Gentilcore, 'Change in Settlement in Ontario (Canada), 1800–50: A Correlation Analysis of Historical Source Materials,' in W. Peter Adams and Frederick M. Helleiner, eds., *International Geography 1972* (Toronto: University of Toronto Press, 1972), I, 419. Kenneth Kelly, 'The Evaluation of Land for Wheat Cultivation in Early Nineteenth Century Ontario,' *Ontario History* 62 (1970), 57–65. A.G. Brunger, 'Analysis of Site Factors in Nineteenth Century Ontario Settlement,' in *International Geography 1972*, I, 269–82.

9 Cronon, *Nature's Metropolis*, xvii. Alfred Schmidt, *The Concept of Nature in Marx*, trans. B. Fowkes (London: New Left Books, 1971), 196, 194, 68. Cronon, *Changes in the Land*, 13. Abraham Rotstein, 'The Mystery of the Neutral Indians,' in R. Hall, W. Westfall, and L.S. MacDowell, eds., *Patterns of the Past: Interpreting Ontario's History* (Toronto: Dundurn Press, 1988), 17–18. Sebastiano Timpanaro, *On Materialism* (London: New Left Books, 1975), 46, 48, 49. Raymond Williams, *Problems in Materialism and Culture* (London: Verso, 1980), 107–8. Raymond Williams, *Marxism and Literature* (Oxford: Oxford University Press, 1977), 87.

10 [Goodspeed] *History of the County of Middlesex, Canada*, new ed. first pub. 1972 (Belleville: Mika Studio, 1972), 214. John Ladell, *They Left Their Mark: Surveyors and Their Role in the Settlement of Ontario* (Toronto: Dundurn Press, 1993), 19–90, 111. Map of the Tract of Land purchased by Government from the Chippewa Indians in the year 1825 in the London and Western Districts ... , M. Burwell, 1828, Canada Company Papers, Archives of Ontario (henceforth AO), C-59; for maps before 1867, I include reference to their number in Joan Winearls, *Mapping Upper Canada, 1780–1867: An Annotated Bibliography of Manuscript and Printed Maps* (Toronto: University of Toronto Press, 1991); this map is number 1028.

11 Ladell, *They Left Their Mark*, 15, 114. Earl G. Harrington, 'Cadastral Surveys for the Public Lands of the United States,' in V. Carstensen, ed., *The Public Lands: Studies in the History of the Public Domain* (Madison: University of Wisconsin Press, 1968), 35–6. William Nolan, *Fassadinin: Land, Settlement and Society in Southeast Ireland 1600–1850* (Dublin: Geography Publications, 1979), 70, 248. William Petty, *The History of the Survey of Ireland, Commonly Called the Down Survey*, first pub. 1851, ed. T.A. Larcom (New York: Augustus M. Kelly, 1967), 47. Robert C. Simington, ed., *The Civil Survey A.D. 1654–1656*, vol. II, *County of Tipperary, Western and Northern Baronies* (Dublin: Stationery Office, for the Irish Manuscripts Commission, 1934), xix, 333.

12 Payson Jackson Treat, 'Origin of the National Land System under the Confederation,' in V. Carstensen, ed., *The Public Lands: Studies in the History of the Public Domain* (Madison: University of Wisconsin Press, 1968), 10.

Norman J.W. Thrower, *Original Surveys and Land Subdivision: A Comparative Study of the Form and Effect of Contrasting Cadastral Surveys* (Chicago: Rand McNally, 1966), 48, 126. Jennie Raycraft Lewis, *Sure an' This Is Biddulph*, (Biddulph Township Council, 1964), 10. 'The Canada Company Agreement of May 23, 1826,' *Western Ontario Historical Notes* 10, no. 1 (March 1952), 21–5.

13 Ladis K.D. Kristof, 'The Nature of Frontiers and Boundaries,' *Annals of the Association of American Geographers* 49 (1959), 269–82. Harrington, 'Cadastral Surveys,' 36. Jones, *History of Agriculture in Ontario*, 56 n 16. L.M. Sebert, 'The Land Surveys of Ontario 1750–1980,' *Cartographica* 17 (1980), 70.

14 R. Louis Gentilcore, 'Lines on the Land: Crown Surveys and Settlement in Upper Canada,' *Ontario History* 41 (1969), 58 n 6. Ladell, *They Left Their Mark*, 33. C.P. Barnes, 'Economies of the Long-Lot Farm,' *Geographical Review* 25 (1935), 298.

15 J.M. McEvoy, *The Ontario Township*, Toronto University Studies in Political Science (Toronto: Warwick & Sons, 1889). Ladell, *They Left Their Mark*, 65, 69, 118. Gentilcore, 'Lines on the Land,' 59. Sebert, 'Land Surveys,' 84, 87. *Ausable Report*, pt 1, 26 n 1.

16 James Scott, *The Settlement of Huron County* (Toronto: Ryerson Press, 1966), 61. Field Notes of a Part of the Townships of Biddulph, McGillivray and Hullett, p. 17; Surveys and Field Notes, Huron Tract, vol. 10, no. 17; both in Canada Company Business Records 1827–1951, Series B-2, F129, AO. *Ausable Report*, pt 1, 'General,' 33–4.

2: Ideologies of Settlement

1 E.G. Ravenstein, *The Laws of Migration*, first pub. 1885, 1889 (New York: Arno Press, 1976), 187, 189, 193. Everett S. Lee, 'A Theory of Migration,' *Demography* 3 (1966), 50. Bruce Elliott, *Irish Migrants in the Canadas: A New Approach* (Montreal: McGill-Queen's University Press, 1988), 99, 115. J. Howard Richards, 'Lands and Policies: Attitudes and Controls in the Alienation of Lands in Ontario during the First Century of Settlement,' *Ontario History* 50 (1958), 193–209. Extracts from the Letters of the Company's Commissioners in Canada, 1 Feb. 1831, 20 n, Colonial Office Papers, Original Correspondence, Upper Canada 1829–1831, Canada Company Directors, Treasury and Others, fol. 88, National Archives of Canada (hereafter NA), CO 42, vol. 410, 20 n.

2 Norman MacDonald, *Canada, 1763–1841: Immigration and Settlement* (London: Longmans, Green, 1939), 23. Helen Cowan, *British Emigration to North America: The First Hundred Years*, rev. ed. (Toronto: University of Toronto Press, 1967), 95, 113. Lillian F. Gates, *Land Policies of Upper Canada*

(Toronto: University of Toronto Press, 1968), 172–3. Aileen Dunham, *Political Unrest in Upper Canada 1815–1836*, first pub. 1927 (Toronto: McClelland and Stewart, 1963), 150.

3 Commissioner Thomas Mercer Jones to Communication Committee, 9 Nov. 1829, 152, Correspondence with the Commissioners, 1826–1951, Letters and Reports, vol. 2, Canada Company Records, AO, A-6-2. Austin Steward, *Twenty-two Years a Slave and Forty Years a Freeman* (Canandaigua, NY: Published by the author, 1867). Fred Landon, 'The History of the Wilberforce Refugee Colony in Middlesex County,' *London and Middlesex Historical Society, Transactions* 9 (1918), 30–44. Fred Landon, 'Wilberforce: An Experiment in the Colonization of Freed Negroes in Upper Canada,' *Royal Society of Canada: Proceedings and Transactions*, 3d series, 31 (1937), 69–78. *Tanner's Universal Atlas* (Philadelphia: H.S. Tanner, 1833–4) (Winearls no. 96). William H. Pease and Jane H. Pease, *Black Utopia: Negro Communal Experiments in America* (Madison: State Historical Society of Wisconsin, 1963), 46–62. T.G. Steward, 'Documents: Banishment of the People of Colour from Cincinnati,' *Journal of Negro History (JNH)* 8 (1923), 331–2. Richard C. Wade, 'The Negro in Cincinnati, 1800–1830,' *JNH* 39 (1954), 43–57. Robin Winks, *The Blacks in Canada: A History* (Montreal: McGill-Queen's University Press, 1971), 155–62. Marilyn Baily, 'From Cincinnati, Ohio to Wilberforce, Canada: A Note on Antebellum Colonization,' *JNH* 58 (1973), 427–40. Jason H. Silverman, *Unwelcome Guests: Canada West's Response to Fugitive Slaves 1800–1865* (Millwood, NY: Associated Faculty Press, 1985), 27–34. 'The Diary of Benjamin Lundy Written during his Journey through Upper Canada, January, 1832' (hereafter 'Lundy Diary'), ed. Fred Landon, *Ontario Historical Society Papers and Records (Ontario History)*, 19 (1922), 114.

4 Fred Coyne Hamil, *The Valley of the Lower Thames* (Toronto: University of Toronto Press, 1951), 313–14. Fred Landon, 'Social Conditions among the Negroes in Upper Canada before 1865,' *Ontario History* 22 (1925), 147. 'Lundy Diary,' 116. Winks, *Blacks in Canada*, 157. Samuel Gridley Howe, *Report to the Freedmen's Inquiry Commission 1864: The Refugees from Slavery in Canada West* (New York: Arno Press and The New York Times, 1969), 40, 69–70.

5 Landon, 'Experiment,' 69. Fred Landon, 'Negro Colonization Schemes in Upper Canada before 1860,' *Royal Society of Canada: Proceedings and Transactions*, 3d series, 23 (1929), 79. Landon, 'History,' 30. Amos J. Beyam, *The American Colonization Society and the Creation of the Liberian State: A Historical Perspective, 1822–1900* (New York: University Press of America, 1991), 6, 7. W.E.B. DuBois, *The Suppression of the African Slave-Trade to the United States of America 1638–1870*, first pub. 1898 (New York: Russell & Russell, 1965), 197. Charles Stuart, *Remarks on the Colony of Liberia and the American Coloniza-*

tion Society: With Some Account of the Settlement of Coloured People at Wilberforce,
Upper Canada (London: J. Messeder, 1832), 4. Early Lee Fox, *The American*
Colonization Society 1817–1840, Johns Hopkins Studies in Historical and
Political Science (Baltimore: Johns Hopkins University Press, 1919), 144.
P.J. Staudenraus, *The African Colonization Movement 1816–1865* (New York:
Columbia University Press, 1961), 192–3.

6 William H. Pease and Jane H. Pease, 'Organized Negro Communities: A
North American Experiment,' *JNH* 47 (1962), 19–20. Pease and Pease, *Black*
Utopia, 22, 28. Frankie Hutton, 'Economic Considerations in the American
Colonization Society's Early Effort to Emigrate Free Blacks to Liberia, 1816–
36,' *JNH* 68 (1983), 385. Clarence Karr, *The Canada Land Company: The Early*
Years, Ontario Historical Research Publication No. 3 (Ottawa: Ontario
Historical Society, 1974), 18.

7 Pease and Pease, *Black Utopia*, 62, 52. Winks, *Blacks in Canada*, 161. Peter
Robinson to Z. Mudge, 4 Dec. 1830, 58791–92, Upper Canada Sundries,
AO, RG 5, A1, vol. 104. N.S. Price to Commissioners, 3 Jan. 1831, 28 Dec.
1831, 222, 270, Correspondence with the Commissioners, Letters and
Reports, vol. 2, Canada Company Papers, AO, A-6-2. H. Clare Pentland,
Labour and Capital in Canada 1650–1860 (Toronto: James Lorimer and Co.,
1981), 6–7. A.L. Murray Papers, J.J. Talman Regional Collection, D.B.
Weldon Library, University of Western Ontario, Box 4450, Diaries and
Scrapbooks of William Porte, Postmaster and Township Clerk, Lucan,
1865–1898, Counting House Diary for 1865, Tuesday, 22 Aug. 1865,
Talman Regional Collection.

8 [Goodspeed] *History of the County of Middlesex*, 461, 462. Biddulph Twp.,
Middlesex Co., 'Old Book,' 57, 154–5, Property Rights Registration Records,
Abstract Index to Deeds, Abstracts before 1866, fols. 151–62, AO, RG 61-33.
'John McDonald,' *Dictionary of Canadian Biography (DCB)*, X, 459. G.R.
Stevens, *Canadian National Railways* (Toronto: Clarke, Irwin & Co., 1960), I,
103–4, 82–3. Deeds, 1847–60, vol. 1–2, 68–69, 79, Biddulph Township,
Middlesex County, AO, GS 424. John Ross, *President's Report: Proceedings of the*
First Meeting of the Shareholders of the Grand Trunk Railway Company of Canada,
held at Québec, 27 July 1854, Sir Alfred Waldron Smithers Papers (1850–
1924), 7, 12, NA, MG 30 A93. Thomas E. Blackwell, Managing Director,
Report to the Directors of the Grand Trunk Railway Company of Canada, Dec.
1859, 1, Smithers Papers, NA, MG 30 A93. 1861 Canada West Census,
Agricultural Census of Huron County, Biddulph Township. R. Louis
Gentilcore and Kate Donkin, *Land Surveys of Southern Ontario, Cartographica*
Monograph No. 8 (Toronto: York University, 1973), 20. Michael J. Doucet,
'Building the Victorian City: The Process of Land Development in Hamilton,

Ontario, 1847–1881,' PhD dissertation, University of Toronto, 1977, 17–28.

9 Peter Baskerville, 'Professional vs. Proprietor: Power Distribution in the Railroad World of Upper Canada/Ontario, 1850–1881,' *Historical Papers* (Ottawa: Canadian Historical Association, 1978), 48. Contract to build Guelph–Sarnia line, 24 March 1857, Gzowski Papers, vol. 2, 24, NA, MG 24 E9. *Lucan* (map), 40p/3, edition 6, Energy, Mines and Resources Canada, 1994. Map of Canada with a part of New Brunswick, Shewing the Line of the Grand Trunk Railway and its connections by Keith Johnston, F.R.S.E.; Talman Regional Collection. Description of the lands intended to be passed over and taken for the purposes of the St Mary's and Sarnia Extension of the Grand Trunk Railway of Canada in the Township of McGillivray in the County of Huron, Talman Regional Collection, Vertical File 235, 2. Blackwell, *Report to the Directors*, 1. W.L. Morton, 'The Significance of Site in the Settlement of the American and Canadian Wests,' *Agricultural History* 25 (1951), 100. [Goodspeed] *History of the County of Middlesex*, 461, 462. Biddulph Township, 'Old Book,' Abstract Index to Deeds, fols. 151–62, 86–90, AO. Village of Lucan (map), *Illustrated Historical Atlas of the County of Middlesex Ontario*, first pub. 1878 (Belleville: Mika, 1972), 35. 1861 Canada West Census, Biddulph, Personal Census. 1871 Dominion Census, District 8, North Middlesex, Biddulph, Division 2, Schedule 1, Nominal Return of the Living. 1881 Dominion Census, Ontario, District 169, North Middlesex, Village of Lucan and Township of Biddulph, Schedule 1, Nominal Return of the Living. William Porte, Counting House Diary for 1865, Saturday, 4 March 1865; Talman Regional Collection. Marx, *Capital*, vol. I, 931–9.

10 Donald Winch, *Classical Political Economy and Colonies* (London: London School of Economics and Political Science/G. Bell and Sons, 1965), 3, 4, 13, 120–1, 99, 107, 103, 150. Gates, *Land Policies*, 152, 305, 180. Fred Coyne Hamil, *Lake Erie Baron: The Story of Colonel Thomas Talbot* (Toronto: Macmillan, 1955). MacDonald, *Canada 1763–1841*, 237. Cowan, *British Emigration*, 85, 87, 84. Marx, *Capital*, I, 932, 939. Leo A. Johnson, 'Land Policy, Population Growth and Social Structure in the Home District, 1793–1851,' *Ontario History* 63 (1971), 57. Pentland, *Labour and Capital in Canada*, 109–13. Gilbert C. Paterson, *Land Settlement in Upper Canada 1783 1840*, Sixteenth Report of the Department of Archives for the Province of Ontario (Toronto: Clarkson W. James, 1921), 160. H.C. Pentland, 'The Development of a Capitalistic Labour Market in Canada,' *Canadian Journal of Economics and Political Science* 25 (1959), 458. R.G. Riddell, 'A Study in the Land Policy of the Colonial Office, 1763–1855,' *Canadian Historical Review* 18 (1937), 398. Edward Gibbon Wakefield, 'A View of the Art of Colonization with Present

Reference to the British Empire: In Letters between a Statesman and a Colonist,' in *The Collected Works of Edward Gibbon Wakefield*, ed. M.F. Lloyd Prichard (Glasgow: Collins, 1968), 766. Karr, *Canada Land Company*, 53.

11 Karr, *Canada Land Company*, 26, 27, 105–7, 120, 121. Scott, *Huron County*, 66. Gates, *Land Policies*, 267, 170. Coleman, *Canada Company*, 114–23, 134, 52–3. *Ausable Report*, pt. 1, 'General,' 40–1. Thomas Mercer Jones, *A Statement of the Satisfactory Results Which Have Attended Emigration to Upper Canada from the Establishment of the Canada Company until the Present Period*, 3rd ed. (London: Smith Elder, 1842), 36.

12 Elliott, *Irish Migrants*, 61, 67, 129–31, 133, 136, 137. Johnson, 'Land Policy, Population Growth and Social Structure,' 42. Coleman, *Canada Company*, 52–3. Biddulph Township, Computerized Land Records Index, vol. 4. Parts of the Brock Western, London, Gore, Niagara, & Home Districts, With the Huron Tract Upper Canada Copied from the original compilation by Colonel Mackenzie Frazer ... (map) (Toronto: QM. Genl Upper Canada, 1840) (NA, National Map Collection [hereafter NMC] 15179; Winearls no. 123). Scott, *Huron County*, 52–3, 57–63. W.H. Smith, *Canada, Past, Present and Future*, first pub. 1852 (Belleville: Mika, 1974), vol. II, 181–2. T.A. Stayner, *Map of Upper and Lower Canada ... Exhibiting the Post Towns & Mail Routes* (Quebec: Govt Post Office, 1839) (Winearls no. 87[2]). Mercer Jones, *Statement*, 36. Huron Tract, 1829–68, vols. 19–21, Register of Contracts, Canada Company Records, Series B-3, MS 729, AO. Biddulph Township Papers, Records of the Ministry of Natural Resources, C-IV, MS 658, AO. Morton, 'Significance of Site,' 99. Biddulph Twp., Assessment & Collectors Rolls for 1862, F1539-3, 24–5, AO. R.W. Hermon, *New Map of the County of Huron Canada West 1862* (Toronto: Hermon, Martin & Bolton, 1862) (Winearls no. 258), AO. J. Rogers, Map of Biddulph Township, in *Illustrated Historical Atlas of the County of Middlesex, Ontario* (Toronto: H.R. Page & Co., 1878), 45.

13 Biddulph Twp., 'Old Book,' fol. 64, AO. Huron Tract, 1829-21, vols. 19-21, Canada Company Records, Series B-3, Register of Contracts, AO. Michael Doucet, 'Urban Land Development in Nineteenth Century North America,' *Journal of Urban History* 30 (May 1982), 301. Randy William Widdis, 'Motivation and Scale: A Method of Identifying Land Speculators in Upper Canada,' *Canadian Geographer* 23 (1979), 340, 348–9. Randy William Widdis, 'Speculation and the Surveyor: An Analysis of the Role Played by Surveyors in the Settlement of Upper Canada,' *Histoire sociale/Social History* 15 (1982), 443–58. Donald H. Akenson, *The Irish in Ontario: A Study in Rural History* (Montreal: McGill-Queen's University Press, 1984), 257. Robert P.

Swierenga, *Pioneers and Profits: Land Speculation on the Iowa Frontier* (Ames: Iowa State University Press, 1968), 6.

14 Doucet, 'Urban Land Development,' 307. *The Agricultural Mutual Assurance Association of Canada* (handbill) (London: Free Press, 1868), 1. N. Omer Côté, *Political Appointments, Parliaments and the Judicial Bench in the Dominion of Canada 1867 to 1895* (Ottawa: Thoburn & Co., 1896), 182. *Upper Canada Law List and Solicitors' Agency Book*, 5th ed., ed. J. Rordans (Toronto: W.C. Chewett, 1866). E.M. Chadwick, *Ontarian Families* (Toronto: Ralph Smith & Co., 1894), vol. II, 69. Biddulph Twp., Computerized Land Records Index, vol. 4, AO. Fred Landon, *Western Ontario and the American Frontier* (Toronto: Ryerson Press, 1941), 55. 'George Jervis Goodhue,' *DCB*, IX, 323–4. Orlo Miller, *A Century of Western Ontario: The Story of London, 'The Free Press,' and Western Ontario, 1849–1949*, first pub. 1949 (Westport, Conn.: Greenwood Press, 1972), 38. *Canada*, Vol. 19, 275, R.G. Dun & Co. Collection, Baker Library, Harvard University Graduate School of Business Administration. Land Papers of George Jervis Goodhue, Series 1: Land Transaction Documents, Folder 4: Biddulph, Mddx., Item 24: Mortgage, Tierney-Goodhue, 6 Oct. 1859, Talman Regional Collection. R.C.B. Risk, 'The Golden Age: The Law about the Market in Nineteenth-Century Ontario,' *University of Toronto Law Journal* 26 (1976), 319–20. Frederick H. Armstrong, 'George Jervis Goodhue: Pioneer Merchant of London, Upper Canada,' *Ontario History* 63 (1971), 226–7, 231. Akenson, *The Irish in Ontario*, 258. Biddulph Twp., Books A–B, Alphabetical Index to Deeds, 1866–1944, AO. David P. Gagan, 'The Security of Land: Mortgaging in Toronto Gore Township 1835–95,' in F.H. Armstrong, H.A. Stevenson, and J.D. Wilson, eds., *Aspects of Nineteenth-Century Ontario* (Toronto: University of Toronto Press, 1974), 148, 150.

15 Gagan, 'Security of Land,' 150. Akenson, *The Irish in Ontario*, 258. Biddulph Twp., 'Old Book,' fol. 60. Karl Marx, *Grundrisse*, trans. Martin Nicolaus (Harmondsworth: Penguin, 1973), 504, 509. Karl Marx, *Precapitalist Economic Formations*, ed. E.J. Hobsbawm (New York: International Publishers, 1964), 113.

16 Joy Parr, *The Gender of Breadwinners: Women, Men and Change in Two Industrial Towns 1880–1950* (Toronto: University of Toronto Press, 1990), 231. Margaret E. McCallum, 'Prairie Women and the Struggle for a Dower Law, 1905–1920,' *Prairie Forum* 18 (1993), 20. Catherine Cavanaugh, 'The Limitations of the Pioneering Partnership: The Alberta Campaign for Homestead Dower, 1909–25,' *Canadian Historical Review* 74 (1993), 202. A.V. Dicey, *Lectures on the Relation between Law and Public Opinion in England*

during the Nineteenth Century, 2nd ed. (London: Macmillan, 1962), 371, 384, 373, 376. Ontario Law Reform Commission, *Report on Family Law*, pt. 4: *Family Property Law* (Toronto: Ministry of the Attorney General, 1974), 26, 19. Constance B. Backhouse, 'Married Women's Property Law in 19th Century Canada,' *Law and History Review* 6 (1988), 217, 218, 222–5.

3: Access and Circulation, Delivery and Through Passage

1 James Scott, *The Settlement of Huron County* (Toronto: Ryerson Press, 1966), 59–63, 52–3. Thomas F. McIlwraith, 'Accessibility and Rural Land Utilization in the Yonge Street Area of Upper Canada,' MA thesis, Department of Geography, University of Toronto, 1966, 114. Thomas F. McIlwraith, 'The Adequacy of Rural Roads in the Era before Railways: An Illustration from Upper Canada,' *Canadian Geographer* 14 (1970), 350. G.P. de T. Glazebrook, *A History of Transportation in Canada* (Toronto: Ryerson Press, 1938), 142.
2 W. Kingsford, *History, Structure, and Statistics of Plank Roads in the United States and Canada* (Philadelphia: A. Hart, 1852), 16.
3 Thomas Roy, *Remarks on the Principles and Practice of Road-Making, as Applicable to Canada* (Toronto: H.& W. Rowsell, 1841), 7. R.W. Packer, 'The Physical Geography of the Fifteen Counties of Southwestern Ontario,' *Western Ontario Historical Notes* 12 (1954), 56. L.J. Chapman and D.F. Putnam, *The Physiography of Southern Ontario* (Toronto: Ministry of Natural Resources, 1984), 94. John Kenneth Galbraith, *The Scotch* (Boston: Macmillan, 1964), 1. Edwin C. Guillett, *Pioneer Travel in Upper Canada*, first pub. 1933 (Toronto: University of Toronto Press, 1966), 4. Fred Coyne Hamil, *The Valley of the Lower Thames* (Toronto: University of Toronto Press, 1951), 16, 34. *Ausable Valley Conservation Report* (Toronto: Conservation Branch, Department of Planning and Development, 1949), pt. IV, 'Water,' 4. C.F.J. Whebell, 'Corridors: A Theory of Urban Systems,' *Annals of the Association of American Geographers* 59 (1969), 6. 'Report on the County of Huron, by Mr. Thomas McQueen of Goderich, *to which a Prize of £15 was awarded*,' *Journal and Transactions of the Board of Agriculture of Upper Canada* (Toronto: Board of Agriculture, 1858), 2, 188. *Upper Canada West Part* (map), compiled and drawn by L.J. Hebert, Lithography Establishment, Quartermaster General's Office, Horse Guards, 1838 (NMC 14021, 14022; Winearls no. 117). A.R.M. Lower, *Settlement and the Forest Frontier in Eastern Canada* (Toronto: Macmillan, 1936), 40, 43 n 12.
4 McIlwraith, 'Adequacy of Roads,' 347, 358. W.H. Breithaupt, 'Dundas Street and Other Early Upper Canada Roads,' *Ontario Historical Society Papers and Records* (hereafter *Ontario History*) 21 (1924), 7–8. Guillett, *Pioneer Travel*, 4, 145.

5 Patrick Sherriff, *A Tour through North America: Together with a Comparative View of the Canadas and United States as Adapted for Agriculture and Emigration* (Edinburgh: Oliver and Boyd, 1835), 180. Guillett, *Pioneer Travel*, 154, 153. McQueen, 'Report on the County of Huron,' 177. T.C. Keefer, 'Travel and Transportation,' in *Eighty Years' Progress of British North America* (London: Sampson Low, Son & Marston, 1863), 117. McIlwraith, 'Adequacy of Roads,' 358, 345, 354, 347.

6 William Johnston, *History of the County of Perth from 1825 to 1902* (Stratford: W.M. O'Beirne, 1903), 100, 99, 43. James J. Talman, 'Travel in Ontario before the Coming of the Railway,' *Ontario History* 29 (1933), 99. Guillett, *Pioneer Travel*, 163. *Ausable Report*, pt. 1, 'General,' 33. W.H. Smith, *Canada, Past, Present and Future*, first pub. 1852 (Belleville: Mika, 1974), II, 193.

7 John McCallum, *Unequal Beginnings: Agriculture and Economic Development in Québec and Ontario until 1870* (Toronto: University of Toronto Press, 1980), 75, 9. McIlwraith, 'Adequacy of Roads,' 354. W.A. Mackintosh, 'Economic Factors in Canadian History,' *Canadian Historical Review* 4 (1923), 16. Lower, *Settlement and the Forest Frontier*, 22. *Ausable Report*, pt. 1, 'General,' 42.

8 McIlwraith, 'Accessibility and Land Utilization,' 121. Guillett, *Pioneer Travel*, 182. Fred Coyne Hamil, 'Early Shipping and Land Transportation on the Lower Thames,' *Ontario History* 34 (1942), 56–7. J. Talman, 'Travel in Ontario,' 90. *Part of the Brock, Western, London, Gore, Niagara & Home Districts, with the Huron Tract Upper Canada* (map), Col. McKenzie Fraser (Toronto: Assistant Quartermaster General, Upper Canada, 1840) (NMC 15179; Winearls no. 123). Smith, *Canada Past Present and Future*, II, map 5, 'Counties of Waterloo, Huron, Perth and Bruce,' facing 90 (NMC 2891; Winearls no. 178[5]). Thomas Roy, *Principles and Practice of Road-Making*, 18, 15, 20. John Loudon McAdam, *Remarks on the Present System of Road Making*, 6th ed. (London: Longman, Hurst, Rees, Orme, and Brown, 1822), 51. [James B. Brown], *Views of Canada and the Colonists by a Four Years' Resident* (Edinburgh: Adam and Charles Black, 1844), 134, 136. Doug Owram, '"Management by Enthusiasm": The First Board of Works of the Province of Canada, 1841–1846,' *Ontario History* 70 (1978), 171–88.

9 Irma E. Pattison, *Historical Chronology of Highway Legislation in Ontario 1774–1961* (Toronto: Department of Highways, 1964), 22–4. Schedule No. 1, District Macadamized Roads in Canada West, 22 April 1843, Board of Works Correspondence re London–Pt. Stanley Road, 1842, RG 11, vol. 82, file 4, NA. J.H. Aitchison, 'Development of Local Government in Upper Canada, 1783–1850,' PhD dissertation, University of Toronto, 1953, 459. Miscellaneous Papers collected by Guy St Denis relating to London roads, c. 1845–50, (newspaper clipping) Talman Regional Collection. Roy, *Principles and*

Practice of Road-Making, 26. J.J. Talman, 'The Impact of the Railway on a Pioneer Community,' *Canadian Historical Association Reports* (1955), 1. Sir Richard Henry Bonnycastle, *Canada and the Canadians in 1846* (London: Henry Colburn, 1846), I, 111; II, 97. Frederic J. Wood, *The Turnpikes of New England* (Boston: Marshall Jones Co., 1919), 39, 40. Guillett, *Pioneer Travel*, 169. Glazebrook, *Transportation in Canada*, 121. [Brown], *Views of Canada*, 135. Hugh G.J. Aitken, *The Welland Canal Company: A Study in Canadian Enterprise* (Cambridge, Mass.: Harvard University Press, 1954), 160 n 9. David J. Hall, 'The Development of the Road System in Elgin County, Ontario, 1850–1880,' *Western Ontario Historical Notes* 26 (1972), 40, 43.

10 William Cronon, *Nature's Metropolis: Chicago and the Great West* (New York: W.W. Norton, 1991), 83, 59. 1815–16 Reconnaissance Survey of the Great Lakes, No. 19: Map of the Area from Grand River to Detroit River and Lake St Clair (NMC 14909; Winearls no. C24). Survey of Lake Erie in the Years 1817 & 1818, Lieut. Henry W. Bayfield, R.N. (map), London: Hydrological Office of the Admiralty, R.B. Bate, Agent, c. 1846 (NMC 16713; Winearls no. C114[2]). John Rolph, Chairman, Report of Select Committee ... relative to ... Kettle Creek, on Lake Erie, *Journal of the House of Assembly of Upper Canada* (hereafter *JHAUC*), 9th Parl., 3rd Sess., 1826–7, Appendix N, 1. Capt. George Phillpotts, R. Eng., Second Report on the Inland Navigation of the Canadas, Cornwall, Upper Canada: 3 August 1840, 93–4, RG 1, E12, vol. 3, NA. A Plan of Lake Erie Detroit River part of Lake St Clair and River La Touche from Actual Surveys made in the Years 1789, 1790 & 1791 ... By Patrick McNiff, Asst Engineer Detroit, May 1791, AO 496 (Winearls no. 910). John Harris, Charles Ingersoll, Evidence to Select Committee on Kettle Creek, Appendix N, *JHAUC*, 1826–7, 1–3. James H. Coyne, 'The Country of the Neutrals,' in *Historical Sketches of the County of Elgin* (St Thomas: The Times Printers, 1895), 28. James Hamilton, President of the Kettle Creek Harbour Commission, to Sir John Colborne, 15 Feb. 1830, *JHAUC*, 11th Parl., 1st Sess., 1831, App., 109. James Hamilton, Report of the Commissioners of the Kettle Creek Harbour, Sundry Reports No. 92, *JHAUC*, 12th Parl., 1st Sess., 1835, Appendix, II, 25.

11 Statements of Exports and Imports from the mouth of Kettle Creek; *JHAUC*, 9th Parl., 3rd Sess., 1826–7, Appendix N, 3. Exports and Imports for 1829, 1830, *JHAUC*, 11th Parl., 1st Sess., 1831, Appendix, 110. Letter to James Hamilton, 3 Dec. 1833, Sundry Reports, *JHAUC*, 11th Parl., 4th Sess., 1833–4, Appendix, 221. Edward Porritt, 'Canada's National Grain Route,' *Political Science Quarterly* 33 (1918), 346. Report of the Committee to whom was referred the subject of Harbours on the North Shore of Lake Erie, *JHAUC*, 1833–4, Appendix, 109. *General Index to the Journals of the House of Assembly of*

the Late Province of Upper Canada; Commencing with the First Session of the Ninth Provincial Parliament (1825) and Ending with the Fifth Session of the Thirteenth Parliament (1839–40) (Montreal: Lovell & Gibson, 1848), 285.

12 J.E. Middleton and F. Landon, *The Province of Ontario: A History 1615–1927* (Toronto: Dominion Publishing Co., 1927), II, 1110. Brown, *Views of Canada*, 24. Correspondence re London–Pt. Stanley Road, 1842, Board of Works, RG 11, vol. 79, file 9, NA. C.S. Gzowski, Report on Works under his Charge, No. 99, 5 Sept. 1842, Board of Works, RG 11, vol. 81, file 8, NA. C.S. Gzowski, Estimate, Port Stanley Piers, No. 15, 7 Sept. 1842, Board of Works, RG 11, vol. 81, file 8, NA. C.S. Gzowski, Semi-monthly Report on the Western Roads, 15 May 1844, RG 11, vol. 83, file 5, NA. Chapman and Putnam, *Physiography*, 94. Map of the London & Port Stanley Plank Road 1840 (NMC 21368; Winearls no. 963). Diagram of Townships in the Vicinity of London, shewing the several Roads diverging therefrom: as constructed and improved by the Board of Works, F. Rubidge Drafted (1844?) (NMC 16965; Winearls no. 972). L. Kos-Rabcewicz-Zubkowski and W.E. Greening, *Sir Casimir Stanislaus Gzowski: A Biography* (Toronto: Burns and MacEachern, 1959), 27. R.L. Jones, *History of Agriculture in Ontario 1613–1880* (Toronto: University of Toronto Press, 1946), 177. Agnes M. Hepburn, *Historical Sketch of the Village of Port Stanley* (Port Stanley: Port Stanley Women's Institute, 1952), 2.

13 Thomas F. McIlwraith, 'Freight Capacity and Utilization of the Erie and Great Lakes Canals before 1850,' *Journal of Economic History* 36 (1976), 865. Samuel Power, Report on information relative to the harbours and roads in this section of the Province, 25 Nov. 1844, Welland Canal, General and Departmental Correspondence Sent, 1844-46, Canal Records 1819–1964, 15–16, Railways and Canals, RG 43, vol. 2248, NA.

14 Cronon, *Nature's Metropolis*, 85, 224. Thomas Odle, 'The American Grain Trade of the Great Lakes, 1825–1873,' pt. I, 'Introduction,' *Inland Seas* 7 (1951), 242–3, pt. VI; *Inland Seas* 9 (1953), 53. Wilgus, *Railway Interrelations*, 35. Robert C. Douglas, *Report to the Hon. J.H. Pope, Acting Minister, Department of Railways and Canals, on the Necessity of Deepening the Welland Canal* (Ottawa: MacLean, Roger & Co., 1884), 70–1, 79. McIlwraith, 'Freight Capacity and Utilization,' 860.

15 Thomas C. Keefer, 'Travel and Transportation,' in *Eighty Years' Progress*. [Samuel Keefer], 'Historical Sketch of the Canals of Canada,' *Letter to the Honourable the Secretary of State, from the Canal Commissioners Respecting the Improvement of the Inland Navigation of the Dominion of Canada* (Ottawa: Canal Commission, 1871). *Report of Canal Commission respecting Improvement of the Inland Navigation of the Dominion of Canada, Sessional Papers*, 4th Sess., 1st Parl.

(Ottawa: Department of State, 1871) VI, 9. Douglas, *Report to the Hon. J.H. Pope.* John N. Jackson, 'The Erie and the Welland Canals: A Comparative Evaluation in Relation to the Niagara Frontier,' in *A Canadian Enterprise: The Welland Canals* (St Catharines: St Catharines Historical Museum, 1984), 52–71. Michelle Greenwald, Allan Levitt, and Elaine Peebles, 'Historical Themes,' in *The Welland Canals: Historical Resource Analysis and Preservation Alternatives,* Heritage Planning Study 1, 2nd ed. (Toronto: Historical Planning and Research Branch, Ontario Ministry of Culture and Recreation, 1979), 11–20. H.A. Innis and A.R.M. Lower, *Select Documents in Canadian Economic History 1783–1885* (Toronto: University of Toronto Press, 1933), 470–86. Capt. George Phillpotts, R. Eng., Report on the Inland Navigation of the Canadas called for by Lord Glenelg's Dispatch to the Earl of Durham dated 23d August 1838, Cornwall, Upper Canada, 31 December 1839, vol. 3, 2, 20, 25–6, RG 1 E12, NA.

16 Cronon, *Nature's Metropolis,* 84, 86, 62. *Sessional Papers,* Legislative Assembly, Canada West, 3 (1863), quoted in Innis and Lower, *Select Documents,* 473. T.C. Keefer, 'Travel and Transportation,' 179. Douglas, *Report to the Hon. J.H. Pope,* 38, 61–8. [S. Keefer], 'Historical Sketch of the Canals of Canada,' 45. Joseph Dart, 'The Grain Elevators of Buffalo,' *Publications of the Buffalo Historical Society* 1 (1879), 400–1.

17 Guy A. Lee, 'The Historical Significance of the Chicago Grain Elevator System,' *Agricultural History* 11 (1937), 21 n 19. Cronon, *Nature's Metropolis,* 83–4, 85. [S. Keefer], 'Historical Sketch of the Canals of Canada,' 45, 38. George G. Tunell, 'The Diversion of the Flour and Grain Traffic from the Great Lakes to the Railroads,' *Journal of Political Economy* 5 (1896–7), 360. Jones, *History of Agriculture in Ontario,* 187. Innis and Lower, *Select Documents,* 495 n 3.

18 Cronon, *Nature's Metropolis,* 85. Innis and Lower, *Select Documents,* 495. M.L. Bladen, 'II. Construction of Railways in Canada to the Year 1865,' *Contributions to Canadian Economics* 5 (1932), 48. Wilgus, *Railway Interrelations,* 108. G.R. Stevens, *Canadian National Railways* (Toronto: Clarke, Irwin & Co., 1960), 120, 479, 485. J.M. Trout and Edward Trout, *The Railways of Canada* (Toronto: The Monetary Times, 1871), 114. McQueen, 'Report on the County of Huron,' 179. James J. Talman, 'The Development of the Railway Network of Southwestern Ontario to 1876,' *Canadian Historical Association: Report of Annual Meeting held at London, June 4–6, 1953, with Historical Papers,* 58. Odle, 'The American Grain Trade,' pt. I, *Inland Seas* 7 (1951), 243.

19 G.R. Stevens, *Canadian National Railways,* I. A.W. Currie, *The Grand Trunk Railway of Canada* (Toronto: University of Toronto Press, 1957). Glazebrook, *Transportation in Canada,* 292. Innis and Lower, *Select Documents.* Bladen,

'Construction of Railways,' 43–5. Carl Vincent, 'Finding Aid,' RG 30, NA.
Lease to Bernard Stanley, 3 June 1873, Executive Committee Meetings,
Minute Book 20, 1872–1875, Grand Trunk Railway of Canada, RG 30,
vol. 1039, 132, NA.

20 Talman, 'Development of the Railway Network,' 57, 53. Breithaupt, 'Dundas
Street,' 7. Middleton and Landon, *The Province of Ontario: A History*, II, 700.
Keefer, 'Travel and Transportation,' 229. J.J. Talman, 'The Great Western
Railway,' *Western Ontario Historical Notes* 6 (1948), 2. T.C. Keefer, *Philosophy of
Railroads and Other Essays*, first pub. 1849, 1850, ed. H.V. Nelles (Toronto:
University of Toronto Press, 1972), 20. Stevens, *Canadian National Railways*,
95. Currie, *The Grand Trunk*, 161.

21 Currie, *The Grand Trunk*, 162, 220–1, 14. Stevens, *Canadian National
Railways*, I, 279–80, 83, 103–4. Glazebrook, *Transportation in Canada*, 167.
Bladen, 'Construction of Railways,' 47. *Map of the Huron District and the
Townships of Bosanquet in the Western and Williams in the Huron Districts*,
Compiled from the Maps of the original Surveyors by Donald McDonald,
Esqr., Toronto, 1846 (Toronto: Scobie & Balfour, 1846) (NMC 21611;
Winearls no. 1056[2]). Louis Bernard Schmidt, 'The Internal Grain Trade
of the United States, 1850–1890,' *Iowa Journal of History and Politics* 18
(1920), 94–124. L.B. Schmidt, 'The Internal Grain Trade of the United
States, 1860–1890,' *Iowa Journal of History and Politics* 19 (1921), 196–245,
414–56; 20 (1922), 70–132. *Report of Israel D. Andrews, Consul of the United
States for Canada and New Brunswick, on the Trade and Commerce of the British
North American Colonies, and upon the Trade of the Great Lakes and Rivers*
(Washington, DC: Robert Armstrong, 1853), 408.

22 Odle, 'The American Grain Trade,' pt. VIII, *Inland Seas* 9 (1953), 168.
Talman, 'The Development of the Railway Network,' 59. Marx, *Capital*, II,
328. Report by George Tunell on the Commerce of the Great Lakes, *U.S.
House of Representatives Documents*, vol. 51, no. 277, 55th Congress, 2nd
Session (1898), 31. Wilgus, *Railway Interrelations*, 157, 109–10. Stevens,
Canadian National Railways, I, 126. Harold Innis, *A History of the Canadian
Pacific Railway* (Toronto: University of Toronto Press, 1971), 67 n 2. Tunell,
'The Diversion of the Flour and Grain Traffic,' 342. Currie, *Grand Trunk
Railway*, 118 20. Bladen, 'Construction of Railways,' 51, 47. J.H. Aitchison,
'The Development of Local Government in Upper Canada, 1783–1850,'
PhD dissertation, University of Toronto, 1953, 323. 'Opportunities Lost,'
London Advertiser, 14 Aug. 1878, 2.

23 Cronon, *Nature's Metropolis*, 233–43. Executive Committee Meetings Minute
Book, 1875–1878, 173, 363, 400, Grand Trunk Railway of Canada 41, RG
30, vol. 1040, NA. Minutes of an Adjourned Meeting of the Executive

Council, 22 Dec. 1881, 203–4, 329, 404, Executive Council Meetings Minute Book, 1878–1882, Grand Trunk Railway of Canada, RG 30, vol. 1042, NA. Minutes of a Meeting between representatives of the New York Central and Hudson River, Boston and Albany, Central Vermont and Grand Trunk Companies, 29 Aug. 1878, 72, Executive Council Meetings Minute Book, 1878–1882, Grand Trunk Railway Company of Canada, RG 30, vol. 1042, NA.

24 Jones, *History of Agriculture in Ontario*, 233. Keefer, 'Travel and Transportation,' 234, 235. Innis, *Canadian Pacific Railway*, 68–9 n 3. Bladen, 'Construction of Railways,' 46. Edward Porritt, 'Canada's National Grain Route,' *Political Science Quarterly* 33 (1918), 370–1, 347. Glazebrook, *Transportation in Canada*, 165. Middleton and Landon, *Province of Ontario*, II, 690. Wilgus, *Railway Interrelations*, 107. Odle, 'The American Grain Trade,' pt. I, *Inland Seas* 7 (1951), 242.

25 Porritt, 'Canada's National Grain Route,' 345, 372–3, 349, 351, 370, 371, 347. A.H. Reginald Buller, *Essays on Wheat* (New York: Macmillan, 1919), 206, 218, 30–2. Charles B. Kuhlmann, *The Development of the Flour-Milling Industry in the United States* (Boston: Houghton, Mifflin, 1929), 113–20. Tunell, 'The Diversion of the Flour and Grain Traffic,' 365, 362 n 1, 360–1.

4: The Trace of the Wheat Staple

1 Harold Innis, *The Fur Trade in Canada* (New Haven: Yale University Press, 1930), 390.

2 *Report of Israel D. Andrews on the Trade and Commerce of the British North American Colonies*, Senate Ex. Doc. 112, 32nd Congress, 1st Session, 408. R.M. McInnis, 'Perspectives on Ontario Agriculture 1815–1930,' chap. 1, 'The Early Ontario Wheat Staple Reconsidered,' *Canadian Papers in Rural History* 8 (1992), 36. Marvin McInnis, 'Marketable Surpluses in Ontario Farming, 1860,' *Social Science History* 8 (1984), 413. R.L. Jones, *History of Agriculture in Ontario, 1613–1880* (Toronto: University of Toronto Press, 1946), 86. Douglas McCalla, 'The Internal Economy of Upper Canada,' *Agricultural History* 59 (1985), 397. Hugh G.J. Aitken, 'Myth and Measurement: The Innis Tradition in Economic History,' *Journal of Canadian Studies* 12 (1977), 96, 99. M.H. Watkins, 'A Staple Theory of Economic Growth,' in W.T. Easterbrook and M.H. Watkins, eds., *Approaches to Canadian Economic History*, first pub. 1963 (Ottawa: Carleton University Press, 1991), 50. Wallace Clement, *The Challenge of Class Analysis* (Ottawa: Carleton University Press, 1988), 71. Daniel Drache, 'Introduction,' in Harold Innis, *Staples, Markets and Cultural Change: Selected Essays* (Montreal: McGill-Queen's

University Press, 1995), xiv. W.T. Easterbrook, 'Problems in the Relationship of Communication and Economic History,' *Journal of Economic History* 20 (1960), 563. Mel Watkins, 'The Political Economy of Growth,' in W. Clement and G. Williams, eds., *The New Political Economy* (Montreal: McGill-Queen's University Press, 1989), 18. Mel Watkins, 'The Staple Theory Revisited,' *Journal of Canadian Studies* 12 (1976), 83–4. Donald Creighton, *The Commercial Empire of the St Lawrence, 1760–1850* (Toronto: Ryerson Press, 1937). Donald Creighton, 'Doctrine and the Interpretation of History,' *Towards the Discovery of Canada: Selected Essays* (Toronto: Macmillan, 1972), 43. William Cronon, 'Boundaries and Ecosystems in U.S. and Canadian History,' *Appalachia* 180 (1985), 23. Donald Creighton, *Harold Adams Innis: Portrait of a Scholar* (Toronto: University of Toronto Press, 1957), 105. W.T. Easterbrook and Hugh G.J. Aitken, *Canadian Economic History*, first pub. 1956 (Toronto: University of Toronto Press, 1965), 396. Fowke, 'Introduction,' 83. V.C. Fowke, 'The National Policy – Old and New,' *Canadian Journal of Economics and Political Science* 18 (1952), 273.

3 Allan Kulikoff, 'The Transition to Capitalism in Rural America,' *William and Mary Quarterly* 3rd series, 46 (1989), 122. McInnis, 'Perspectives on Ontario Agriculture,' 38, 47, 18–20. Donald N. McCloskey, 'Editor's Introduction,' *Essays in a Mature Economy: England after 1840* (London: Methuen, 1971), 9, 10. Douglas McCalla and Peter George, 'Measurement, Myth, and Reality: Reflections on the Economic History of Nineteenth-Century Ontario,' *Journal of Canadian Studies* 21 (1986), 72. C.B. Schedvin, 'Staples and Regions of Pax Britannica,' *Economic History Review* 2nd series, 43 (1990), 534.

4 McInnis, 'Perspectives,' 29, 26, 31, 35, 46. Douglas McCalla, 'The Wheat Staple and Upper Canadian Development,' *Canadian Historical Association: Historical Papers* (1978), 43. McCloskey, 'Editor's Introduction,' 10. Donald N. McCloskey, 'The Achievements of the Cliometric School,' *Journal of Economic History* 3 (1978), 15, 21.

5 David McNally, 'Staple Theory as Commodity Fetishism: Marx, Innis and Canadian Political Economy,' *Studies in Political Economy* 6 (1981), 41, 45, 47. David McNally, 'Technological Determinism and Canadian Political Economy: Further Contributions to a Debate,' *Studies in Political Economy* 20 (1986), 161–9. Marx, *Capital*, I, 165, 167. Drache, 'Introduction,' in Innis, *Staples, Markets and Cultural Change*, xix, xx. Marx, *Capital*, III, 455.

6 Marx, *Capital*, I, 167, 174 n 34. Marx, *Capital*, II, 303. McCalla and George, 'Measurement, Myth and Reality,' 76. McInnis, 'Perspectives,' 88, 94, 50. Mel Watkins, 'The Innis Tradition in Canadian Political Economy,' *Canadian Journal of Political and Social Theory* 6 (1982), 16.

7 Vernon C. Fowke, *Canadian Agricultural Policy: The Historical Pattern* (Toronto: University of Toronto Press, 1947), 79, 80. Innis, *Select Documents*, I, 568. R.T. Naylor, 'The Rise and Fall of the Third Commercial Empire of the St Lawrence,' in G. Teeple, ed., *Capitalism and the National Question in Canada* (Toronto: University of Toronto Press, 1972), 13–14. Innis and Lower, *Select Documents*, II, 231, 236, 315, 237.

8 Drache, 'Introduction,' in Innis, *Staples, Markets and Cultural Change*, xxxviii. Kenneth Buckley, 'The Role of the Staple Industries in Canada's Economic Development,' *Journal of Economic History* 18 (1958), 443. Marx, *Capital*, III, 444, 448.

9 Innis and Lower, *Select Documents*, II, 231, 236, 315, 237. Easterbrook and Aitken, *Canadian Economic History*, 111, 150. Innis, *Select Documents*, I, 568. Gilbert Norman Tucker, *The Canadian Commercial Revolution 1845–1851* (New Haven, Conn.: Yale University Press, 1936), 218–19. L.H. Officer and L.B. Smith, 'The Canadian–American Reciprocity Treaty of 1854 to 1866,' *Journal of Economic History* 28 (1968), 614. Jones, *History of Agriculture in Ontario*, 187–8, 177, 190–1, 197. O.J. McDiarmid, *Commercial Policy in the Canadian Economy* (Cambridge, Mass.: Harvard University Press, 1946), 51, 18–19, 23, 25, 32, 34, 43, 46, 42, 56–60. Harold Innis, 'Toronto and the Board of Trade,' in *Commerce Journal: Annual Review* (University of Toronto Commerce Club, 1939), 20–1. Harold Innis, 'Decentralization and Democracy in the Atlantic Basin' [1943], in Innis, *Staples, Markets and Cultural Change*, 42. Cohen, *Women's Work*, 34. Peter Baskerville, 'Transportation, Social Change, and State Formation, Upper Canada, 1841–1864,' in Allan Greer and Ian Radforth, eds., *Colonial Leviathan: State Formation in Mid-Nineteenth-Century Canada* (Toronto: University of Toronto Press, 1992), 239.

10 *Journal and Transactions of the Board of Agriculture of Upper Canada*, 2, 'Transactions of the Tenth Year, 1855–56' (Toronto: Board of Agriculture, 1858), 11, 182. *Report to the Ontario Agricultural Commission* (Toronto: C. Backett Robinson, 1881), II, Appendix B, 358.

11 Kulikoff, 'The Transition to Capitalism,' 123, 122. *Huron Expositor*, 15 Jan. 1869, 3; 5 Feb. 1869, 3, 6; 22 Jan. 1869, 2. *Exeter Times*, 28 May 1873, 2; 20 Jan. 1874, 2; 19 Aug. 1875, 2; 11 Oct. 1877, 8; 27 Jan. 1876, 2. *St Marys Argus*, 27 Feb. 1873, 3. Harriet Bertha Friedmann, 'The Transformation of Wheat Production in the Era of the World Market, 1873–1935: A Global Analysis of Production and Exchange,' PhD dissertation, Harvard University, 1976, 56.

12 'Lucan,' in *Lovell's Province of Ontario Directory* (Montreal: John Lovell, 1871). 'Lucan,' in *Lovell's Business and Professional Directory of the Province of Ontario* (Montreal: John Lovell & Son, 1882). *Mitchell's Canada Gazetteer and Business*

Directory for 1864–65 (Toronto: W.C. Chewett, 1864), 341, 748, 175, 569, 762. Scrapbook, 20 Sept. 1862, Diaries and Scrapbooks of William Porte, Talman Regional Collection. *Anderson's Province of Ontario Gazetteer and Directory* (Toronto: Robinson & Cook, 1869), 291. Letters from Edward Ermatinger, 10 Feb., 27 Feb., and 9 Mar. 1843, Papers, Letters, Accounts of George R. Williams, Forwarding Merchant, Port Stanley, 1842–1859, Talman Regional Collection. Hepburn, *Port Stanley*, 16.

13 *Mitchell's Directory*, 1864–5, 748. *Anderson's Directory*, 1869, 291. *Lovell's Directory*, 1871, 'Lucan,' 'Granton.' C.F. Wilson, *A Century of Canadian Grain: Government Policy to 1951* (Saskatoon: Western Producer Prairie Books, 1978), 13–14. Jones, *History of Agriculture in Ontario*, 107. *St Marys Argus*, 8 Feb. 1871, 2. Marx, *Grundrisse*, 488.

14 Marx, *Capital*, III, 401–2. William Cronon, *Nature's Metropolis: Chicago and the Great West* (New York: W.W. Norton, 1991), 107, 109, 111.

15 Cronon, *Nature's Metropolis*, 113, 114, 115, 118, 116. Thomas S. Ulen, 'The Regulation of Grain Warehousing and Its Economic Effects: The Competitive Position of Chicago in the 1870s and 1880s,' *Agricultural History* 56 (1982), 194–210. Arthur Harvey, 'The Grain Trade: Extract from a Paper on the Graphical Delineation of Statistical Facts,' read before the British Statistical Society, 21 Jan. 1863. S.J. Daly, *Grain* (London: Oxford University Press, 1928), 83. Marx, *Capital*, III, 445.

16 Friedmann, 'Transformation,' 79. Wilson, *Canadian Grain*, 13–20. D.A. MacGibbon, *The Canadian Grain Trade* (Toronto: Macmillan, 1932), 25–38, 183–6. *St Marys Argus*, 17 Oct. 1872, 3. *Exeter Times*, 1 Feb. 1877, 6. 'Weighing Grain,' *Farmer's Advocate* (Feb. 1871), 19. *An Act to make better provision, extending to the whole Dominion of Canada, respecting the Inspection of certain Staple Articles of Canadian Produce*, 37 Vict. 1874, chaps. 4, 5, pp. 2, 36. Jones, *History of Agriculture in Ontario*, 237.

17 Fire insurance plans: *St Marys* (Toronto: Chas. E. Goad, 1885); *St Thomas* (Toronto: Chas. E. Goad, 1882); *Exeter* (Toronto: Chas. E. Goad, 1890). *Currie's County of Huron Directory for 1876–77* (Goderich: J.C. Currie, 1876), 102. *Canadian Merchants' Magazine and Commercial Review* 1 (April 1857), 2. *Canadian Agriculturist* 15 (May 1863), 198. Jones, *History of Agriculture in Ontario*, 235. Douglas McCalla, 'The Commercial Politics of the Toronto Board of Trade, 1850–1860,' *Canadian Historical Review* 50 (1969), 56. William J. Pattison, *Statements Relating to the Home & Foreign Trade of the Dominion of Canada ... for 1872* (Montreal: The Gazette, 1873), 38; *Statements Relating to the Home & Foreign Trade of the Dominion of Canada ... for 1875* (Montreal: Lovell, 1876), 19. Orlo Miller, *The Point: A History of the Village of Point Edward* (Point Edward: The Village of Point Edward, 1978), 27.

Memories of Goderich, 2nd ed. (Goderich: Jubilee 3 Committee, 1979), 50. Nick and Helma Mika, *Mosaic of Kingston* (Belleville: Mika Silk Screening Ltd., 1969), 139. *The Province of Ontario Gazetteer and Directory* (Toronto: Robertson & Cook), facing 672. *Might's Directory for 1892–93*, 1645. 'Trade and Commerce of Lucan Station for the Year 1863,' Scrap Book, Diaries and Scrapbooks of William Porte, Talman Regional Collection.

18   *1871 Dominion Census*, Province of Ontario, District 8 – North Middlesex, Biddulph Township, Schedule 1 – Nominal Returns of the Living. *Anderson's Province of Ontario Gazetteer and Directory*, 1869. *Lovell's Province of Ontario Directory*, 1871. Karl Marx, *The Eighteenth Brumaire of Louis Bonaparte*, in D. Fernbach, ed., *Surveys from Exile* (Harmondsworth: Penguin, 1973), 179. Donald Swainson, 'The Personnel of Politics: A Study of the Ontario Members of the Second Federal Parliament,' PhD dissertation, University of Toronto, 1968, 469 n 30.

19   Gordon Darroch and Lee Soltow, *Property and Inequality in Victorian Ontario* (Toronto: University of Toronto Press, 1994), 47, 81. Elliott, *Irish Migrants in the Canadas*, 146. S. Armitage-Stanley, Lucan's Grain Buyer and Banker was Robert H. O'Neill (typescript), Lucan, 20 May 1934; S. Armitage-Stanley, Some More Pioneer Business Men of Lucan (typescript), Lucan, 25 Sept. 1935; both in Spencer Armitage-Stanley Papers, Misc. Box B4718, Stanley of Biddulph, Talman Regional Collection. Middlesex East and North (London) No. 33, Registration Nos. 1–78, 1870–1933, Middlesex County Partnership Registrations, AO. 1851 Canada West Census, Huron County, Township of Biddulph, Personal Census, District 8, 15. 1871 Dominion Census, District 8, North Middlesex, Biddulph Division 2, Schedules 1, 6. Canada, Vol. 17, p. 43, 60Q, 60DD, 60R, R.G. Dun & Co. Collection, Baker Library, Harvard University Graduate School of Business Administration. David G. Burley, '"Good for all he would ask": Credit and Debt in the Transition to Industrial Capitalism – the Case of Mid-Nineteenth Century Brantford, Ontario,' *Histoire sociale/Social History* 20 (1987), 91, 98, 97. Risk, 'The Golden Age,' 329. Biddulph Township, 'Old Book,' Abstract Index to Deeds, fol. 168, Lots 157, 158; Abstracts 1831–1866, fols. 87, 88, Lots 157, 158, AO.

20   Tucker, *The Canadian Commercial Revolution*, 215. *Farmer's Advocate*, 12 (Feb. 1877), 12. Jones, *History of Agriculture in Ontario*, 248. William Davison Butt, 'The Donnellys: History, Legend, Literature,' PhD dissertation, University of Western Ontario, 1977, 97. Ray Fazakas, *The Donnelly Album*, first pub. 1977 (Willowdale, Ont.: Firefly Books, 1995), 94. D.A. Lawr, 'The Development of Ontario Farming, 1870–1914: Patterns of Growth and Change,' *Ontario History* 64 (1972), 274. McCalla, 'The Changing Structure,' 198. Kulikoff, 'The Transition to Capitalism,' 123.

5: Biddulph Township in the 1870s: Social Formation and Conjuncture

1 David Harvey, *Justice, Nature and the Geography of Difference* (Oxford: Blackwell, 1996), 112, 208, 262. Nicos Poulantzas, *Political Power and Social Classes* (London: New Left Books, 1973), 15.

2 David Harvey, 'Globalization in Question,' *Rethinking Marxism* 8 (1995), 6, 7.

3 Marx, *Grundrisse*, 509. Marx, *Eighteenth Brumaire*, 179.

4 'Trade and Commerce of the Lucan Station for the Year 1863,' Scrapbook, Diaries and Scrapbooks of William Porte, Talman Regional Collection. 'Lucan,' Dun & Bradstreet Reference Books, 1864–July 1871, AO.

5 Marx, *Capital*, II, 471–2. Marx, *Capital*, I, 571. Ernest Mandel, *Marxist Economic Theory* (London: Merlin, 1962), 155.

6 'Lucan,' Dun & Bradstreet Reference Books, 1864–July 1871, AO. Canada, vol. 19, 60EE, R.G. Dun & Co. Collection, Baker Library, Harvard University Graduate School of Business Administration. Butt, 'The Donnellys,' 150.

7 Cohen, *Women's Work*, 35, 32, 33–4, 36, 37.

8 Marx, *Eighteenth Brumaire*, 238–9, 240, 241, 242, 244.

9 Harriet Friedmann, 'Household Production and the National Economy: Concepts for the Analysis of Agrarian Formations,' *Journal of Peasant Studies* 7 (1980), 158, 160, 176–7.

10 Ibid., 159, 174. Harriet Friedmann, 'Simple Commodity Production and Wage Labour in the American Plains,' *Journal of Peasant Studies* 6 (1978), 71, 73. Harriet Friedmann, 'World Market, State, and Family Farm: Social Bases of Household Production in the Era of Wage Labor,' *Comparative Studies in Society and History* 20 (1978), 548.

11 Friedmann, 'Household Production,' 176, 175. Harriet Bertha Friedmann, 'The Transformation of Wheat Production in the Era of the World Market, 1873–1935: A Global Analysis of Production and Exchange,' PhD dissertation, Harvard University, 1976, 331–2, 25. Friedmann, 'World Market,' 562, 559.

12 Friedmann, 'World Market,' 545, 564. Friedmann, 'Transformation,' 79.

13 1861 Census, Biddulph Township, Agricultural Census. Friedmann, 'Simple Commodity Production,' 76, 78. Cohen, *Women's Work*, 36ff.

14 Friedmann, 'Simple Commodity Production,' 78–9, 1871 Census, Biddulph Township, Division 4, 2, 4, 6, Schedules 1, 4, 7. Ray Fazakas, *The Donnelly Album*, first pub. 1977 (Willowdale, Ont.: Firefly Books, 1995), 43–5.

15 *Exeter Times*, 18 Feb. 1875, 2; 1 Feb. 1877, 10. Fazakas, *The Donnelly Album*, 51–124. William Davison Butt, 'The Donnellys: History, Legend, Literature,' PhD dissertation, University of Western Ontario, 1977, 74. Friedmann, 'Simple Commodity Production,' 83. Louis Althusser, 'Ideology and Ideo-

logical State Apparatuses,' in *Lenin and Philosophy* (London: New Left Books, 1971), 152ff. Paul Phillips, 'Staples, Surplus and Exchange: The Commercial–Industrial Question in the National Policy Period,' in Duncan Cameron, ed., *Explorations in Canadian Economic History* (Ottawa: University of Ottawa Press, 1985), 30–1. Lynne Marks, *Revivals and Roller Rinks: Religion, Leisure and Identity in Late-Nineteenth-Century Small-Town Ontario* (Toronto: University of Toronto Press, 1996), 81–91.

16 Edgar Packard Dean, 'How Canada Has Voted: 1867 to 1945,' *Canadian Historical Review* 30 (1949), 236, 238. David Lee, 'The Dominion General Election of 1878 in Ontario,' *Ontario History* 51 (1959), 172, 184. Phillips, 'Staples, Surplus and Exchange,' 33. Ben Forster, *A Conjunction of Interests: Business, Politics and Tariffs 1825–1879* (Toronto: University of Toronto Press, 1986), chap. 4, 173, 174, 193. G.T. Orton, Speech in Parliament, *Debates of the House of Commons of the Dominion of Canada*, 5th Sess., 3rd Parl., 41 Vict. 1878, vol. 4 (Ottawa: McLean, Rogers & Co., 1878), 1166–7. J.B. Plumb, Speech in Parliament, in *Home Industries: Canada's National Policy: Protection to Native Products, Development of Field and Factory: Speeches by Leading Members of Parliament* (Ottawa: Publishers Tariff Speeches, 1876), 68. Jones, *History of Agriculture in Ontario*, 350. L.A. Wood, *A History of Farmers' Movements in Canada* (Toronto: University of Toronto Press, 1924), 93.

17 Fazakas, *The Donnelly Album*, 126. W.B. Graham, 'Liberal Nationalism in the Eighteen-Seventies,' *Canadian Historical Association Reports* (1946), 109. Frank H. Underhill, 'Political Ideas of the Upper Canadian Reformers, 1867–78,' *Canadian Historical Association Reports* (1942), 106, 115. Charles Tupper, Speech in Parliament, 22 Feb. 1878, *Debates of the House of Commons* (1878), 451, 452, 454, 461, 547. Forster, *Conjunction of Interests*, 177, 75–6, 79. Ralph Heintzman, 'Efficiency and Community: The National Policy and National Unity,' *Journal of Canadian Studies* 14 (1979), 144. John A. Macdonald, Speech in Parliament, 7–8 March 1878, *Debates of the House of Commons* (1878), 855. 'North Middlesex,' *Advertiser*, 11 May 1878, 3. 'The Debate on the Address Ended,' *Free Press*, 18 Feb. 1878, 2.

18 'A Farmer on Protection,' *Farmer's Advocate* (April 1876), 78. 'John Stuart Mill on Protection,' *Advertiser*, 18 May 1878, 2. Macdonald, Speech in Parliament, 7–8 March 1878, *Debates of the House of Commons* (1878), 858. Wood, *Farmers' Movements*, 92–3. 'John Granger,' 'Free Trade Vs Protection,' *Farmer's Advocate* (April 1876), 78.

19 Macdonald, Speech in Parliament, 7–8 March 1878, *Debates of the House of Commons* (1878), 855, 861–2. Fazakas, *The Donnelly Album*, 145-8. David Glass, *Address to the Electors of East Middlesex 27 July 1878*, 7, 4.

20 'A National Policy,' *Exeter Times*, 11 April 1878, 4. 'Mr Porter in Exeter,' *Exeter Times*, 30 May 1878, 4. 'Mr Porter at Dashwood,' 'Messrs Porter and Greenway,' *Exeter Times*, 6 June 1878, 1, 4. 'Canadian Reciprocity with the United States,' *Free Press*, 24 June 1878, 2. A.H. Dymond, Speech to Parliament, 8 March 1878, *Debates of the House of Commons (1878)*, 887.

21 'West Middlesex,' *Free Press*, 28 June 1878, 3. 'The Anniversary,' *Free Press*, 1 July 1878, 2. Lee, 'Election of 1878,' 174. 'The Session,' *Advertiser*, 11 May 1878, 3.

22 'Liberal-Conservatives in Accord,' *Free Press*, 14 March 1878, 4. 'A National Policy,' *Free Press*, 18 March 1878, 1. 'A National Policy,' *Free Press*, 19 March 1878, 1. 'North Oxford,' *Free Press*, 20 March 1878, 1. 'Conservative Reaction,' *Free Press*, 22 March 1878, 1. 'The People Alive,' *Free Press*, 25 March 1878, 2. 'Conservatism in Woodstock,' *Free Press*, 1 April 1878, 3. 'Campaign Points,' *Advertiser*, 30 April 1878, 2.

23 Fazakas, *The Donnelly Album*, 130, 244–5. 'Northern Sparks,' *Advertiser*, 19 Aug. 1878, 3. 'North Middlesex,' *Free Press*, 13 May 1878, 3. 'Northern Sparks,' *Advertiser*, 14 May 1878, 3. 'Northern Sparks,' *Advertiser*, 23 May 1878, 3. 'Nomination at Ailsa Craig Yesterday,' *Advertiser*, 11 Sept. 1878, 3.

24 'Centralia,' *Exeter Times*, 30 May 1878, 5. *Exeter Times*, 6 June 1878, 8. Fazakas, *The Donnelly Album*, 151. James Reaney, 'James Donnelly,' *DCB*, X, 234–5. 'Lucan,' *Free Press*, 22 May 1878, 3. 'North Middlesex,' *Free Press*, 4 July 1878, 1. 'Biddulph,' *Free Press*, 27 June 1878, 3. 'West Middlesex,' *Free Press*, 28 June 1878, 3. 'More Biddulph Bulldozing,' *Free Press*, 3 Aug. 1878, 4. 'Northern Sparks,' *Advertiser*, 19 Aug. 1878, 3. 'Northern Sparks,' *Advertiser*, 28 May 1878, 3. 'Northern Sparks,' *Advertiser*, 9 July 1878, 3.

25 'A Fatal Day for the Grits,' *Free Press*, 18 Sept. 1878, 2. 'Celebrating the Victory,' *Free Press*, 24 Sept. 1878, 4. Fazakas, *The Donnelly Album*, 148–53. Lee, 'Election of 1878,' 185.

26 Carolyn Strange and Tina Loo, 'Spectacular Justice: The Circus on Trial and the Trial as Circus, Picton, 1903,' *Canadian Historical Review* 77 (1996), 160, 161. David H. Flaherty, 'Writing Canadian Legal History: An Introduction,' in D.H. Flaherty, ed., *Essays in the History of Canadian Law* (Toronto: University of Toronto Press, 1981), I, 15. W.R. and G. de N. Clark Cornish, *Law and Society in England 1750–1950* (London: Sweet & Maxwell, 1989), 19. Morton J. Horwitz, *The Transformation of American Law* (Cambridge, Mass.: Harvard University Press, 1977), 30. Richard C.B. Risk, 'The Law and the Economy in Mid-Nineteenth Century Ontario,' in Flaherty, ed., *Essays in the History of Canadian Law*, I, 125. J.D. Blackwell, 'William Hume Blake and the Judicature Acts of 1849: The Process of Legal Reform in Upper Canada,' in Flaherty, ed., *Essays in the History of Canadian Law*, I, 166.

27 Paul Romney, 'From the Rule of Law to Responsible Government: The Transformation of Political and Legal Culture in Nineteenth Century Ontario,' in *Papers Presented at the 1987 Canadian Law in History Conference* (Ottawa: University of Ottawa, 1987), 370–2. Paul Romney, 'From Constitutionalism to Legalism: Trial by Jury, Responsible Government and the Rule of Law in Canadian Political Culture,' *Law and History Review* 7 (1989), 124, 141, 130, 139, 131–2, 133. Cornish, *Law and Society*, 19. J.M. Beattie, *Crime and the Courts of England 1660–1800* (Princeton, NJ: Princeton University Press, 1986), 322. Paul Romney, 'Upper Canada (Ontario): The Administration of Justice,' *Manitoba Law Journal* 23 (1996), 209.

28 Strange and Loo, 'Spectacular Justice,' 160. Butt, 'The Donnellys,' 293–6. 'The Biddulph Tragedy,' *Globe*, 7 April 1880, 2. 'The Biddulph Murder,' *Globe*, 13 April 1880, 4. 'A Change of Venue Required,' *Globe*, 6 March 1880, 2. 'The Change of Venue,' *Globe*, 22 March 1880, 2. 'The Donnelly Massacre,' *St Marys Argus*, 5 Feb. 1880, 2. 'Changing the Venue,' *St Marys Argus*, 11 May 1880, 2. 'The Lucan Tragedy,' *Ingersoll Chronicle*, 12 Feb. 1880, 2. 'The Biddulph Tragedy,' *Mail*, 6 Feb. 1880, 2. 'The Biddulph Tragedy,' *Mail*, 23 March 1880, 2. 'The Biddulph Tragedy,' *Western Dispatch*, 18 Feb. 1880, 2. 'Horrible! Brutal Butchery Near Lucan,' *Western Dispatch*, 11 Feb. 1880, 2. 'The Biddulph Tragedy,' *Free Press*, 3 March 1880, 2. 'The Biddulph Troubles,' *Free Press*, 21 Feb. 1880, 3. 'Changing the Venue,' *Free Press*, 23 March 1880, 2. 'Howling with the Globe,' *Free Press*, 24 March 1880, 2. 'A Common-Sense Letter from Justitia,' *Free Press*, 19 March 1880, 2. 'A Very Esteemed Contemporary,' *Advertiser*, 21 Feb. 1880, 2. 'Editorial Dashes,' *Advertiser*, 16 March 1880, 2. 'Editorial Dashes,' *Advertiser*, 25 March 1880, 2.

29 Fazakas, *The Donnelly Album*, 263. 'A Clever Boy,' *Exeter Times*, 19 Feb. 1880, 4; 'The Biddulph Murder,' 4. 'The Biddulph Tragedy,' *Globe*, 26 May 1880, 6. 'The Biddulph Prisoners,' *Globe*, 14 April 1880, 4. Butt, 'The Donnellys,' 255–6, 261. 'The Donnelly Butchery,' *Mail*, 14 April 1880, 4. 'Northern Sparks,' *Advertiser*, 22 March 1880, 2.

Index

emigration to Canada, 31–3; and
women, 55
Erie Canal: geography and construction of, 75
exchange value of land, 51–2

Fazakas, Ray: *The Donnelly Album*, xii,
144, 146
Friedmann, Harriet: on excess labour,
141; on farm demographics, 139–
40; on independent household
production, 137–8; on the peasantry, 134–6; on pre-capitalist
agricultural production, 136

gender, 119, 122–3; division of farm
labour, 139–40; on the Roman
Line, 133–4; and 'rough culture,'
145–6; as structural limitation,
145–6
geography, 3–4; landscape, 7–10;
moraines, 8–10; soil, 8–10, 13–16;
timber and soil, 15–16
glaciers: pause, 7–8; stadial oscillations, 7
Goodhue, George Jervis, 52–3, 54–5,
68, 71, 83, 122
grain elevators: in Canada, 116–18;
technology and ideology, 114–16
grain trade: and 1878 election, 150;
and gender, 119; in Lucan, 118,
119–21; and protection, 147–8; *see
also* American Grain Trade; wheat
staple
Grand Trunk Railway: adaptation to
Chicago traffic, 87–91; and Chicago
beef trade, 89–91; competition with
Great Western, 84–6; and Lucan,
38–41; route across Biddulph

Township, 40–1; St Marys–London
branch line, 82, 86
Great Western Railway, 38, 83–5;
competition with the Grand Trunk,
84–6, 89; and New York Central, 86,
89; and Through Passage, 84

Harvey, David: on constitutive
moment, 127; on space, 126
Huron Tract, 19–20; settlement of,
49–51; survey of, 20, 23–9; *see also*
Biddulph Township

ideology: Althusser on, 146n15; and
1878 election, 152–3; and 1878
election in Biddulph Township,
160–1; and the issue of venue,
168–9, 171; and the law in the
Donnelly murder trials, 171–4; and
the law in Upper Canada, 161–5;
of masculinity, 145–6
Innis, Harold, 98; empiricism of,
103–4; and staple theory, 100

Keefer, Thomas: *Philosophy of Rail-
roads*, 83–4; on railways and the
Great Lakes, 91–2
Kelley, Thomas P.: *Black Donnellys;
Vengeance of the Black Donnellys*, xi
Kettle Creek: exports/imports, 71–2

Lake Erie, 70–1
land grants, 43
land speculation, 40–3, 51–4; effects,
55; in Lucan, 41–2
land surveys: American practice, 23;
and Biddulph Township, 23–5, 28–
9; double-front township system,
28; general types of, 20; of the